PSYCHOSOMATIC DISORDERS:
A BEHAVIORISTIC INTERPRETATION

APPROACHES TO
BEHAVIOR PATHOLOGY SERIES

Brendan Maher—Series Editor

PSYCHOSOMATIC DISORDERS: A BEHAVIORISTIC INTERPRETATION

SHELDON J. LACHMAN

Wayne State University

John Wiley & Sons, Inc.
New York · London · Sydney · Toronto

Library of Congress Cataloging in Publication Data

Lachman, Sheldon Joseph, 1921–
    Psychosomatic disorders: a behavioristic interpre-
tation.

    (Approaches to behavior pathology series)
    Bibliography: p.
    1. Medicine, Psychosomatic.   I. Title.
RC49.L27   616.08   78-37936
ISBN O-471-51145-5
ISBN 0-471-51146-3 (pbk)

Printed in the United States of America.

10 9 8 7 6 5 4 3 2 1

To
Grace Ann Preston Lachman
with deepest affection

SERIES PREFACE

Abnormal psychology may be studied in many different ways. One traditional method of approach emphasizes the description of clinical syndromes with an extensive use of case histories to illustrate the central phenomena and the psychological processes believed to underlie them. Another common position is found in the adoption of a systematic theory (such as psychodynamic or behavioral) as a framework within which important problems of abnormal psychology may be delineated and interpreted.

Whether systematic or eclectic, descriptive or interpretive, the teaching of a course in abnormal psychology faces certain difficult problems. Just as in other areas of science, abnormal psychology has exhibited a rapid increase in knowledge and in the rate at which new knowledge is being acquired. It is becoming more and more difficult for the college teacher to keep abreast of contemporary developments over as wide a range of subjects as abnormal psychology encompasses. Even in the areas of his personal interest and special competence the instructor may be hard pressed to cover significant concepts and findings with real comprehensiveness.

Adding to this spate of new knowledge is the fact that, in the field of abnormal psychology, we are witnessing a resurgence of enthusiasm for empirical research of an experimental kind together with a growth of interest in deviant behavior on the part of other scientists, notably the geneticists, neurobiologists, biochemists on the one hand and epidemiologists, anthropologists and social scientists on the other. It is less and less possible to claim mastery of a topic area in abnormal psychology when approaching it purely from the standpoint of a single psychological theory. An adequate understanding of any central topic now depends on familiarity with literature coming from many quarters of the scientific community.

Knowledge multiplies but time does not. Working within the limits of forty to fifty lecture hours available for the usual course in general abnormal psychology, it has become necessary for the student to turn more and more often to specialized outside reading to acquire the depth that cannot be given by any one textbook or by any one instructor. Although much can be gained by reading a range of selected reprints, these are often written originally for audiences other than the undergraduates and for purposes too narrowly technical to be entirely suited to instruction.

The present volume is one of a series developed to meet the need for depth of coverage in the central topic areas of abnormal psychology. The series is prepared with certain criteria in mind. Each volume has been planned to be scientifically authoritative, to be written with the clarity and directness necessary for the introductory student, but with a sophistication and timeliness of treatment that should render it of value to the advanced student and the fellow-specialist. Selection of the topics to be included in the series has been guided by a decision to concentrate on problem areas that are systematically and empirically important: in each case there are significant theoretical problems to be examined and a body of research literature to cast light on the several solutions that are adduced. Although it is anticipated that the student may read one or more of these volumes in addition to a standard text, the total series will cover the major part of a typical course in abnormal psychology and could well be used in place of a single text.

We are in a period of exciting growth and change in abnormal psychology. Concepts and hypotheses that have dominated the field for over half a century are giving place to new and provocative viewpoints. Much of this has been accomplished in one short decade: it is clear that the character of the field will be changed even more radically in the decades to come. It is the hope of the editor and the contributors to this series that they will play a useful part in preparing the coming generation of psychopathologists for the challenge of the years that lie ahead.

BRENDAN MAHER

PREFACE

Psychosomatic disorders are a widely varied, highly interesting and, in many ways, most perplexing kind of pathology. Here I provide a framework of concepts for organizing information about psychosomatic relationships, particularly relationships regarding psychosomatic disorders. I do this by proposing, as a central concept, the idea that emotional behavior consists of general reaction constellations extensively involving autonomic response mechanisms, that is, smooth muscles and glands.

Several principles are associated with this nuclear idea:

1. Various patterns of autonomic reaction may be learned.

2. Originally ineffective stimuli may later provoke autonomic reactions.

3. Organs vary in their vulnerability to pathology and such vulnerability is at least, in part, genetically determined.

4. The frequency, duration, and intensity of autonomic reactions, depending on their nature and patterning, may produce a variety of constructive as well as disordered conditions.

This book has several goals: to provide an objective perspective of psychosomatic phenomena, with special emphasis on psychosomatic disorders; to briefly consider significant ideas in the province of psychosomatics; to survey the range of psychosomatic disorders; to examine research evidence, particularly experimental evidence, concerning the genesis and development of psychosomatic events; and to provide a rationale or general theoretical framework for considering psychosomatic disorders.

Throughout the book I have expressed preferences for the following:

1. An objective position concerning emotion, emphasizing behavior rather than subjective experience.

2. Systematic research investigations of psychosomatic pathology, involving many subjects and preferably involving measurement procedures and controls rather than case studies of a single or very few individuals with minimal measurement and control—that is, a preference for experimental over clinical research.

3. Conceptual schemes firmly anchored to stimulus and response variables rather than conceptual schemes that are more abstract.

4. Parsimonious and simple speculation rather than complex and superelaborate theoretical networks.

5. A single general theory with broad applicability rather than many specific theories for specific psychosomatic disorders.

The book is arranged in the following way. The introductory chapter defines the field and specifies some basic concepts. Fundamental ideas relating to biological principles, emotional behavior, and learning are found in the next three chapters. The fifth chapter considers various theories including the theoretical conceptualizations that serve as the basis for organizing the book. Each of the several chapters that immediately follow reviews the general structure and functioning of a particular organ system; it also considers the various psychosomatic disorders relating to that system, including empirical evidence and suggested mechanisms for the development of various disorders. The last chapters concern psychotherapy relevant to psychosomatic disorders and provide perspectives of the horizon with regard to future developments.

Several case histories or (since they are incomplete and hence highly abbreviated) case history vignettes are presented in association with the discussion, particularly in Chapters 6–14. They are intended to be exemplary or illustrative material rather than evidence for a particular theoretical position.

I thank Mrs. Arlene Sue Fox and Serje Seminoff of Wiley for the direction, instruction, and many useful ideas that they provided during the course of completing this manuscript; their help was of substantial value to me and to the manuscript. Several professional colleagues and associates have also reviewed the manuscript and have made suggestions. I gratefully acknowledge their generosity in sharing critical evaluations and suggestions, which have resulted in improvement of the manuscript. Robert H. Berman reviewed Chapter 6. Gerald J. Briskin reviewed Chapters 4 and 5. Ross Stagner reviewed the first five chapters. And Kenneth S. Davidson and Brendan A. Maher reviewed the entire manuscript. Of course, I assume responsibility for the shortcomings.

SHELDON J. LACHMAN

Ann Arbor, Michigan, 1972

CONTENTS

PSYCHOSOMATIC DISORDERS:
A BEHAVIORISTIC INTERPRETATION

CHAPTER ONE

INTRODUCTION: BASIC PSYCHOSOMATIC CONCEPTS

The following case history has been modified from the original report to emphasize specific stimuli and behavior rather than hypothetical or intra-psychic processes. The case is representative of many psychosomatic case histories and illustrates concretely the kinds of variables believed to be relevant in the development of a psychosomatic disorder.

THE CASE OF MR. A—GENESIS AND DEVELOPMENT
OF A DUODENAL ULCER

Background. As a child, Mr. A was quiet and obedient, whereas his brother who was three years older was aggressive and independent. Socially, Mr. A was very close to his brother and his brother's companions and was always under the protection of his brother. Mr. A also spent much time with his parents, who provided him with much attention.

Emotion-Arousing Situations. When Mr. A was 13 his brother died; about two years later his father also died. Both of those events were of major significance in Mr. A's young life. Following the death of his father, his mother became psychologically dependent on him, consulting him about important problems and requiring him generally to substitute for both his older brother and his father, a situation for which Mr. A was completely unprepared intellectually and otherwise. While maintaining a secure outer appearance, Mr. A was aroused emotionally, and his emotional reactions were repeatedly intensified by the excessive expectations of his mother.

Symptoms and Treatment. At age 18, Mr. A experienced a short period of stomach discomfort that was followed by the initial hemorrhaging of a duodenal ulcer. When psychotherapy began about five years later, x-ray findings and general symptoms indicated an active ulcer. Psychoanalytic treatment involving in part discussion of his emotional relationships, particularly with his mother, resulted in his improved understanding of his attitudes and emotional reactions and gradually also succeeded in producing more mature attitudes and presumably less-severe emotional reactivity. At about the same time he established for the first time in his life an extended and satisfying relationship with a young woman whom he later married. Stomach symptoms diminished, and Mr. A was able to get along on a *normal* diet with only occasional and mild gastrointestinal discomfort.

Follow-Up. Follow-up study during a three-year period after conclusion of this initial psychotherapy disclosed the following facts. Mr. A had a mild relapse shortly after his marriage when he accepted a very strenuous assignment abroad and had an unsuitable diet; a second mild relapse occurred immediately prior to the birth of his first child, which corresponded in time with his mother's considering remarriage. A few psychotherapeutic consultations at that time involved examination of the existing emotion-provoking problems and apparently resulted in the resumption of more stable functioning. At the end of the three-year period (following conclusion of initial psychotherapy), Mr. A was on a normal diet with minimal daily medication (Alexander, 1950).

Interpretation. Apparently several emotional situations—for example, the death of Mr. A's brother, of his father, and the demands of his mother on Mr. A—provoked intensive internal behavior including unusual secretion of the gastric glands, which liberated acid to engender a gastrointestinal ulcer and to foster its maintenance and development. The theoretical structure for this idea is elaborated particularly in the section of Chapter Five titled "Autonomic Learning Theory." An examination of this case later will probably make this book's theoretical position more cogent and meaningful. One or more of the principles considered in Chapter Five will also apply to each of the case-history vignettes cited in later chapters.

PSYCHOSOMATIC CONCEPTS

The term psychosomatic is derived from the Greek words *psyche* and *soma*. Psyche in ancient times meant soul or mind and more recently has come to mean behavior; soma typically refers to the physical organism—the body. The term psychosomatic, therefore, indicates relationships between psychological processes or behavior on the one hand and somatic structures or bodily organs on the other. As a technical term, psychosomatic is currently used in at least two ways. First, it sometimes indicates the wholeness, the organization, or the integration of an organism. Essentially, the single word conveys the idea that psychological being and biological being are not separate, but rather are a unit. Second, the term indicates that although an organism is unitary, psychological and somatic aspects can be distinguished, can be studied separately and independently, and can be considered in terms of the relationships between them. Both proposed uses of *psychosomatic* are accepted in the present work; however, the focus of attention is on the second one.

Systematic consideration and careful analysis are necessary for research progress. More specifically, according to the second perspective, the term psychosomatic refers to the influence of psychological processes on biological processes. The influence of biological processes on the psychological ones, that is, on behavior, may more appropriately be called *somatopsychic*.

Somatopsychic Relationships

Although they are important in their own right, I shall consider somatopsychic relationships only briefly here. They are, perhaps, more obvious than psychosomatic relationships. Somatopsychic relationships concern effects of biological factors, including organic structure, on behavior. Behavior means all actions of the organism; it includes internal and directly unobservable physiological responses such as movements of the stomach or beating of the heart, as well as external directly observable responses such as talking, smiling, running, and applauding. A basic principle, broadly applicable to relationships between biological structure and behavior, may be summarized as follows. *Behavior is a function of structure; structure sets a ceiling on behavior and thereby limits behavioral possibilities.* The examples cited below all involve some kind of somatic pathology, but the principle also holds for the normal or nonpathological. Normal or nonpathological organic structure is a range of structures, not a single fixed point on an anatomical continuum. Assume, for the moment, that there is no organic pathology, that men have adequate nourishment, surroundings, and background influences, and that they function optimally. They will differ, nevertheless, in their running speeds, reaction times, muscular steadiness, maximum speech volume, and so forth, as a consequence of biological differences—that is, differences in behavior are directly dependent on differences in the anatomy and physiology of individuals.

It is obvious that a person with a broken arm or broken finger has difficulty manipulating objects, a person with a fractured leg has difficulty in running, a man with a glandular deficiency may not be able to sustain vigorous activity very long, and a man with brain damage may not be able to solve problems requiring effective abstract thinking. Destruction of brain tissue as in syphilis produces slurred speech, tremulous writing, and uncoordinated locomotion. Inflammation of the brain, as in encephalitis, may produce somnolence, disorientation, and delirium. A bullet wound in the brain may produce speech and language impairment, perceptual distortions, and problems in executing skilled acts.

Profound undersecretion of the thyroid gland—hypothyroidism—as a consequence of damage to that gland may manifest itself in a generally reduced activity level; a tumor of the adrenal medulla, producing increased secretion of epinephrine, may be manifested in increased heart rate, increased liberation of carbohydrate by the liver, and changes in the respiratory pattern. Ossification of the tympanic membrane (hardening of the eardrum) or fusion of the middle-ear bones may make auditory discrimination more difficult; a hemorrhage that destroys a cerebral motor area may produce a paralysis. Pressure in a sensory area of the brain may lead to reports of overt sensory stimulation in the absence of such stimulation— that is, a hallucination. Irritation or inflammation of various motor centers may instigate convulsive actions. This is a partial, but perhaps representative, list; all may be considered somatopsychic effects—influences of somatic structure on behavior.

There are also some noteworthy *indirect* psychological consequences of somatic damage. Perhaps a single example will illustrate the point. A man whose arm has been amputated may change substantially psychologically as a consequence of such loss. Not only can he no longer perform as he once did, and as most men can, but he may have to accept a lower-level job; his self-attitudes may change substantially, perhaps in part because of feelings of inadequacy or inferiority. He may perceive the world and his relationships to it differently than he once did—for example, he may expect condescension, or he may reject friendly offers of aid. As a consequence of a somatic change, then, there may be extensive and profound *indirect* psychological effects—perhaps via social interaction—in addition to *direct* consequences.

Organic Disorders and Psychosomatic Disorders

Organic disorders are structurally based. They are caused by parasites of various kinds (such as tapeworms or microorganisms), by proximity to or ingestion of toxic substances (e.g., carbon monoxide, various lead compounds, cyanides, or hydrochloric acid), by severe mechanical contact with people or objects or penetration by inanimate objects like bullets or shrapnel, or by a vast array of similar physical agents.

Psychosomatic disorders are physiological dysfunctions and structural aberrations that result primarily from psychological processes rather than from immediate physical agents like those involved in organic disorders. Psychological processes include frustrating circumstances, conflict situations, and other emotion-provoking stimulation and the internal behavior resulting therefrom.

Emotional behavior of a living organism may produce durable structural changes in that organism. The physiological arousal produced by emotional stimulation may, for example, facilitate increased quantity and concentration of acid secretion in the stomach, leading to the development of ulcers in the digestive tract; it may involve increased blood pressure and cardiac activity, and if such activity is sufficiently intense and persistent, it may produce coronary damage. It may also result in rupture of blood vessels; in promoting or retarding the periodic breakdown of tissues in the uterus; in damage to the colon; or in certain kinds of enlargement of the thyroid gland. Again, such structural changes in the organism are the effects of internal or emotional behavior, *elicited psychologically* by stimulation of the sense organs and not as a consequence of physical pathology. Structural changes psychologically induced may be constructive, but attention has been focused primarily on their destructive aspects, that is, on psychosomatic disorders. In current psychiatric literature, psychosomatic disorders are sometimes called psychophysiologic disorders, but the word psychosomatic is still more generally used.

Conversion Reactions and Psychosomatic Disorders

Psychosomatic disorders must be distinguished from conversion reactions. Conversion reactions (once called hysteria) are neurotic disorders characterized by development of an illness symptom, typically a loss or alteration of a sensory or motor function (e.g., deafness, blindness, or paralysis). There is no physical damage; in fact, there is no detectable tissue change. The condition is usually temporary, and the symptom appears to solve a problem for the individual. A man who knows that someone is guilty of a crime may be fearful of the consequences if he testifies against that person; he may become mute until the trial is over. A soldier who cannot express his fears may develop a paralysis of an arm or leg and therefore not be required to return to the battle lines. An individual may develop a conversion blindness or deafness to get out of a particular job or to avoid an unpleasant or painful situation. These symptoms relate to the motives and conflicts of the persons who display them, but they are not deliberate; the individuals are not malingering. Neither is the psychosomatic patient producing his symptoms deliberately nor malingering; but the psychosomatic patient does directly suffer real tissue damage, whereas the conversion-reaction patient does not.

Comparing Organic Illness, Conversion Reactions, and Psychosomatic Disorders.

Table 1.1 indicates some distinctions among organic illness, conversion reactions, and psychosomatic disorders. It should be remembered that psychosomatic disorders are closely associated with activity of the autonomic nervous system (see Chapters 2 and 3 for discussions) and that a disorder should be considered psychosomatic only if emotional factors can be identified among its major determinants.

SOMA-MODIFYING BEHAVIOR

Soma-modifying behavior is in a sense psychosomatic, but differs substantially from matters relating to the central theme of this book. Soma-modifying behavior is self-modification of the body with varying degrees of deliberation and self-control. It may result in damage or mutilation to the body or in bodily improvement or perceived improvement, but it need not be either.

Destructive Soma-Modifying Behavior

Destructive soma-modifying behavior is exemplified by beating oneself to the extent of inducing bruises or discoloration; by excessively scratching the skin, perhaps with a comb or knife; by pulling out the hair; or by picking at incompletely healed wounds. More severe examples include such forms of self-mutilation as perforation of the skin with acid or mechanical instruments; burning oneself; branding oneself with a hot iron; and amputating a finger, nose, ear, arm, hand, breast, penis, or the scrotum.

Enhancing or Constructive Soma-Modifying Behavior

Soma-modifying behavior in which the goals are constructive or intended to be so include piercing the ears or the nose for adornments; mechanical stretching of the neck; plucking the eyebrows; use of cosmetics; tattooing; using false fingernails or eyelashes; cutting the hair; and cutting the nails. Developing muscles by exercise, changing bodily contour by diet or by use of mechanical equipment, or even changing the shape of limbs by binding them are other examples.

Soma-modifying behavior can be distinguished from psychosomatic effects in several ways. Soma-modifying behavior is deliberate or intentional, or at least can readily become so. It is accomplished primarily by the skeletal musculature rather than by the visceral musculature or other structures

TABLE 1.1 Distinctions between Organic Illness, Conversion Reaction, and Psychosomatic Disorder[a]

Distinguishing Characteristic	Organic Illness	Conversion Reaction	Psychosomatic Disorder
1. Determinants			
General	Physiogenic	Psychogenic	Psychogenic
Specific	Microorganisms, laceration, concussion, contusion	Difficult situation Earlier familiarity with symptoms	Stimuli provoking physiological changes (i.e., emotional reactions)
2. Structures involved	Any part of organism	Typically sensory or motor systems	Typically structures involved in or closely associated with autonomic nervous system innervations
3. Tissue pathology	Present	Absent	Present
4. Effect of suggestion	Pathology unchanged	Symptoms can be modified	Pathology unchanged (usually)
5. Effect of motivation on symptoms	Usually none obvious	Important; plays a determining or selective role	Usually none obvious
6. Reactions	Physical incapacity	Selective functional incapacity	Physical incapacity
7. Physical treatment	May have positive effect	Typically no effect	May have positive effect
8. Patient's typical attitude	Concern	Belle indifference	Concern
9. Consistency and anatomical feasibility of symptoms	Anatomically consistent and dependent on nature of the damage	May not correspond to feasible anatomical patterns (e.g., glove anesthesia, shoe paralysis)	Anatomically consistent and dependent on the nature of the damage

[a] Terms such as "usually," "typically," or "generally" should qualify each characteristic suggested, since there are occasional exceptions to almost every property indicated.

controlled by the autonomic nervous system. Many if not all soma-modifying effects can be directed toward or accomplished on others as well as on oneself. They may involve intermediate use of tools or chemical substances.

There is no question that these behaviors often are the overt accompaniments of the extensive physiological changes of emotion. The apparently cruel and self-punishing behaviors in this general category also relate to what others have termed sadomasochistic and self-aggression responses. The consequences of such behavior can be serious. For example, repeated scab-picking can result in more severe illness via irritation. Self-burning or other self-inflicted injury also can lead to infection resulting in serious illness or death. Overeating or refusal to eat in the absence of any structural or physiological aberration can have similar consequences. Biological changes as a function of smoking, alcohol consumption, or narcotics use are also in this category.

THEORIES OF PSYCHOSOMATIC DISORDER

In a disorder that is strictly psychosomatic, as earlier mentioned, there is no exogenous toxin, no penetrating inanimate object, and no specifiable microorganism or other parasite to be identified. Rather, significant emotional stimulus situations that may be highly evanescent are implicated. It is, therefore, very difficult to detect, isolate, examine, and study the determinants of psychosomatic illness. Obviously, it is still more difficult to quantify the amount of what is only uncertainly detected. Further, to complicate the situation, a clinician may not be consulted until many years later—long after the psychologically significant event has taken place, if indeed there is *but one* psychologically significant event.

Because of these and other problems it has been difficult to know with any degree of certainty the precise conditions leading to particular psychosomatic disorders. As a consequence, much speculation has been engendered and many theories have been developed. Some of those theories have been highly specific, involving the formulation of groups of conceptions to account for only one particular kind of psychosomatic disorder. Such theories have often taken one of three common forms.

1. Personality-profile theories. Personality-profile theories propose that particular sets of personality characteristics are related to particular psychosomatic disorders.

2. Emotional reaction-pattern theories. Emotional reaction-pattern theories maintain that different physiological patterns of emotion are responsible for different psychosomatic disorders, that is, that particular emotional reaction patterns are responsible for particular disorders.

3. *General emotional-arousal and genetically determined organ-vulnerability theories.* Those theories hold that emotional reactions are fundamentally similar, and the structure likely to be involved in a psychosomatic disorder is the one that is genetically weakest. This kind of theory analogizes an organ or the organism to a rubber band or a length of wire; under stress conditions, the rubber band breaks where the rubber is thinnest or of poorest quality; the wire "snaps" or the rope parts where it is weakest.

One problem with the *personality-profile theories* is that psychological evaluation procedures are notably weak in appraising personality; certainly it is difficult to make meaningful predictions about personality on the basis of standard psychological tests of personality. A major difficulty with the *emotional reaction-pattern theories* is that there have been very few dependable differences in physiological patterns for the allegedly different emotional states. And an obvious criticism of the *genetically determined organ-vulnerability theories* is the fact that structures are weakened as a consequence of nongenetic factors also.

In this book I hope to provide a new set of theoretical perspectives based on empirical principles, anchored in observable events, and capable of yielding hypotheses that are objectively testable. These speculations, collectively called an *autonomic learning theory,* are related most closely to the third category of theory indicated, but do not exclude the possibility that various hypotheses relating to type 1 and type 2 theories may also be useful.

The conceptual framework of the *autonomic learning theory* permits incorporating many of the highly specific psychosomatic hypotheses proposed by others at various times; and perhaps it also increases the value of those theories by suggesting psychobiological mechanisms by means of which psychosomatic disorders develop. The *autonomic learning theory* is outlined in Chapter Five.

CHAPTER TWO

BIOLOGICAL FOUNDATIONS

FUNDAMENTAL BIOLOGICAL CONCEPTS

Living things are characterized by the presence of a complex substance called protoplasm, which consists largely of water that contains a variety of chemical compounds, many of them highly complex and colloidal in form. The chemical composition of protoplasm varies from organism to organism and even in different parts of the same organism. However, the general type of mixture is common to all living things, so protoplasm is regarded as the physical basis of life.

In general, protoplasmic materials display characteristics that distinguish them from inanimate materials. In animals these characteristics include metabolism (internally regulated chemical processes whereby protoplasm maintains itself), intussusceptive growth (growth by assimilation or incorporation rather than by addition), irritability (responsiveness or sensitivity), and reproduction (processes whereby protoplasm creates new protoplasmic units).

Protoplasm is organized into units known as cells, which vary greatly in size and in shape. Essentially a cell is the *unit of structure* of an organism; living things are built of cells. It is the *unit of function* of an organism; each cell carries on basic life functions. It is the *unit of development* of an organism; organisms grow either by an increase in the size of existing cells or by the addition of new cells. And it is the *unit of heredity;* the new members of the species, no matter how large and complex they ultimately become, begin as single cells. Some organisms are made of a

10

single cell, but most species are multicellular. Humans have billions upon billions of cells.

A group of cells similar in structure and specialized for a *general* function is called a *tissue;* examples are connective tissue, glandular tissue, muscle tissue, and nervous tissue. A group of tissues specialized for a *particular* function is an organ; the stomach, liver, adrenal gland, heart, and cerebrum are organs. A group of organs generally related to each other and involved in the same general function is called a *system.* It is sometimes convenient to organize the human body into about nine systems: cardiovascular, gastrointestinal, respiratory, integumentary, musculoskeletal, genitourinary, endocrine gland, sensory, and nervous. Each of these systems will be considered in a later section of this book; I shall also discuss normal functions and psychosomatic disorders pertinent to each.

PRINCIPLES OF GENETICS

Any contemporary and comprehensive introductory textbook in biology or psychology will provide the major elements of present knowledge concerning mechanisms of heredity. A variety of books present details concerning genetics.[1] My intent in this section is to consider concepts relating to the overall relationships between genetic determinants, biological structure, and behavior.

Fundamental individual differences in biological structure are inherited. Evidence indicates that eye color, taste mechanisms, and height are largely determined by genetic factors. Assuming an environment that permits optimal expression of heredity potential, some individuals inherit a quality of cardiac muscle that will permit that heart to beat for over 100 years, others for 70 years, others for 30 years, and still others for not more than 3 years, despite the best efforts of physicians. Different individuals inherit livers, kidneys, thyroid glands, intestines, adrenal glands, and other organs of varying structure and effectiveness, that is, with the capacity to perform competently for varying lengths of time. There are, then, genetically determined differences in biological structures that very much influence their functional effectiveness, their durability, and their vulnerability to various agents of potential damage.

[1] An excellent introduction to genetics is C. Stern's *Principles of Human Genetics* (2d ed.), San Francisco: W. H. Freeman, 1960. Areas of genetics of special interest to psychology are cogently discussed in J. L. Fuller and W. R. Thompson's *Behavior Genetics,* New York: Wiley, 1960. Various findings in genetics relevant to medical practice are found in C. A. Clarke's *Genetics for the Clinician,* Philadelphia: F. A. Davis, 1964.

Differences in inherited structures provide the biological foundations for differences in behavior. There are also, of course, environmental influences on structure; obviously, modifications of biological structure by the environment correspondingly influence behavior.

Systematic animal research involving successive generations has clearly established the fact that selective breeding can develop distinct strains of rats that are (1) bright and dull with respect to maze-learning ability (Tryon, 1942), (2) emotional and nonemotional (Hall, 1938), (3) active and inactive (Rundquist, 1933), and (4) seizure-prone and seizure-resistant (Maier and Glaser, 1940). Similar statements can be made concerning other species based on more recent evidence.

Such psychological characteristics depend on inherited structural characteristics of these animals. For example, it may be that brightness and dullness relate to the density or arrangement of nerve cells in the brain or to microanatomic characteristics of brain cells. Perhaps activity levels and degrees of emotionality relate to structural and functional characteristics of particular endocrine glands. In fact, Yeakel and Rhoades (1941) did discover that emotional rats have larger adrenal glands than nonemotional rats. And seizure-proneness may relate to idiosyncratic structural features of auditory, endocrine, and neural organs. While well-controlled studies with careful measurement regarding genetic influences on behavior have been accomplished primarily with experimental animals, there is reason to believe that the general principles discovered are applicable to man.

In humans there appear to be differences in potential for developing musical ability, mechanical ability, and intellectual ability. These, likewise, depend on biological differences, which set capacity limits and put ceilings on behavior functions.

Other things being equal, the ability to make fine tonal distinctions will differ greatly in an unselected population given prolonged and intensive training; presumably such differences very much depend on characteristics of the sensory apparatus for hearing and of the central nervous system auditory analyzer. Highly motivated individuals given prolonged and intensive training in developing fine mechanical skills will differ widely in the mechanical skills that they thereby acquire. Probably much in the way of such differences is determined by bone structure, muscle structure, central coordinating mechanisms, and structural differences in nerve-muscle relationships. Similarly, highly motivated people who are exposed to optimal opportunities to acquire conceptual knowledge or mathematical proficiency will differ in their consequent attainments and, in part, such differences are functions of biological differences, perhaps primarily in the structure of higher brain centers.

The general rationale proposed here may be extended to all psychological and physiological functions of the organism: *Functions depend on organismic structures, which in turn are fundamentally determined by hereditary factors.* Behavior itself is not inherited, but biological structures are inherited that influence (a) the predisposition to apprehend certain stimulation, (b) characteristics of neural processing, and (c) properties of reactivity.

From the standpoint of pathology, the resistance of a biological structure to damage by cold, heat, mechanical pressure, parasitic organisms, and other such assaultive agents is in part a function of the quality of that organ, which in turn is genetically determined.

It should be remembered that behavior is not inherited. What is inherited is structure. Characteristics of biological structure set limits on individual behavior and on the potential for developing behavior. Behavior is always dependent on environmental opportunity as well as inherited structure. The environment does not merely limit opportunities for behaving, but can also deleteriously modify biologically inherited structures and by that means impose additional limitations on behavior. The following examples illustrate the point.

1. A man who inherits defective color receptors is color-blind. This means that he cannot distinguish between stimuli that differ only in color; therefore, that man cannot learn to react differentially to such stimuli. However, the individual with normal receptors for color vision can make appropriate color-stimulus discriminations and may learn differential reactions to them.

2. The size of an endocrine gland—the adrenal gland or the thyroid gland, for example—depends in part on heredity. Further, the size of such a structure is typically related to its level of secretion, which in turn is related to the activity level of the organism. Thus, differences of individuals in ability to provide vigorous and sustained reactions to particular situations (assuming, of course, adequate nutritive substances to insure normal growth and operation) very much depend on glandular functioning and size, which in turn depend on genetic factors.

3. Synaptic connections of low threshold may be inherited to constitute critical aspects of the reflex arc; but reflexive behavior itself depends on an instigating stimulus. Stimuli derive from the environment and appropriate stimuli may or may never occur. *Behavior potential,* then, not behavior, is inherited.

4. How rapidly an individual can move or otherwise react depends very much on the speed of conduction in his nervous structures, in the efficiency of his muscular contractions, and in the nature of his bone structure. Those biological foundations of behavior—nervous structures,

striated muscles, and bone structure—are, of course, all inherited. The behavior itself depends on a variety of circumstances that are not inherited, including the eliciting stimulus situation.

One must also be wary of the prevalent notions that whatever is present at birth is inherited and whatever occurs later is acquired. Those ideas are fallacious. What occurs at birth may be a function of the prenatal environment as well as of heredity; and what occurs long after birth may be primarily a function of hereditary factors. To illustrate these points, consider the following.

1. Unusual chemical or mechanical conditions in the environment prior to birth can produce various aberrations. For example, unusual intrauterine chemical conditions may lead to modification in bone structure and perhaps alter the shape of the head; consider those unfortunate youngsters with defective appendages born to mothers who during pregnancy had used the drug thalidomide. Another example: if a developing infant's appendage should become entangled with the umbilical cord, it may lead to the infant's being born with a withered limb. Thus, the prebirth environment may modify organismic structure. After birth, potentially deleterious influences of the environment are almost limitless.

2. The normal course of development of a structure regulated by hereditary factors is termed maturation. Teeth are rarely present in a human at birth; they will, however, erupt and develop at a later time. Muscles of the limbs are not sufficiently developed to support the weight of the infant immediately after birth, but structural changes regulated by heredity to permit such support will occur in time. The sex glands are not completely developed nor completely functional at birth; but within a dozen or so years after birth, guaranteed an adequate environment, those glands and accessory organs will undergo structural differentiation to permit dependable functioning. Maturation, then, refers to those processes whereby biological structures develop and become functional as a mere consequence of internal differentiation.

BIOLOGICAL FOUNDATIONS OF BEHAVIOR: RECEPTOR, INTEGRATOR, AND EFFECTOR

Psychologists in general concern themselves with three kinds of biological structure—receptors, integrators, and effectors.

Receptors, or sense organs, are structures that are sensitive to various kinds of energy—for example, structures in the eyes are sensitive to light; in the ears to sound; in the tongue to a variety of chemicals; in the skin to temperature changes and to mechanical deformation; and in muscles and joints to pressure.

Effectors are response mechanisms—structures by means of which behavior is accomplished. They are of two kinds, muscles and glands. Muscles are specialized for contracting and glands for secreting. There are three kinds of muscle: striated muscle operates in locomotion and manipulation; smooth muscle accomplishes movements ordinarily not under the direct control of an individual, such as movements of the stomach or intestines; and cardiac muscle is the muscle of the heart. Glands are of two kinds: exocrine (duct) and endocrine (ductless). Exocrine glands pass their secretions through a tube either into a body cavity or onto the body surface; the gastric glands pass their secretions into the stomach, the salivary glands into the mouth, the lacrimal or tear glands onto the surface of the eye, and the sweat glands onto the skin surface. Endocrine glands lack a duct or tube and pass their secretions directly through the organ wall into the bloodstream. The thyroid, pituitary, and adrenal are representative endocrine glands.

Integrators serve a basic function; they mediate between sense organs and effectors. The nervous system is specialized as an integrator.

Although psychologists are interested in the behavior of an entire organism, they tend to focus on these three kinds of structure. The properties of the environment to which a person may respond are limited by the structural properties of his receptors. Motor dexterity, including locomotion and manipulation, are present in an individual only to the degree permitted by the structure of his effectors, particularly muscles. The major integrating structure, the nervous system, limits and makes possible opportunities for (1) flexibility in behavior, (2) the individual's ability to benefit from his past experience, that is, learning, and (3) developing symbols, that is, neural representations of persons, objects, events, and situations.

GENERAL FUNCTIONS OF THE NERVOUS SYSTEM

The nervous system integrates the behavior of the organism and regulates rather directly all other systems of the body. The nervous system, like other systems of the body, is composed of cells called neurons.

Neurons are specialized for conduction. Energy effects in the form of impulses, which are electrochemical in nature, are mediated from sense organs and to effector structures by means of the nervous system.

Anatomically, the nervous system is made up of central and peripheral components. The central nervous system, so called because it is located centrally in the vertical axis of man, consists of the brain and the spinal cord. The peripheral nervous system consists of all the nerves of the body, of which 12 pairs known as cranial nerves connect to the brain and 31 pairs known as spinal nerves connect to the spinal cord. The nerves connect the central nervous system with more peripheral structures—sense organs, glands, and muscles. (See Figure 2.1.)

The brain, a gigantic mass of nerve cells protected by the skull, consists of many organs. The part of the brain that is largest, most complex, most recently developed in the course of evolution, and most responsible for many of the unique psychological qualities of man is the cerebrum.

The cerebrum is incompletely divided by a deep fissure into right and left halves known as the cerebral hemispheres. The cerebrum contains a number of primary sensory centers; impulses reaching such centers are interpreted as light, sound, warmth, taste, pressure, or kinesthetic sensations. It contains centers concerned with voluntary motor activity such as movements of the shoulders, arms, hands, fingers, trunk, leg, foot, and toes. There are centers in the cerebrum that are important in perception, in the performance of skilled acts, and in language functions. Further, the cerebrum is apparently very much involved in imagining, comparing, evaluating, planning, learning, thinking, and reasoning.

The second-largest part of the brain, the cerebellum, is primarily concerned with smoothing out activity—with coordinating movements and sequences of movements so that they are executed in an organized way. It also has a major role in the maintenance of muscle tone. The cerebellum is located beneath and toward the rear part of the cerebrum.

All of the other parts of the brain—excluding the two largest, the cerebrum and the cerebellum—make up the brain stem. Among the major structures of the brain stem are the thalamus, hypothalamus, midbrain, pons, and medulla. Two other brain stem structures of special significance to psychology, and particularly to the psychology of emotion in view of knowledge about them acquired in recent years, are the limbic system and the reticular system.

The limbic system consists of a group of structures in midline regions encompassed by the cerebral hemispheres which influences emotional expression. The reticular system which in part consists of networks of neurons radiating upward through the core of the medulla and midbrain operates to influence arousal, wakefulness and alertness.

The above description briefly characterizes the nervous system *anatomically*. However, these same structures may be considered in another way, by organizing them in terms of their functions—what they do. *Functionally*, there is a somatic nervous system and an autonomic nervous system.

The somatic nervous system consists of all nervous structures, whether

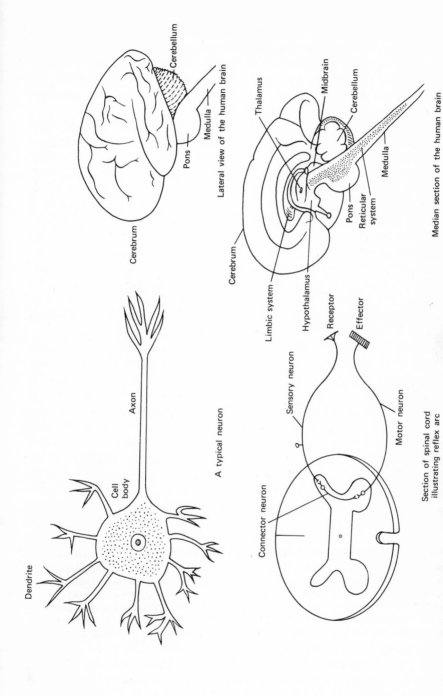

Dendrite

Cell body

Axon

A typical neuron

Cerebrum

Cerebellum

Medulla

Pons

Lateral view of the human brain

Thalamus

Midbrain

Cerebellum

Medulla

Pons

Reticular system

Hypothalamus

Limbic system

Cerebrum

Median section of the human brain

Receptor

Effector

Sensory neuron

Motor neuron

Connector neuron

Section of spinal cord illustrating reflex arc

FIGURE 2-1. Nervous system structures.

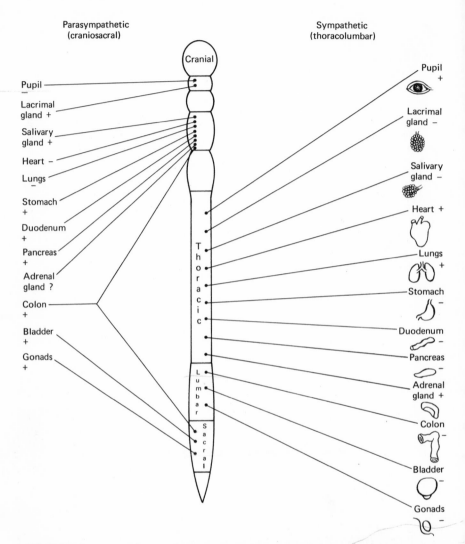

FIGURE 2-2. A simplified and schematic representation of the autonomic nervous system. The parasympathetic nervous system and structures innervated by it are indicated at the left. The sympathetic nervous system and structures innervated by it are indicated at the right. "Positive" reactions, including dilation, vasodilation, contraction, secretion, acceleration, and motility are designated with a plus (+) sign. "Negative" reactions, including constriction, vasoconstriction, relaxation, deceleration, and inhibition of motility are designated with a minus (−) sign.

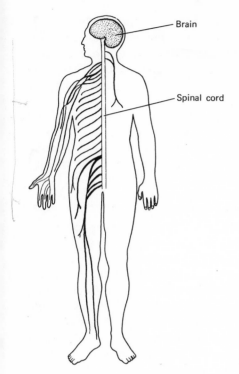

FIGURE 2-3. Nervous system.

central or peripheral, concerned with mediating impulses from receptors and with directing impulses to striated muscles. The autonomic nervous system consists of all nervous structures, whether central or peripheral, concerned with regulating the internal environment, more specifically the heart, smooth muscles of the viscera, and the glands.

The autonomic nervous system is of special concern because it is by means of that system that the extensive bodily changes that characterize emotional behavior are mediated. The system consists of a number of structures that are located in the central nervous system. Some of these, which have to do with a variety of reflexes such as those involving the intestines, the stomach, and blood vessels of the lower trunk and lower limbs, are found in the spinal cord, while other reflex centers and centers of integration are found at levels of the medulla and the midbrain. The highest centers for integrating activities of the autonomic nervous system are in the hypothalamus. (See Figure 2.2.)

The autonomic nervous system has two components, the sympathetic nervous system and the parasympathetic nervous system. While each of these subdivisions has centers in the spinal cord and brain as indicated, the two systems can be more readily distinguished peripherally. Fibers leading from the thoracic and lumbar regions of the spinal cord to effectors make up the sympathetic nervous system; fibers leading from the brain and from the sacral part of the spinal cord to effectors make up the parasympathetic system.

For the most part, both systems innervate the same structures of the body such as the heart, the intestines, the adrenal medulla, and the iris. But their effects are opposite. Sympathetic innervation serves to increase cardiac activity, inhibit intestinal motility, facilitate secretion of epinephrine (adrenalin), and dilate the pupil of the iris. Parasympathetic innervation serves to reduce cardiac activity, increase intestinal motility, reduce secretion of epinephrine, and constrict the pupil of the iris.

Reflexes involving many structures of the body including the blood vessels, the heart, the endocrine glands, the digestive tract, and other organs of the viscera, serve to maintain basic vegetative functions and conditions of internal equilibrium; such reflexes are mediated by the autonomic nervous system. Common patterns of physiological reaction to emotional stimulation are also mediated by means of the autonomic nervous system.

A general characteristic of the brain that is of major biological and psychological significance is its functional plasticity. This is mainly due to the brain's cellular (neural) components and their arrangements. It is by means of changes taking place in the brain that man learns—that in the course of his behavior, stable and dependable changes in relationships between stimulation and reaction develop. Man, of all animals, has the most prodigious capacity to learn.

A second significant function of the brain is its capacity to develop and manipulate symbols. Certain neurological changes in the brain may represent particular objects, events, persons, or situations in the absence of such objects, events, persons or situations from the stimulus field; other neurological changes in the brain may represent *aspects* or *categories* of objects, events, persons, or situations. Such neurological changes are neural symbols. They are of great relevance because neural symbols underlie thinking and because once established, those symbols themselves have a fundamental role in influencing behavior. Such symbols, of course, may trigger emotional behavior.

Man, of all animals, because of his facility in developing and manipulating neural symbols, has the greatest capacity to think. His autonomic responsiveness *to those neural symbols* that represent past external events, anticipated external events, fear situations, anger situations, or other emotional situations, real or imagined conflicts, and a variety of other problems and difficulties may be related to his tendency to develop psychosomatic disorders.

The nervous system has several roles in emotional behavior. Certainly the effects of emotion-provoking stimuli are transmitted by the nervous system, and the conscious or awareness states related to emotion that have been reported—assuming for the moment their validity and relevance—depend directly on the brain. The interpretation of certain stimulus events as having emotional significance may depend much on the cortex. Likewise, the overt or explicit behaviors that follow and accompany emotional stimulation are mediated by the nervous system. But most important, *the physiological changes*—changes in cardiac activity, blood-vessel diameter, movements and secretions of the gastrointestinal tract, and glandular secretions, among a constellation of other changes—*that are emotion* are regulated by the nervous system, particularly the autonomic nervous system. Thus, some understanding of the role of the autonomic nervous system in emotional states is of critical importance in understanding the more specific mechanisms and concepts relating to the development of psychosomatic disorders.

CHAPTER THREE

EMOTIONAL BEHAVIOR

A psychosomatic disorder is a pathological condition elicited primarily by emotional behavior. For that reason it is necessary to review certain fundamental ideas about emotional behavior. That is the purpose of this chapter.

DEFINITION OF EMOTION

Emotional behavior refers to extensive and intensive changes in physiological functioning that are psychological in origin (Lachman, 1969). The essential difference between emotional and nonemotional behavior is that emotional behavior is characterized by *multiple* and *intensive* changes in physiological functioning of the autonomic effectors, including alterations in heart rate, rate of stomach or duodenal movement, and gastric or adrenal-gland secretion, among other activities. Often emotional reactions are engendered suddenly, and often they are brief, but not necessarily. The changes may involve any or all parts of an organism via blood vessels, glands, and other structures widely distributed and broadly influencing bodily function. They may represent either an increase or a decrease in activity and may be vigorous deviations from the nonemotional base line. The physiological reactions comprising emotional behavior are psychological in origin; this means that they are responses to environmental stimulation of sense organs or to central nervous surrogates, that is, symbols, of such stimulation. The phrase "psychological in origin" distinguishes the physiological changes in emotion from very similar changes that may be a consequence or concomitant of violent exercise, tissue pathology, ingested drugs, parasitic infection, or other such conditions (Lachman, 1969). Physiological reactions are also called *covert, internal,* or *implicit* reactions.

Of course, *explicit, external,* or *overt* behaviors may or may not accompany the essential implicit reaction pattern—for example, clenching the teeth, screaming, laughing, shaking a fist, smiling, frowning, or running toward or away from a stimulus. Such reactions may be violent or moderate, or they may not be apparent at all—a person need not indicate overtly the fact that potent internal changes are in progress. Occasionally an individual may be petrified, that is, immobilized, in a fear situation. Further, in the course of social development, people learn to suppress overt expression of emotion under certain conditions, as well as to display overt expression of emotion under other conditions. Emotion must not be identified with any single set of responses either internal or external.

The term emotion means measurable behavior—implicit behavior. Various writers, philosophers, and psychologists have used the term to refer to a state of awareness, but such definitions make emotion subjective, private, and not accessible directly to the research observer. This leads to problems of independent confirmation and difficulty in communication, and occasionally even to a kind of mysticism concerning the nature of emotion. Dealing with emotion as behavior rather than subjective experience should reduce ambiguity and confusion; further, progress in scientific research depends much on dealing with what is observable and measurable.

ASPECTS OF EMOTIONAL BEHAVIOR

The boundary lines between explicit behavior and implicit behavior are not sharp, definite, and distinct, but rather vague, indefinite, and indistinct. For example, how should blushing—facial flushing—be classified? The increasing coloring or redness of the face is an explicit reaction. But if approached in terms of blood-vessel dilations, it is also an implicit reaction. Pallor or blanching also falls within the questionable group, since the surface paling is related to blood-vessel constriction. Likewise, occasionally pulsations of blood vessels, particularly in the neck, temple, or forehead, are visible. Respiratory movements and many other reactions also have both explicit and implicit manifestations. Nevertheless, for the sake of convenience in research investigation and in discussion, it is desirable to dichotomize emotional behavior into an implicit behavioral sphere and an explicit behavioral sphere and further to categorize and specify varieties of

Physiological Measure	Graphic Record	Recording Instrument
	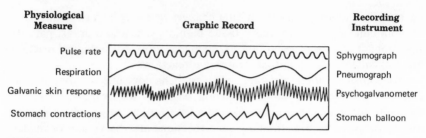	
Pulse rate		Sphygmograph
Respiration		Pneumograph
Galvanic skin response		Psychogalvanometer
Stomach contractions		Stomach balloon

FIGURE 3-1. A graphic record of physiological activity.

response within each of these aspects. Some of the common reactions are briefly considered below within each of these two major categories of response.

The Implicit Behavioral Aspect

The implicit aspect of emotional behavior refers to internal or covert behavior, to involuntary behavior, and to physiological activity. This category includes behavior that involves autonomic effectors—the glands and visceral musculature—and consists essentially of movements and secretions of the internal organs, particularly the soft organs of the viscera. Reactions classifiable within the sphere of implicit behavior may be differentiated further into subcategories such as the following: *cardiovascular activity* (includes modifications in rate and amplitude of heart beat, diameter of blood vessels, blood pressure, pulse rate, and chemical composition of the blood), *gastrointestinal activity* (includes changes in rate and amplitude of stomach contraction, peristalsis and reversed peristalsis, and secretions of salivary and gastric glands), *respiratory activity* (includes variations in rate, depth, and regularity of breathing), *genitourinary activity* (includes various changes in sexual potency and in rate of formation and chemical composition of urine), and *endocrine activity* (includes changes in the rate and nature of secretion of the pituitary, thyroid, adrenal glands, and other endocrine structures). Ordinarily such internal behaviors are not directly observable. However, indices of such activities may be obtained by means of specialized techniques and instruments. (See Figure 3.1.)

Sometimes instrumentation is organized to permit recording a group of physiological reactions simultaneously. In fact, procedures have been developed not only for simultaneously recording several physiological effects but also for preparing records permitting immediate tabulations of performance, including the specification of ratios and the comparison of various physiological indices with each other.

The Explicit Behavioral Aspect.

The explicit aspect of emotional behavior—external or overt behavior, the superficial or surface manifestations—is often but not always an accompaniment of the implicit; it is often, although certainly not always, "voluntary" behavior. This behavior includes primarily the somatic or striated musculature and consists for the most part of movements that are readily observable. Much of it is learned as a consequence of social and cultural interaction. Behavior classifiable as explicit may be categorized as follows. *Facial expression* includes activity of facial effectors and is exemplified by such movements as frowning, smiling, weeping, grimacing, and dilation of the nostrils. *Postural orientation* involves the general bodily musculature; it consists for most part of gross positional changes: slumping, stretching, crouching, cringing, and bending are typical. *Gestural reactions,* usually reactions of appendages but also of the trunk and head, generally have communicative significance; for example, a clenched fist, a pointing finger, wringing the hands, and clapping of the hands as in applause. *Vocal expression* includes the utterance of voice sounds, regardless of whether such sounds are of linguistic significance. Sobbing, swearing, scolding, shouting, stammering, moaning, groaning, and screaming are examples. *Locomotor responses* move an organism from place to place. Brisk, long strides, short, slow steps, irregular and apparently random walking, pacing movements, crawling, jumping, staggering, running, and climbing are forms of such response. *Manipulatory responses* ordinarily involve the grasping and movement of objects by the hands as well as defensive and attacking movements. Tactual exploration or manipulation of objects as well as kneading, pinching, probing, slapping, pulling, pushing, squeezing, striking, and caressing exemplify this category. The mouth may also be used in making manipulatory responses as in licking, sucking, or nibbling. *Substitutive reactions,* a group of responses that does not appear to be as cohesive as the other subcategories and perhaps is not really distinct from them, embraces explicit reactions that often are particularly *symptomatic or indicative of autonomic arousal.* It incorporates repetitive or perseverative responses or automatisms such as pulling at the earlobe, thumb-sucking, drumming the fingers, picking at a scab, and biting the nails. Certain ticlike movements may also be included. It is frequently difficult to distinguish responses classifiable in the first six subcategories from responses classifiable in the last; however, because of their apparently dependably close association with autonomic responses, such "substitutive responses" are of special significance. Records of explicit behavior may be obtained via still cameras, motion-picture cameras, audiorecorders, techniques of assessing bodily balance, coordination, steadiness and tremor, sensory discrimination, rate of movement, and a wide variety of rating scales and psychological tests.

GENERAL ROLE OF THE NERVOUS SYSTEM IN EMOTION

General functions of the nervous system in emotion may be briefly summarized as follows.

1. The physiological reactions that constitute emotional behavior are mediated by the autonomic nervous system.

2. Perception of situations as emotional depends on the brain and is related to learning. This includes overt representation of emotional stimuli such as a casket, flag, swastika, spoken or written word, or picture of a train wreck. Not only are *most stimuli* that serve to engender emotional reactions learned, but *various aspects of response* to such stimuli, including particularly overt responses, are also learned.

3. The neurological processes of the brain that underlie thought— presumably at the cortical level—may be considered neural symbols. These may function to permit recall of emotional situations, anticipation of emotional situations, and imagining or fantasying of emotional situations, all of which may trigger autonomic reactivity. Certain neural symbols representing stimulus situations may evoke overt behavior tendencies perceived by the reactor as incompatible; these are the neural equivalents of conflict situations and of course may be further manifested in autonomic reactions as well as in more overt behavior.

STIMULUS SITUATIONS INDUCING EMOTIONAL BEHAVIOR

The stimuli that originally elicit emotional reactions are not known with absolute certainty. However, it has been observed that early in life, certain kinds of stimuli dependably tend to elicit emotional reactions: stimuli that are unexpected or introduced suddenly; stimuli that are relatively intense; and stimuli that are unfamiliar or strange. Several other kinds of stimulus situation also produce emotional reactions frequently. One of these is the frustration or blocking of goal-directed behavior. It is suggested that the stronger the motivation toward a goal, the greater the intensity of any emotional reaction to blockage or frustration. Threat of frustration produces similar reactions. Another stimulus situation producing emotional reactivity—typically emotional reactions tinged with positive affective tone—is one in which motives are unexpectedly gratified or are gratified with much greater intensity than anticipated. Time-performance pressures or conditions in which excessive demands are made for effective performance within specific periods of time—usually relatively brief and insufficient periods of time—may produce emotional reactions.

Conflicts may foster emotional reactions. Conflicts are problem situations in which an individual is confronted with alternatives requiring action or at least decision. Three kinds of conflict may be distinguished: approach-approach conflict, in which an individual is attracted to two or more goals that are mutually exclusive; avoidance-avoidance conflict, in which an individual is repelled by two or more behavioral alternatives but must choose one; and approach-avoidance conflict, in which an individual is both attracted and repelled by the same object or stimulus situation. When these approach and avoidance tendencies have increasingly higher but equal values, decision is increasingly difficult, and emotional reactivity is increasingly likely to occur during the decision-making period, which is frequently characterized by overt vacillation. The decision-making period may last only a few seconds, or it may endure over many years. Overt representations, that is, *external symbols* or *stimulus symbols* of situations that were effective in producing emotional reactions in the categories mentioned, may themselves produce such emotional reactions.

Neural symbols, or implicit representations of emotion-eliciting situations (as well as overt symbols of such situations), may also induce emotional reaction. Such neural symbols or implicit representations presumably are anatomical or physiological changes in the brain. Thinking involves a processing or manipulation of those symbols. In the course of thinking, therefore, certain symbols may provoke emotional behavior. Neural symbols such as those representing real or imagined threat situations, or of overt surrogates of threat situations, may trigger or sustain emotional reactions.

On the basis of temporal contiguity with stimuli in those categories indicated above that are initially effective in producing emotional behavior, other stimuli, originally neutral or indifferent, can become associated so as to effectively elicit such behavior. Thus, in time, a wider range of stimuli may become capable of eliciting emotional responses.

PHYSIOLOGICAL REACTIONS
TO EMOTIONAL STIMULATION

With intense, unexpected, or unusual stimulation (and perhaps also in response to the other stimulus situations specified above), a large group of implicit activities is set into operation. Similar patterns of reaction may also be set into operation under conditions of great somatic activity, such as in exercise, or under conditions of fever or of infection, for example. This integrated and extensive internal complex of adjustments, which mobilizes the energy resources of the body, constitutes a generally adaptive set of reactions that involves the autonomic nervous system and the endocrine gland system. The pattern, described in detail by the great physiologist Walter B. Cannon, is regarded as adaptive because it is frequently elicited in times of *emergency*—under conditions of injury or potential injury—and it is believed to have value in preparing the organism for dealing with such situations. The changes making up the pattern are largely cardiovascular, but respiratory and glandular as well as other systems are also pertinently involved. A basic component of the pattern is secretion of the adrenal gland, and it is believed that such secretion is independently capable of eliciting, reinforcing, and sustaining various components of the emergency reaction that normally are engendered primarily by the sympathetic part of the autonomic nervous system. The adrenal gland, then, apparently cooperates with the sympathetic nervous system in effecting the adaptive set of physiological responses.

Following are some of the frequent constituents of this adaptive pattern, the emergency reaction of the sympathetic nervous system. (1) Epinephrine (adrenalin) is liberated by the adrenal gland into the blood stream. (2) Epinephrine causes carbohydrates that have been stored in the liver in the form of glycogen (animal sugar) to be released into the bloodstream. Hence, the sugar content of the blood is increased. The released sugars provide energy materials necessary for the functioning of nerve and muscle, which store very little of such fuel materials. (3) The bronchioles of the lungs are dilated; this facilitates respiration, that is, provides for accelerated or deeper respiration. In the utilization of fuel material by muscle and nerve, oxygen is required. The accumulation of acid as a consequence of muscular activity enhances dangers of acidosis and nervous impairment. Oxygen combusts nonvolatile lactic acid, changing it to volatile carbonic acid, which can be eliminated as carbon dioxide and water vapor. Acceleration of respiration results in increased amounts of oxygen inspired and of carbon dioxide and other gases expired. (4) More red blood corpuscles are liberated into the circulatory system. This increases the oxygen-carrying capacity and also the carbon dioxide transportation capacity of the bloodstream. (5) Blood vessels of the digestive tract constrict, and in general there is a depression or cessation of digestive processes, including decreased salivation; blood vessels of the periphery dilate, and blood is directed toward the striated muscles of the periphery—particularly the large muscles of the limbs—and also to the heart, lungs, and nervous system. In that way, blood that contains the ingredients necessary for intensive and sustained muscular and nervous activity is directed away from various visceral structures and toward other structures—structures likely to be intensively involved in defending the organism from injury or the threat of injury. Digestive functions may best be postponed in emergency situations. (6) Cardiac rate and vigor of cardiac contraction increase; this serves to propel oxygen-suffused blood to structures in need of it. (7) Through chemical changes, blood is rendered more coagulable, that is, the blood-clotting process is accelerated. This reduces the likelihood of serious blood loss through injury. (8) Along with peripheral vasodilation, sweating is accelerated and increased perspiration permits ready release of heat generated by increased muscular activity. (See Figure 3.2.)

The biological utility or adaptive function of each component in this reaction is obvious. The reaction pattern is one in which *energy resources are mobilized* and one that *prepares the organism for sudden, extensive activity—for the violent expenditure of energy* needed to fight or flee— activities of a defensive or protective sort. It renders the organism capable of expending vast quantities of energy, sometimes over long periods of time; that is, it provides the resources for vigorous, and prolonged activity. In these ways, the pattern or reaction is generally—not specifically— adaptive.

The behavior described is of intrinsic interest. Since this implicit reaction influences rate, quality, and intensity of explicit behavior, it is of special psychological significance. Its biological significance is that the preparations for explicit activities are generally effective and serviceable to the organism in emergency situations—situations of danger or stress; it has survival value for the organism and the species.

On the basis of original research and careful analysis, Hans Selye has amplified and extended this fundamental idea of Cannon, namely, that a variety of situations may provide a constellation of autonomically mediated physiological changes that are of adaptive value to the organism. Selye uses the terms stress and stressor to refer to a wide variety of physical factors and psychological stimuli—including emotional stimuli—that provoke extensive adaptive patterns of reaction. While indicating many of the responses pointed out by Cannon, Selye has emphasized and elucidated the role of the adrenocorticotropic hormone (ACTH), a substance liberated by the pituitary gland (which in turn activates the adrenal gland), in the general adaptation syndrome. The general adaptation syndrome involves three successive phases: the alarm reaction, the stage of resistance, and the stage of exhaustion.

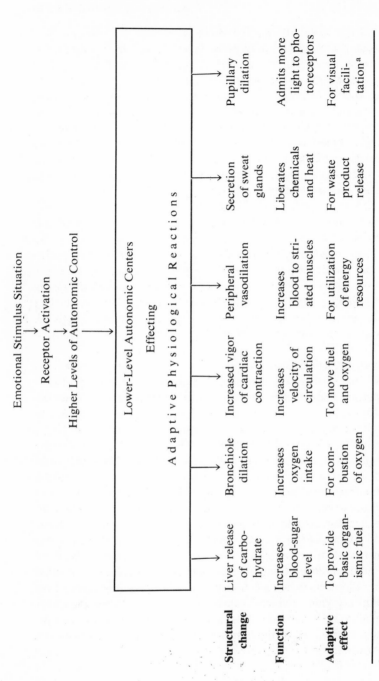

Emotional Stimulus Situation
→
Receptor Activation
→
Higher Levels of Autonomic Control
→

Lower-Level Autonomic Centers

Effecting

Adaptive Physiological Reactions

	Liver release of carbo-hydrate	Bronchiole dilation	Increased vigor of cardiac contraction	Peripheral vasodilation	Secretion of sweat glands	Pupillary dilation
Structural change						
Function	Increases blood-sugar level	Increases oxygen intake	Increases velocity of circulation	Increases blood to stri-ated muscles	Liberates chemicals and heat	Admits more light to pho-toreceptors
Adaptive effect	To provide basic organ-ismic fuel	For com-bustion of oxygen	To move fuel and oxygen	For utilization of energy resources	For waste product release	For visual facili-tation[a]

[a] Especially in dim illumination; serves to forewarn of danger.

FIGURE 3-2.1   Common physiological mechanisms of adaptation in response to emotional stimulation

The physiological reactions to emotional stimulation specified above are representative, not exhaustive. However, the adaptive significance of each reaction is apparent. Further, receptor activation via the stimulation presented, may simultaneously lead to cognitive arousal and to overt behavior.

DEVELOPMENT OF EXPLICIT REACTIONS
TO EMOTIONAL STIMULATION

From an overt behavioral point of view, the development of emotional re-actions can be characterized as originating in the newborn or young infant, with *general excitement,* which within a few months becomes further dif-ferentiated into *distress,* a negative or withdrawal response, and *delight,* a positive or approach response (Bridges, 1932). Each of these—*excitement, distress,* and *delight*—is further differentiated in time, and eventually the mature adult becomes capable of expressing a wide variety of kinds and nuances of emotional reaction.

If the constellations of overt behaviors of human adults that accom-pany emotions (defining emotion in physiological terms as has been done) were to be given distinctive names, our present language would prove in-sufficient. A wide variety of subtleties of emotional expression occur. Among the more frequent of the general categories of terms used are fear, anger, hate, love, affection, elation, jealousy, sorrow, grief, and shame. More specifically, a variety of terms may be used to indicate varying in-tensities or kinds of reaction within each category. For example, instead of the generic term fear, words such as apprehension, trepidation, terror, dis-may, or horror may be more precise for particular situations involving somewhat different reactions.

Two broad categories of factors obviously underlie the development of emotional behavior. These are maturation and learning. From the stand-point of psychology, maturation refers to the functioning of a structure as a mere consequence of internal biological growth and development. Tears cannot be shed until the lacrimal glands are sufficiently developed; various sounds cannot be made until teeth have erupted; smiling cannot occur until there is sufficient development of facial muscles. Maturational variables are much influenced by genetic factors. Assuming an adequate environ-ment of nutrition, temperature, pressure, and other sustaining conditions, structural development (much as a result of maturation, which in turn de-pends substantially on genetic variables) tends to occur in an orderly se-quence for a particular species. In the human, certain structures develop within the first few weeks following birth and many, of course, even prior to birth; on the other hand, certain structures—the sex glands, for example—mature and become functional only many years after birth.

Most emotional behavior—for example, biting, swinging a club, run-ning away, and saying "Ye angels and little fishes!" or something more colorful—depends on both maturation and learning.

The differently named emotions may be distinguished in terms of (1) consistent aspects of the eliciting stimulus situation, (2) consistent explicit

TABLE 3.1 Stimulus Situations and Reaction Patterns Characteristic of Variously Named Emotions[a]

Emotion[b]	Aspects of Adequate Stimulus Situation	Representative Explicit Reaction Pattern
Fear	Intense pain or threat of pain	Abient response (withdrawal, escape, avoidance), perhaps inactivation or concealment
Anger	Blockage of strong motive	Vigorous, hostile approach
Elation	Unexpected and perhaps prolonged and intense motive gratification	Adient response. Enthusiastic movement and approach
Disgust	Distasteful, repugnant, loathsome stimulus (e.g., rotting meat, garbage, observation of person blowing nose without handkerchief, etc.)	Rejecting and aversive behavior. Casting away, spurning, repelling the stimulus or withdrawing from it
Lust or sex (in male)	Attractive, acceptable, encouraging female. Also kissing, stroking, light pressure on erogenous zones	Movements of tactual exploration and manipulation of stimulus object. Penis erection and vaginal insertion. Movements to maximize active stimulation of the penis
Lust or sex (in female)	Attractive, acceptable, encouraging male. Also kissing, stroking light pressure on erogenous zones	Erection of nipple tips and of clitoris. Secretion from Bartholin glands. Movements to retain and maximize stimulation of vaginal canal by penis. Rhythmic contraction of constrictor muscles of vagina (during coitus)

[a] Common physiological reactions to each of the emotions in the table include: Changes in cardiac rate, cardiac amplitude, blood pressure, respirational pattern, adrenal-gland secretion, digestive activities, sweating, and GSR. It is hoped that with further research, distinctive physiological reactions will be thoroughly itemized (in addition to the common reactions) and that better terms will be developed for designating discrete emotional patterns.

[b] Emotion is a generic term for "emotional reaction-constellation."

response patterns, and (3) the physiological reaction-constellation consistencies that coexist. A sample of a few such patterns is outlined in Table 3.1.

The reactions specified are general, although for particular emotional stimuli, one or more components of the physiological pattern may be unique. Physiological changes may differ in kind, in direction, and in degree from person to person and from time to time in the same individual for very similar stimulus situations. There are likewise vast individual differences in the explicit behavior patterns; for each "emotion," mention has been made of only a few core responses that are encountered with great frequency. There are, of course, characteristic gestures, facial expressions, and verbal reactions in addition to the reactions specified in Table 3.1.

CHAPTER FOUR

LEARNING

A fundamental point in my position is that with few exceptions *psychosomatic disorders are learned*. This chapter considers some central ideas in the field of learning with particular reference to psychosomatic disorders.

DEFINITION OF LEARNING

In the course of development, human beings display increasing potential for plasticity and versatility in behavior. They tend to modify their behaviors periodically, particularly as circumstances change. Some of these behavioral modifications are merely of a temporary nature. Others are more permanent and may be considered learned.

In other words, on the basis of man's fundamental capacities, (a) *for distinguishing* various aspects of his environment, (b) *for reacting* to that environment, (c) *for varying his behavior* in response to stimulation and to changes in stimulation, and (d) *for preserving the effects of such stimulus sensitivity and reactivity,* humans display high-grade learning competence.

More specifically, *learning is a relatively stable modification in stimulus-response relationships as a consequence of functional interaction with the environment by means of the senses, rather than as a consequence of structural growth and differentiation.* The phrase *relatively stable* suggests that whatever is acquired is relatively durable or persistent. The phrase *modification in stimulus-response relationships* distinguishes between the innate and the acquired, and suggests that in learning changes or alterations in stimulus-response relationships occur. Such changes may involve (a) associating new stimuli with old responses, (b) associating old stimuli with new responses, or (c) apprehending and associating new stimuli and new responses, that is, combining the effects of stimulation with reactions in new ways. The phrase *as a consequence of interaction with the environment by means of the senses* distinguishes learned changes in behavior from other changes in behavior such as those that may result from brain damage, fatigue, or drug ingestion. Learning, then, involves not only responsiveness but also sensitivity to and discrimination of environmental energies. And, the final phrase, *rather than as a consequence of structural growth and differentiation,* distinguishes learned phenomena from behavioral modifications that are consequences of innate structural change, that is, the consequences of maturation.

PRINCIPLES OF LEARNING

A number of principles can be formulated to indicate major influences on learning processes. Perhaps several such principles can be summarized into a single, brief statement. *Stimuli and responses contiguously and frequently associated with each other and with rewarding circumstances in the appropriately motivated organism tend to be learned.* This general statement can be analyzed and qualified and extended by specifying a small group of more elementary principles.

1. Motivational principle. Other things being equal, the most efficacious learning occurs when the organism is motivated. Relatively little learning occurs without it. For example, a man motivated to learn to speak Spanish in order to qualify for a job he desires as a sales representative to a Latin American country, learns to speak Spanish in short order. Without such motivation it is unlikely that Spanish would have been studied or learned. Or as another example, a young man strongly motivated to enter a religious seminary to become a minister, studies the Bible carefully in order to pass an entrance examination.

2. Principle of reinforcement and nonreinforcement. Other things being equal, reactions that satisfy or reinforce the organism's motivating conditions tend to persist or become strengthened so that on recurrence of the motivating or stimulating conditions, those responses will reappear; reactions that fail to satisfy or reinforce the organism's motivating conditions tend to disappear or become weakened, so that on recurrence of the stimulating or motivating conditions, those responses are less likely to appear. For example, a youngster who successfully gains candy, money, toys, and similar desired items from other youngsters by threatening, bullying, and hitting them is thereby reinforced and learns to replicate that kind of behavior. If such behaviors are met with lack of success or with punishment, such delinquency behavior is not rewarded and such learning is thereby discouraged. Another example: through trying a variety of cosmetics, in terms of compliments elicited from friends, a young woman learns which combination provides the effects she desires. By being ridiculed, scolded, or punished for certain behavior—eating habits, dressing habits, working habits, and the like—the learning of such behavior is often discouraged.

3. Principle of contiguity. Other things being equal, stimulating conditions and organismic responses that occur close together temporally tend to be organized together. In walking to a friend's home several times with that friend, a right turn is made at a particular corner where there is a brown frame house. Eventually the house is identified with the corner and is also "associated" with a right turn at that point—that is, brown frame house (stimulus) and right turn (organismic response) become associated.

4. Principle of frequency. Historically this has also been called the principle of practice, repetition, exercise, or use. Other things being equal, the more frequently a reaction follows a particular stimulating condition, the more likely it is to recur at some future time under similar stimulating conditions. For example, if the word "doggie" is said in the presence of a four-legged furry animal a number of times, the infant or young child eventually learns to associate the spoken word "doggie" with that four-legged furry animal. An adolescent touched a hot radiator on several different occasions and after receiving stimulation from it each time, quickly withdrew from the radiator. Now mere sight of the radiator leads to withdrawal reactions on the part of the youngster.

Much in the way of learning can be accounted for in terms of the brief set of principles outlined above, although a variety of other determinants may also be formulated as principles.

FOUNDATIONS OF LEARNING

Explicit and Implicit Stimulation and Reaction

Theoretically, any stimulus that the organism can apprehend may lead to any response of which the organism is capable. Corollaries to this general statement would include at least the following.

1. An explicit stimulus may produce an implicit reaction. For example, the sight of a wild animal rapidly approaching a man may lead to an

increase in the heart rate of that man or an increase in his blood pressure or the secretion of his adrenal glands; any of these reactions is implicit.

2. An implicit stimulus may produce an explicit reaction. For example, a pressure sensation from the stomach of a man who has recently consumed a heavy meal may lead to his going to the medicine chest and taking a pill to aid digestion or to his drinking a glass of water that he believes will have a similar effect or to his commenting, "I should not have eaten so much." The stimulus indicated is implicit; all of the reactions cited are explicit.

Obviously, implicit stimuli may induce implicit responses and explicit stimuli may induce explicit responses also. Our principal questions—the ones whose answers we are most interested in elucidating because of their relevance for the psychosomatic area—are: What stimulus leads to what responses? Why does a particular stimulus lead to a particular response? What are the major determinants of particular responses?

Changes in stimulus-response relationships that occur in time via environmental interaction as indicated are much a function of learning. What is the nature of the learning process?

Kinds of Learning

Two basic forms of learning are sometimes distinguished, (1) classical conditioning and (2) operant learning, which is also sometimes called instrumental or trial-and-error learning.

Classical conditioning is essentially stimulus-substitution learning and in its pure form is rare. It is a kind of *connection* learning. In conditioning, a neutral stimulus is paired with a stimulus that elicits a particular response. As a consequence of such paired presentation—often of several such paired presentations—the originally neutral stimulus becomes effective in evoking the response. In other words, a new stimulus produces an old response—a new stimulus is substituted for an old one. In experimental situations the stimuli are deliberately presented at about the same time and therefore both are in close temporal proximity to the response; this kind of learning—stimulus-substitution learning—depends very much on contiguity.

Operant learning—selection-and-connection learning—is much more versatile. It involves the organism's *actively discriminating and selecting stimuli* from the constellation of stimuli constantly present *and associating with such stimuli a particular response or group of responses* from the multiplicity of responses that occur. For simplicity consider a rat in a 30-blind maze. The animal inspects his surroundings, using vision, smell, touch, temperature, and perhaps even taste and hearing; in the process, it makes many movements, examining the walls, the floor, and the wire-mesh ceiling, and it enters into dead-end blinds. It may spend many hours doing this, each time finding food in the food box far distant from the starting point. Eventually, after much such exploration, manipulation, and locomotion, the animal runs directly from the start box to the goal box in minimum time and without entering any blind alleys. The animal has discriminated and related certain stimuli in the situation and has associated those stimuli with certain responses that have also been selected and differentiated from the variety earlier exhibited. Thus, a crack in the floor of the initial stem of the maze becomes associated with a right turn, and a paint spot on the wall in the next passageway is associated with a subsequent left turn; a particular shadow in the succeeding alley is related to another left turn, and a particular odor or sound or unevenness of the floor in the next alley comes to be associated with the next right turn. In that way, stimuli and responses become associated in sequence.

As a second and perhaps even simpler example, let us consider a kitten in a Skinner box. This is a boxlike structure having in it a lever that can be depressed and a food trough into which a pellet of food is released after the lever is depressed. The hungry kitten in this device explores; it examines and paws the sides and ceiling as well as the floor. Sooner or later in exploring the lever area, it depresses the lever and a food pellet appears, which the hungry animal eats. With further exploratory movements, the lever is again depressed, each time followed by the appearance of food, which the animal eats. Eventually the lever is discriminated and reacted to more directly with the appropriate "depress" movement. The stimulus, sight of the lever, and the response, depression of the lever, have been selected from the large number of stimuli and responses that occur in the situation, and the two have become linked or associated. (See Figure 4.1.)

Most human learning is a function, at least in part, of operant learning, including learning to make speech sounds, to read, to write, to operate machinery, to play a musical instrument, to dress, to dance, and to perform most overt behavior. Humans also learn why, when, and how to conceal overt actions accompanying emotional behavior as well as why, when, and how to express them. Such learned responses that accompany emotional reactions are developed gradually; they are acquired by a process of gradual change through successive approximations or modifications. Autonomic responses—the essence of emotional behavior—are typically subject to much less direct control but may in part be acquired in a similar way.

Although classical conditioning and operant learning will be of particular value in subsequent discussion, it is probable that other kinds or vari-

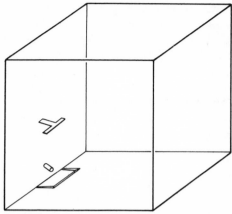

FIGURE 4-1. The Skinner box—a chamber used in experimental studies of learning with animals.

eties of learning can also be distinguished, at least in terms of content and method.

In one type of learning, two or more discriminated aspects of the stimulus situation are associated; this may be called *perceptual* learning. In another kind of learning, two or more discriminated aspects of a stimulus situation are related to each other and to a response to solve a problem; this has been called *insightful* learning. Also, learning based fundamentally on replicating observed responses has been called *observational* learning or learning by *imitation*. In addition, new learning may be achieved by internal manipulation of cognitions earlier acquired via the more basic learning procedures.

Another classification distinguishes *between* three broad categories of learning—S-S (stimulus-stimulus), S-R (stimulus-response), and R-R (response-response) learning. Of the three, least attention has been paid to R-R learning.

Response-response learning is concerned with the simultaneous learning of two separate responses or with the learning of two responses in sequence.

Three mechanisms may be suggested for R-R learning, particularly when the Rs appear to occur in close temporal proximity or simultaneously. More specifically, these include the simultaneous occurrence (1) of an autonomic response with an autonomic response, (2) of a somatic response with a somatic response, and (3) of an autonomic response with a somatic response.

Theoretically, any overt act and any physiological act may be linked together. Representative of overt acts are frowning, groaning, crouching, shaking the fist, trembling, running away, pulling at one's clothing (such as twisting a button or belt buckle), or drumming the fingers. Representative of autonomic or physiological acts are changes in secretion of salivary, gastric, or adrenal glands and changes in rate of cardiac contraction, in patterns of vasomotor response, in bronchiole dilation or bronchiole constriction, in digestive movements, in relaxations or tightenings of the anal sphincter, and in liver releases of carbohydrates.

Typically, patterns of activity in both the overt and physiological realms are likely to be linked rather than single acts, although the principle remains the same.

A youngster may associate his slender, craggy-faced, red-haired uncle, a particular room in his uncle's home, a set of framed pictures there, a group of toys, certain accents, tones, and spoken words, the odor of furniture polish, the taste of chocolate, and excessive pressure from his (the youngster's) stomach *with* circumstances in which severe punishment was administered by the uncle, in turn eliciting trembling, struggling to get away, unusual breathing patterns, screaming, clenching the fist, and a variety of autonomic responses (including increased heart rate) on the part of the youngster. Let us consider just one aspect of the stimulus situation and two responses. The stimulus is the uncle who administered severe physical punishment to the youngster's posterior; the responses we select are clenching the first and increased heartbeat.

At least three relatively distinct concepts of linkage in relationships between the two acts—clenching the fist and accelerating rate of cardiac contraction—may be proposed.

1. The simplest notion is that a single stimulus such as sight of the uncle leads to clenching the fist, and that same stimulus also simultaneously leads via other nervous system structures to cardiac acceleration.

2. A second viewpoint holds that in response to sight of the uncle, one of the two responses first occurs, let us say clenching the fist. However, kinesthetic or tactual or other sensations from clenching the fist then reach the central nervous system and trigger central nervous mechanisms, resulting in cardiac acceleration. This, then, involves a sensory feedback device by which one response is linked with another. Sensory stimulation from the heart presumably could also lead to the clenched fist.

3. A third concept suggests that the sight of the uncle—via central structures concerned with visual perception—mediates impulses to one or both of the motor centers responsible for the behaviors, and that there are *in addition neural linkages in the central nervous system between these two neuromotor centers* so that excitation of one leads to activation of the

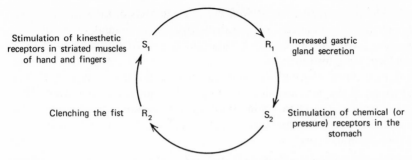

FIGURE 4-2. Recurrent stimulus-reaction circuit involving explicit and implicit responses.

other. In time, then, because of central nervous connections functionalized between the respective motor centers involved, the responses will occur simultaneously, or at least in very rapid and overlapping succession. Excitation of the motor center for either response directs impulses that excite the motor center for the other response.

A point to be noted is that responses themselves produce stimulation. Movement of muscles activates kinesthetic receptors in the muscles; changes in blood pressure or digestive activity may activate chemical or pressure receptors in the circulatory or digestive systems. Such response-induced stimulation may serve to elicit new reactions.

Now suppose that stimulation induced by the second response served to elicit the first response. Under such conditions a persistent or sustained circle of activity could be developed. S_1 evokes R_1, which produces S_2 evoking R_2, which produces S_1 to reinitiate the cycle. Recurrent stimulus-reaction circuits may be represented in this way. (See Figure 4.2.)

The concept of *response-induced stimulation* as an elicitor of subsequent responses—perhaps a succession of them—helps account for chains of acts and for complex behavior sequences.

Analysis of the Stimulus Situation

The stimulus situation is the total complex constellation of energies impinging on an organism at a particular time and place. Several aspects of such a situation may be distinguished, including the critical or eliciting stimulus, major associated stimuli, and concomitant stimuli.

1. The critical or *eliciting stimulus* is the aspect of the stimulus situation that is most significant in provoking or producing a particular response.

2. The major *associated stimuli* are those aspects of the stimulus situation closely associated temporally—from the standpoint of the organism—with the critical eliciting stimulus. (These are *major* immediate or adjacent stimulus aspects.)

3. *Concomitant stimuli* (or stimulus accompaniments) are the remaining aspects of the stimulus situation that appear to be less significant; they may be incidental or chance stimuli or regular accompaniments of the critical eliciting and major associated stimuli. (These are *minor* immediate or adjacent stimulus aspects.)

As an example let us consider the child—previously cited—who displayed a variety of responses to punishment administered by his uncle. The *critical stimulus* may be the uncle and his various sensory properties. The *associated stimuli* may be sight of the stick that the uncle used as a weapon, words the uncle used, and certain conspicuous features of the room in which punishment occurred—perhaps the odor of furniture polish, the set of framed pictures, and the oversized and outdated furniture. *Concomitant stimuli* may include other minor features of the room, excessive pressure from the stomach due to earlier overconsumption of chocolate, sounds of a train passing by, and noises of the youngster's dog scratching at the door.

Basic Concepts

Phenomena relating to learning have been organized under a number of concepts including redintegration, generalization, and symbol learning.

1. Redintegration. The principle of redintegration is based on the idea that the stimulus situation is made up of many elements. When a group of such elements—A, B, C, D, E, and F—have formed a whole, the recurrence of any one tends to reinstate the others. The redintegration concept proposed by Hollingworth (1928) maintains that a single element of a former complex event tends to revive the total stimulus situation and the behavior associated with it. Thus, a few musical notes played on a single instrument may tend to revive implicitly many of the *sensory experiences and reactions* to them of a Schubert concert—a full orchestration—heard many years before, including recollections of the place, the decor, the season, the sight of the musicians on stage, the many instruments and their sound systems, the perfumed fragrance of one's escort, and a variety of other details, *including autonomic sensations and explicit reactions.*

Consider the youngster punished by his red-haired uncle and the withdrawal reaction and physiological responses engendered. According to the *redintegration principle* any stimulus aspect of the situation—the punishment room, the framed picture, the toys, the furniture, the uncle's accent and words, pressure from the stomach, the furniture polish odor—any single one of them may serve to revive the others and also the resultant emotional reaction.

2. Generalization. Generalization refers to the phenomenon in which learning extends from a specific stimulus to all the stimuli of a class, category, or type. Thus, Pavlov's dog, conditioned to respond to a tone of a particular frequency, would also respond to tones of other frequencies, both higher and lower. A youngster who has learned to pet a particular rabbit may display a similar reaction to other rabbits and also to cats, dogs, hamsters, fur pieces, and perhaps a variety of similar stimuli.

Again, consider the youngster punished by his red-haired uncle and the ensuing negative reaction. According to the *generalization concept* the youngster may display a negative reaction not only to his red-haired uncle but also to all men with red hair, to rooms similar to the punishment room, to many different framed pictures, to toys resembling those present in the punishment situation, to all oversized furniture, to all accents similar to that of the uncle, to a variety of visceral pressures, and to many furniture-polish odors. Each of these constitutes a relatively independent generalization continuum.

In terms of probability and quantity of response, the greater the similarity of the new or "generalized" stimulus to the one originally associated with the response, the more effective the stimulus in producing the response. Generalization seems to be based in part on a failure to detect stimulus differences. It may also be based on detecting stimulus similarities.

3. Symbol learning. Two kinds of symbols may be distinguished: neural symbols, which are implicit and stimulus symbols, which are explicit. In the human, as a consequence of exposure—in some cases repeated exposure—to a particular situation, a modification takes place within the organism, presumably within the brain, which serves then to represent the stimulus situation. This neural modification functions as an implicit representation of the stimulus situation and is called a neural symbol. Once established, it may operate in the absence of the original stimulus situation, not only to represent it, but also to produce the responses originally associated with the explicit stimulus. In the case of emotion-provoking stimulation, this of course means the physiological reactions of emotion. Thus, to return to our example, a *neural symbol* of the red-haired uncle (i.e., an intrabrain event in the absence of the uncle or any overt representation of him) may serve to reactivate the constellation of physiological responses of emotion, though probably in attenuated form.

Stimuli that represesent events of a happy holiday—for example, the words "motorboat race," "dinner with Katie," "swimming with Deanna," or the sight of a tennis racket, a Gibson Lake Theater ticket, or a swimming trophy—insofar as they represent various happy events, may be considered explicit symbols and may serve to elicit the physiological effects and affects associated with that holiday. The explicit symbol or stimulus symbol of a cat—a drawing, a silhouette, a photograph, or a shadow of a cat or the word "cat"—may revive a different set of physiological effects and different affects in a youngster who earlier was painfully scratched by the now-symbolized cat. A neural symbol (or implicit surrogate) of an employer by an employee who two hours before was severely and unfairly reprimanded by the employer may elicit a still-different set of physiological effects and affects.

Neural symbols may be combined and associated with each other in various ways, and the term "thinking" is given to the process whereby the world is considered by manipulating such symbols. Neural symbols are responsible for recall memory, and those associated with well-practiced explicit (as well as implicit) responses also trigger such responses as relatively automatic behavior. Other symbols are less directly associated with overt behavior.

Learning Visceral and Somatic Pathological Reactions

A man with a headache due to extensive vasoconstriction of blood vessels within the brain may attribute this condition to concomitant circumstances, for example, to loud noises or disharmonious sounds, and may say "That gives me a headache." Saying this, thinking it, hearing the noise stimuli, having the extensive pattern of vasoconstrictions, and "experiencing" a headache—since these events occur simultaneously—tend to be associated together. Saying later, then, that a certain circumstance "gives me a headache" (or even thinking it via symbolic representations) may directly lead to the vasoconstrictive pattern and the resulting headache report.

Parallel developments may be cited. Vomiting concomitant with, preceded by, or followed by a stimulus pattern (such as a pain in the stomach, an unpleasant voice, a conflictful or difficult situation) may lead the involved person at a later time to respond to similar circumstances by reviving the neural equivalent—the symbol or engram—of "That makes me want to throw up" which, as earlier associated, is related to vomiting.

There may be conditions of increased blood pressure and increased body surface temperature that lead a person to say, in response to a situation, "That makes my blood boil." Such physiological reactions and their accompanying labeling stimuli together with the verbal responses and the stimuli accompanying all the reactions tend to become associated. Later, then, the person may say, after observing or hearing about an emotional situation, "That makes my blood boil." Merely saying it may, as a consequence of prior contiguity and frequency of association, lead to replication —perhaps, but not necessarily, in diminished intensity—of the physiological response. Or the individual need not actually say the words; simply reviving the symbol, the engram, the neural equivalent of the symbol situation, that is, the thought, may lead to the physiological reaction and its consequences.

Learned Behavior in General

Normally, behavior that is acquired or learned is in the direction of what is socially approved or at least socially permitted; typically, such behavior contributes to more effective living or more efficient performance or to the avoidance of pain and difficulty. Sometimes, however, people do develop behaviors that are socially disapproved and that contribute to inefficient performance and the creation of personally painful and difficult conditions; these latter categories of behavior are often regarded as abnormal. One point worthy of note, then, is that the same principles operate in the development of both normal behavior and maladjustive or abnormal behavior. The determinants of deviant behavior are generally to be understood in terms of unusual magnitudes and combinations of influences; no new or unique principles are necessary for understanding abnormal, deviant, or pathological behavior.

Walking is gradually acquired in the developing infant. The many falls that the youngster experiences in the course of its attempting to remain erect and to locomote are gradually reduced, and in time the efficiency of his locomotor behavior is progressively increased. In attempting to talk, the first sounds are only very crude approximations to the precisely articulated sequences of sound that, in time, are gradually differentiated. Walking and talking, as well as many other somatic behaviors, are readily accepted as involving learning. The learning of autonomic responses may not be quite so obvious. Nevertheless, such responses also are learned; and the sequential differentiation is also similar.

The principles cited earlier apply particularly to learning that involves the somatic musculature. These principles, however, also apply in varying degrees to autonomic learning—learning involving smooth muscle and glands, including the soft internal organs that are collectively termed the viscera. On the other hand, there may also be some additional principles necessary in order to facilitate understanding of special characteristics of autonomic learning.

Let us consider autonomic learning and its nature and also the question of to what extent autonomic learning and autonomic control are within the capabilities of the normal functioning of the individual organism.

Autonomic Learning

The work of Ivan P. Pavlov (1928) in conditioning dogs to salivate to an auditory stimulus is illustrative of autonomic learning. A brief review of the method and results discloses operation in conditioning of the four basic principles of learning already specified—motivation, reinforcement, contiguity, and frequency. The fact of autonomic learning is so clearly established that the classical work of Pavlov with autonomic learning has often been used as a paradigm for somatic learning.

Learning and Emotion—
Characteristics of Emotional Learning

Following are half a dozen principles concerning learning and emotion. (1) *Stimuli eliciting emotional reactions may be learned in a single trial on occasion.* Many reports indicate that certain vivid, dramatic, and sometimes traumatic situations may become strongly associated with emotional reactions in but a single trial. Learned stimuli involving intense fear reactions may remain viable over a period of many years, even though there is no further contact with the original evoking stimulus situation. Sometimes only a few trials are required. (2) *Explicit emotional reactions tend to be persistent.* Explicit behaviors in reaction to stimulus situations provoking emotional reactivity tend to be persistent. Often stereotyped overt reactions are firmly established in a single trial. (3) *Implicit emotional reactions tend to be persistent.* Implicit behavior in response to emotion-provoking stimulating situations once established tend to persevere (Lacey et al., 1953). (4) *Affect—or at least reports of affect—to certain elements of earlier encountered emotion-provoking stimulus situations tends to be persistent.* (5) *Recall of specific details of traumatic emotion-provoking stimulus situations is frequently very poor, despite the fact that various stimulus aspects of the situation may serve effectively to revive the implicit behavior, the explicit behavior, and the affect originally associated with the situation.* Certain general characteristics or conspicuous stimulus elements, however, may be recalled. (6) *There may be generalization effects from the original stimulus situation engendering affective responses to similar situations.* Such generalization is not substantially different from generalization that occurs in nonaffective learning.

In summarizing these principles, it is evident that emotional reactions are associated readily with new stimuli (and symbols) and that such reactions including not merely the essential physiological changes, but also the accompanying explicit behaviors and affect if any, are also extremely persistent. Further, although details of the eliciting stimulus situation are not readily recalled, stimulus elements may still be effective in eliciting the emotional reaction; and principles of stimulus generalization apply as well to emotional responses as to other responses. There is a substantial array of clinical evidence, as well as some experimental evidence, to support these principles. The following examples may be illustrative:

Case 4.1. Mr. A, who as a youngster was severely and painfully hurt when hit by a truck after he ran into the street at a small resort town, displays negative affect and profound autonomic arousal to the mention of the name of that resort town or to the word "truck."

Case 4.2. Mr. B, as a soldier during World War II with his infantry squad while pinned down by overwhelming machine-gun fire in an unprotected area, was dive-bombed and strafed by enemy aircraft, during which time all other members of his squad were killed and he was severely wounded, responds with negative affect and autonomic activation to words such as war, battle, and machine gun, and refuses to ride in or even approach airplanes. He also displays profound autonomic arousal to loud staccato sounds resembling machine-gun fire.

Case 4.3. Mr. C many years ago, as a passenger, was in a serious train accident and, although he was uninjured, witnessed the pain, suffering, and death of many others. Now he is emotionally aroused by sounds of a moving train or a train whistle and by other aspects of the simulus situation, such as the name of the place at which the accident occurred.

Case 4.4. Miss D, when about three years old, was lost for almost two days in a woods near Ishpeming, Michigan, during which time she had nothing to eat, was frightened by the dark and by sounds of wild animals, and was badly scratched and bruised by the sharp thorns and burrs of the vegetation and by frequently falling down, reacts with affect to mention of woods or Michigan and is very fearful of darkness and of animals.

Although all of the examples illustrate anxiety or fear-provoking situations, the same principles appear to operate for other negative emotional reactions and for positive affective reactions also.

EVIDENCE OF AUTONOMIC LEARNING

Autonomic responses, including the autonomic responses involved in emotional behavior, are typically not much under the control of the reacting individual, although sometimes they may be regulated by, that is, brought under the control of, external stimuli.

There are, however, several lines of evidence that suggest that autonomic response mechanisms can be brought under the direct immediate control of external stimulation or of implicit symbols representing such stimulation. Four lines of evidence are cited below: (1) evidence based on observation of normal psychological development, (2) evidence provided by yogis, (3) evidence from studies in hypnosis, and (4) experimental evidence of autonomic learning.

Evidence Based on Observations of Normal Psychological Development

Lacrimal gland secretion—in this case crying—may occur immediately as a reflex to the fumes of onions or of ammonia or other volatile chemical irritants assaulting the eyes, or it may be the result of a foreign agent, such as a tiny speck of real estate, impinging on the surface of the eye, or it may be a response to painful tissue damage. On the other hand, some people can *learn* to cry on a number of different bases. Here are a few of them.

1. A youngster cries, perhaps because it is being stuck with a pin. Mother reacts by picking up the infant and removing the pin; this is a reinforcing state of affairs. Further, mother may cuddle the infant, stroke and fondle it, talk to it, and otherwise give it special attention. Crying behavior, then, has been multiply rewarded. Later, the youngster under other conditions in which it strives to acquire an attractive stimulus object— perhaps a toy or a piece of candy or a pillow or whatever—and fails to do so, engages in various behaviors including crying. If crying results in persons in the environment providing the youngster with the toy or candy or pillow, again crying behavior has been rewarded. The youngster may thereafter use crying behavior in a variety of situations. Assuming that crying results in acquisition of the desired goal frequently, it is likely to become firmly established in the youngster's behavioral repertoire, and to be readily employed. Here learning occurs largely because *the crying response has been rewarded.*

2. A handsome one-year-old human infant is attracted to a handsome one-year-old cat. The cat responds to the youngster's effort to play with it by severely scratching the youngster and causing her to cry. The infant's contact with the cat a few months later again results in the youngster's crying in reaction to its being promptly and painfully scratched by the cat. And a few weeks later the infant again provides a vigorous crying response after being scratched and bitten by the cat. Thereafter, the infant may begin to cry at merely seeing the cat. Here learning occurs on the basis of *association of the cat with physical stimulation that resulted in crying.* With regard to crying also, accomplished actresses may learn to cry

—to shed tears on cue. And some youngsters learn to shed tears in anticipation of punishment.

Examples to indicate the development of trembling responses and
changes in heart rate, adrenal gland secretion, sweating, muscle tension,
blood pressure, thyroid gland activity, and blood chemistry, among others,
could be developed by specific application of the same set of principles to
a variety of situations associated with each of the reactions listed; crying
reactions are not unique, merely illustrative. Apparently some individuals
learn to reverse peristaltic movements to various stimulus situations, and
a few have even achieved independent control over reversed peristaltic
movements of such magnitude as to produce vomiting (in response to internal as well as external stimulus cues).

Let us consider blinking and breathing. Blinking is a response that occurs periodically and rather automatically, but blinking may be learned.
Conditioned response research in which a puff of air directed against the
eyeball elicits a blinking response indicates that such a response can be
conditioned to a buzzer stimulus. Patterns of rapid or exaggerated blinking
may also be learned in everyday life, however, perhaps as an attention-
getting device.

Breathing is also normally a relatively automatic and periodic response. However, various aspects can be learned. A gasp initiated by a
sudden unexpected stimulus can come to be elicited by new stimuli that
earlier had been associated with the unexpected stimulus. Also, complex
patterns of breathing behavior can be learned and functionalized as independent responses, perhaps to express sexual passion or the pretense of it.

Interested husbands and wives can learn control over genital contractions and secretions in coitus to achieve mutually desired levels of reci-
procity in responding. In part, of course, this is done by cooperative
regulation of critical eliciting aspects of the stimulus situation and via concomitant interpersonal regulation of somatic activity. The point is, however, that the fundamental reflexes involved are autonomic, and *originally*
they are not so readily "controlled" or directed by the individuals concerned. A learning process is involved.

Bladder and bowel responses that in early life are not under the direct
and immediate control of the infant are brought under such control
through a learning process. The bladder and the intestine are smooth muscle structures. In very early life, when the bladder becomes filled with
liquid wastes, it reflexly discharges; in early life, when the intestine is sufficiently distended by the accumulation of semisolid waste products, it too
reflexly empties. In time, however, the youngster comes to develop increasing
control over bladder and bowel discharges. Learning, formal and informal,

is involved in the process and, within quite narrow limits, only certain restricted circumstances and stimulus conditions become appropriate for bladder and bowel responses; the youngster learns when, where, and how to control eliminatory behaviors. It is not merely the discomfort produced by the consequences of random release of bladder and bowel wastes that leads to these modifications in the stimulus-response relationship; there are, in addition, the avoidance of punishment, which should not be underestimated, and the granting of rewards provided by society as represented at first by the youngster's parents or parent surrogates and later by authority figures as well as peers. However, our major point is that autonomic responses that originally function relatively autonomously, in a reflex fashion, can be brought under the control of the individual via sequences of adaptive responses to internal stimulation, and in the course of normal development many of them are typically brought under such control.

Evidence Provided by the Performances of Yogis

Several reports and observations from India suggest that the yogis, through their techniques of meditation and contemplation, have been successful in controlling physiological activities that ordinarily are not directly controlled by those unacquainted with practice of the yoga techniques. These phenomena include substantial reduction in respiratory activity, cessation of auditorily detectable heartbeat, reduction in basal metabolic rate, control of gastrointestinal activity, and other perhaps less dramatic reactions. Unfortunately, there are few careful research studies in the area, and most of the reported observations are uncorroborated. Nevertheless, there seems to be a sufficiency of information to suggest the authenticity of extensive personally regulated or self-controlled direct manipulation of physiological processes by at least certain individuals (Yeats-Brown, 1937; Behanan, 1937). Lowered rates of carbon dioxide production indicative of lowered basal metabolic rate (Rao et al., 1958), reduction in heart-rate audibility, and reduction in pulse intensity (Wenger et al., 1961) have also been demonstrated by yogis.

Apparently the practice of yoga involves, in the beginning, adopting a sitting posture and engaging in waking activity that involves little movement. These very behaviors are likely to bring certain autonomically influenced reactions such as breathing and heart rate to a minimal level. It is possible that such reactions may then be associated with concomitant internal stimulation, with stimuli from somatic activity, with external stimulation, and with concurrent symbolic processes. On that basis, such modifications in physiological behavior may later be reinstated by replication of the overt stimuli or neural symbols that were earlier associated with that behavior.

Evidence from Studies in Hypnosis

Hypnosis may be conceived as a state of hypersensitivity and hyper-reactivity. The hypnotized individual apparently can make certain responses more readily than he ordinarily does. In hypnosis there appears to be a reduction in inhibitory or restraining activities; that is, the intermediate processing between stimulation and response is reduced. Waking suggestions produce similar reactions.

The idea that autonomic reactions not normally within the control of the individual can be subject to the influences of external stimulation, even to the extent of generating reactions of such intensity as to produce structural pathology, is supported by a number of independent clinical and research reports concerning the effects of hypnotic suggestion. Skilled practitioners of hypnosis have demonstrated rather startling control of autonomic processes during the hypnotic trance, including the following:

1. The production in prescribed localized areas of the skin in selected subjects of erythema, blisters, wheals, urticaria, tumefaction, congestion, and hemorrhage (Pattie, 1941). Apparently, allergic reactivity of otherwise sensitized skin can also be substantially modified by hypnotic suggestion.

2. Increase in metabolic rate from 8 to 25 percent following the suggestion of "anxiety and fear producing experiences" (Gorton, 1959).

3. Increase in heart rate of from 75 to 120 beats per minute as disclosed by electrocardiographic tracings following the suggestion of strong "anxiety and anger," and reversion to the normal rate within 60 to 90 seconds after the subject had been reassured (Gorton, 1959).

4. Reduction of blood calcium level in one subject from 10.6 to 8.4 percent through a quieting suggestion (Gorton, 1959).

5. Alteration in spasticity of the bowel by suggestions of symptom relief (Gorton, 1959).

6. Increase in gastric acidity in subjects to whom the suggestion was made that they were eating a given food with enjoyment; while a decrease in gastric acidity was associated with the suggestion of eating a given food with strong disgust (Gorton, 1959).

7. Effective direct hypnotic suggestions concerning respiratory and circulatory changes (Gorton, 1959).

8. Significant influence on the action of the heart via induced suggestions of emotionality (Gorton, 1959).

9. The reduction or termination of asthmatic and allergic reactions (Gorton, 1959).

10. Increased pancreatic secretion of pepsin and trypsin to suggested protein ingestion, increased secretion of lipase to suggested fat ingestion,

and increased maltase secretion to suggested carbohydrate ingestion (Gorton, 1959).

The inhibition of gastric contractions to appropriate suggestion during hypnosis is reported as directly related to the degree of hypnosis. The study on which this result is based (Lewis and Sarbin, 1943) has been cited as illustrating the degree to which normal physiological functions may be altered through hypnotic suggestion.

Many of the cited observations and investigations were not well controlled, at least in the sense of having waking control groups for comparison. However, for our purposes, this deficiency is not critical, since our intent is merely to demonstrate that physiological reactions may be rather systematically and sometimes profoundly related to particular explicit stimulus situations, verbal or otherwise.

One can only speculate about the neural mechanisms involved in the manipulation of physiological reactions through explicit stimulation. The critical idea in such speculation, whatever form it may take, is that the effects of explicit stimulation can be channelled via central nervous mechanisms into routes of significance for autonomic functioning.

Experimental Evidence of Autonomic Learning

Among the best-known research work in psychology is that of Ivan P. Pavlov, who is credited with being the modern discoverer of conditioning. In those classical research studies, Pavlov conditioned the salivary response in dogs to auditory stimuli. This was done by presenting, first, a bell; in close temporal proximity immediately thereafter food was put on the dog's tongue; the food on the tongue produced salivation. After several such combinations of bell-food followed by salivation, the bell alone was effective in producing salivation. The salivary response is regulated by the autonomic nervous system, and so the classical research of Pavlov involved autonomic learning. The animal learned to salivate to a stimulus that did not initially elicit salivation.

In the human, it is likely that the salivary response can be elicited by a wide variety of different learned stimuli. For example, for some people salivation may occur in response to a number of cooking aromas emanating from the kitchen, to a picture of one's favorite food, or perhaps even to certain words, written or spoken, such as "a thick succulent broiled steak, with mushrooms, green peas, and french-fried onions, followed by one's favorite dessert, perhaps pecan pie a la mode." Such stimuli, particularly those involving the use of language, are relatively complex, involving as they do symbolic processes. Also, in harmony with the principles of motivation proposed earlier, they are likely to be more effective when the individual has been without food for an extended period.

Autonomic learning occurs much more often than is commonly supposed. Even in the learning of what appear to be strictly striated muscle responses (that is, responses of structures under the direct immediate control of the organism), autonomic learning very likely occurs simultaneously, although the psychologist typically either does not measure it or ignores it completely. Let us consider first animals learning a relatively long maze—say a maze with 40 blind alleys.

1. Naive animals first put into the start box of such a maze display many signs of heightened autonomic activity. For example, at first defecation and urination are frequent in the start box. As the animal becomes proficient in negotiating the maze, such responses diminish and disappear.

2. Frustration for the animal occurs in the course of learning. Entering a blind alley is such a frustration, and it may augment adrenal gland secretion, change heart rate, decrease digestive system activity, or produce respiratory alterations. In any case, modifications in autonomic reactions accompany modifications in more overt reactions. Such autonomic reactions have largely been ignored in the study of maze learning.

Certainly after a subject is given electric shock as punishment for a response, he learns more than avoidance of that response under similar circumstances in the future; autonomic reactions are also associated with the shock situation. Liddell, for example, has observed that in the process of conditioning limb withdrawal in sheep, he was also simultaneously conditioning changes in respiratory pattern. The water-deprived animal who finally reaches the water reward not only displays the consummatory response of drinking, but in the process alters autonomic responses also. In fact, it would be altogether surprising if such responses did not occur. And there are, of course, investigations indicating that such responses do occur in controlled laboratory situations.

A number of other studies through the years demonstrate that autonomic responses can be conditioned. For example, Jones (1924), using one-year old infants, conditioned the galvanic skin response (GSR) to dim lights and faint sounds. Darrow and Heath (1932) conditioned the GSR in naive adults. Cason (1922) conditioned dilation and constriction of the pupil. Menzies (1937) produced vasoconstriction to a buzzer stimulus. Roessler and Brogden (1943) conditioned vasomotor responses to a nonsense syllable or to thinking the syllable. Razran (1960) has reported researches of Russian investigators in which reports of intensity of the urge to urinate has been conditioned to the position of an indicator on a dial.

CHAPTER FIVE

PSYCHOSOMATIC PERSPECTIVES

HISTORICAL BACKGROUND

The great French physiologist of the last century, Claude Bernard (1813–1878), delineated the role of the "milieu interne" or internal environment in sustaining life. That environment is composed largely of internal fluids such as lymph and blood; these fluids regulate many biological processes, and they must remain relatively constant for the maintenance of life.

Later in that century, Charles R. Darwin (1809–1882) discussed the role of behavior and its adaptive significance for organismic survival. In his discussions, Darwin pointed out that under conditions of emotional stimulation, constellations of inner behavioral changes or physiological deviations from the normal steady state were apparent. Among the many autonomic structures noted by Darwin as involved in such reactions were the heart, sweat glands, salivary glands, respiratory mechanisms, anal sphincter, and pupil of the eye (Darwin, 1872).

The conceptualizations and research of Walter Bradford Cannon (1871–1945), an outstanding American physiologist of the early twentieth century, extended the ideas of Bernard and of Darwin. Two of his concepts, *homeostasis* and the *emergency reaction,* are relevant and deserve citation.

Homeostasis was the name given to the dynamic tendency in living organisms to maintain conditions of internal constancy—to maintain certain physiological variations within narrow limits. Simple examples are the following. When the body temperature falls, among other changes, shivering occurs. This has the same effect as massage; it promotes the circulation of warm blood and thereby raises body temperature. When body temperature rises, sweating occurs, which involves the deposition of liquid on the surface of the skin, the evaporation of which has a cooling effect. A fall in the blood-calcium level promotes mobilization of calcium from bone to raise the blood calcium level, while an excess of blood calcium leads to the excretion of calcium from the body. In recent years, work of the cyberneticists, who clarified the concept of servomechanisms or feedback mechanisms, particularly negative feedback mechanisms, has contributed to understanding of a variety of internal bodily processes such as those described above as aspects of homeostasis.

The emergency reaction of the sympathetic nervous system was described in great detail by Cannon. It was conceived as a reaction pattern promoted by emotional circumstances and by situations potentially dangerous to an organism. The pattern that is mediated primarily via the sympathetic nervous system includes secretion of epinephrine, accelerated cardiac activity, bronchiole dilation, reduction in digestive activities, peripheral vasodilation, and sweating, among other concomitant changes. The sum total of these conditions mobilizes the energy resources of an organism to deal with an emergency situation, particularly to prepare it for fight or flight. It therefore has a *defensive* or *protective* or *adaptive* function.

More recently, Selye has made empirical contributions and has elaborated another set of ideas relating to concepts of homeostasis and reactions to various harmful or threatening situations (Selye, 1946; 1956). According to Selye's *stress-reaction theory,* a great variety of harmful and threatening situations or *stressors*—and these include infectious agents, toxic substances, physical trauma, extreme temperature conditions, fatigue, x-rays, and emotional circumstances—result in a set of rather stereotyped reactions. This reaction pattern is termed by Selye the *general adaptation syndrome.* It consists of three stages.

1. *The alarm reaction stage.* The adrenal cortex, as a consequence of excitation via a hormone liberated by the pituitary gland—the adrenocorticotropic hormone (ACTH)—becomes hyperactive, overproducing hormones that help the body to cope with the effects of the stressor. This may result in the restoration of a bodily balance and therefore operates to achieve a kind of physiological equilibrium or condition of homeostasis.

2. The resistance stage. During this period, the biological changes generated serve to defend the organism generally and also against the specific stressor in the particular situation; a new level of physiological balance is achieved.

3. The exhaustion stage. Under conditions of prolonged exposure to the stressor, resistance cannot be maintained and bodily resources are depleted; if the stressor is maintained for sufficient time, death will ensue.

MORE RECENT DEVELOPMENTS

The writings of Helen Flanders Dunbar, Franz Alexander, and Roy R. Grinker, among others in recent decades, effectively extended thinking about emotional behavior into the realm of psychosomatic disorders.

A case can be made for the position that the recent era in the development of perspectives and ideas concerning psychosomatic disorders began with the publication of a reference work by Dunbar titled *Emotions and Bodily Change*. The first edition, published in 1935, contained an annotated survey of the literature and listed over 2000 references; although there were four subsequent editions, with the explosion of research investigations in a variety of psychosomatic subfields, later editions did not endeavor to maintain such a comprehensive reference survey. Dunbar suggested that various personality characteristics were associated with particular psychosomatic disorders and provided, even in her first book, statistical evidence concerning relationships between personality profiles and various disorders.

Alexander did much research in the area, and in his book *Psychosomatic Medicine* (1950), he presented ideas concerning the origin and development of psychosomatic disorders from the standpoint of psychoanalytic theory. The book also summarized his own research work and that of the Chicago Institute for Psychoanalysis. Alexander subscribed to the idea that specific emotional states provoke specific physiological disturbances or specific structural pathology.

Grinker has maintained that the same kind of visceral disorder may result from widely different life situations and that different disorders may result from similar life situations. He has also subscribed to the view that the biological vulnerability of an organ is a function of its earlier physiological involvement in reactions to stress.

Contributions, empirical as well as theoretical, have been made to various subfields of psychosomatic disorders by many specialists, including internists, endocrinologists, gynecologists, urologists, psychiatrists, and psychologists. Empirical contributions will be considered in appropriate places throughout the text. An overview of the major classes of theoretical position is presented in the next section.

CLASSES OF CONTEMPORARY THEORY

The various contemporary theories of psychosomatic disorders, regardless of their differences, for most part subscribe to the following oversimplified general paradigm.

Stimulus —————→ Physiological —————————→ Psychosomatic
situation   reactivity   disorder

Stimulus situations, whether explicit or implicit, provoke a variety of internal conditions, including those physiological activities that are conceived as the essential aspects of emotional behavior. If the reaction pattern generated (or some part of it) is sufficiently intense and prolonged, a relatively permanent kind of structural or physiological alteration may occur as a direct consequence.

With a focus on the question of which structure will manifest psychosomatic pathology, theories concerning the genesis and development of psychosomatic disorders may be classified into the five major groups listed below; these groups are not absolutely discrete, but suggest different areas of emphasis in theorizing.

1. Constitutional-vulnerability (weak-link) theories. These theories hold that the most vulnerable organ becomes malfunctional or is damaged in response to stressful stimulation. Such theories may analogize such malfunction to the breaking of a link in a chain or the blowing out of an inner tube; the chain breaks at the weakest link, and the inner tube "blows" where the rubber is thinnest. These theories focus on genetic vulnerability, but the effects of injuries, diseases, and other earlier influences may also contribute to biological vulnerability.

2. Organ response learning theories. These theories maintain that the major determinant of biological malfunctioning or damage is a specific organ reaction to emotional stimulation that is learned. Such theories hold that as a consequence of earlier association between emotional stimulation and the response of an organ—particularly if that response has been rewarded—new stressful situations come to arouse the same organ response, and when they do so with sufficient frequency, persistence, and intensity, engender malfunction or damage to that organ.

For example, each time Mr. Jones yelled at his wife, her heart rate and pulse pressure sharply increased, she trembled visibly, and there were pronounced constrictions of the bronchioles that led to her gasping for breath, among other responses. The first time this happened, her husband was so concerned about her welfare—particularly about her breathing difficulties —that he immediately stopped his tirade, gave her sympathetic attention, and called a physician. Intermittent tirades of Mr. Jones over the years, with similar subsequent compassion on his part expressed immediately thereafter to his wife's breathing problems, eventually resulted in the gasping pattern being established as a reaction of the wife, while changes in heart rate, pulse rate, trembling and other responses tended to diminish and disappear. Further, she then displayed the gasping pattern—which was repeatedly rewarded by the solicitous attention of her husband as well as by other personal gains—very frequently, not only to her husband when he yelled at her, but even when he was present and did not yell at her. And it was also elicited by people who resembled her husband in some way, and to a variety of stimuli associated with her husband—his job, his automobile, his family, his associates, his favorite activities. In short, an asthmalike reaction was developed.

A parallel could be drawn with respect to the man who in response to an emotional situation develops vigorous cardiac contractions and as a consequence reports pain and other uncomfortable stimulation from within the upper thoracic region; should that symptom be rewarded by compassionate attention and by diminished family or vocational responsibilities, the overly vigorous cardiac contraction and subsequent pain could become a well-established reaction to stressful situations, which might also lead in time to cardiac damage.

As a third example, suppose a man suffers a major frustration and reacts with a profound physiological arousal of anger that manifests itself in part in gastrointestinal pain about which he complains and for which he gains solicitous attention from others. That kind of arousal and the reaction to it may become associated with the people, the circumstances, the place, and the time of the original occurrence, as well as with any other aspect of the provoking situation. Therefore, in future encounters with those people, that place, and stimuli relating to or similar to the frustration situation (as well as thinking, i.e., processing neural symbols about them) may lead to emotional arousal—let us say particularly of increased gastric secretion and decreased gastrointestinal motility, which have in the past been selectively reinforced—and eventually to duodenal ulcers.

3. *Stimulus-situation theories.* Stimulus-situation theories maintain that different emotional stimulus situations lead to different patterns of physiological reaction and that such patterns differentially promote damage in different organic structures. There is often the implication in

this kind of theory that innate relationships exist between various patterns of stimulation and various patterns of physiological reactivity in emotion.

4. Emotional reaction-pattern theories. Emotional reaction-pattern theories hold that different patterns of physiological reaction in emotion engender malfunction or damage in different organ structures. These theories appear to be similar to the stimulus-situation theories. However, two differences in the theoretical positions may be cited. First, as far as emotional reaction-pattern theories are concerned, objectively identical or very similar patterns of stimulation can produce different physiological reactions in different people, and different emotional stimulus patterns can produce similar physiological reactions in the same person. Second, the emotional reaction-pattern theories often imply some kind of cognitive-affective factor or central component that intervenes between stimulus and response and that influences or processes the pattern of reaction.

5. Personality-profile theories. Personality-profile theories maintain that particular sets of personality characteristics are related to particular personality disorders. In other words, temperament, attitudes, habits, reaction tendencies, and other components of personality have major roles in influencing the development of particular psychosomatic disorders. Different personality structures presumably lead to different reaction inclinations and, therefore, predispose the individual to different kinds of biological pathology.

One criticism of the *weak-link theories* is the fact that it is difficult to ascertain the relative strength or vulnerability of a particular organ. Even if an objective estimate of vulnerability were obtained, there is the further problem of comparing the resistance level of that organ to the level of resistance of other biological structures. On the other hand, *weak-link theories* have some support from a variety of studies such as that of Sines (1961), who found that certain strains of rat had a greater tendency toward the development of ulcers than other rats and that this tendency was apparently genetically determined.

The major advantage of *organ response learning theories* is that there is a ballast of supportive evidence for the general paradigm of autonomic learning. Further, learning theories readily generate testable hypotheses. With cooperation between specialists in biology and psychology, there are excellent possibilities for testing hypotheses relating to learning processes in the development of psychosomatic disorders.

A major criticism of both *stimulus-situation theories* and *reaction-pattern theories* is that, with few exceptions, the physiological reaction patterns of emotion are very similar in gross terms for a wide variety of differently named emotions and for different eliciting situations; at least there are wide overlaps in physiological activity. Both of these classes of theory would predict discrete emotional reaction patterns. However, empirically very few dependable differences in physiological patterns have been determined for different stimulus situations and for the allegedly different emotional states.[1]

Further, it has been demonstrated by Lacey and his associates (Lacey, Bateman, and VanLehn, 1953) that autonomic reactions to stressful situations for individuals constitute stable, consistent, and idiosyncratic patterns of activity. If an individual's characteristic reaction in one stressful situation is a rise in blood pressure, it is likely to be a rise in blood pressure in other stress situations, even though the specific details of each situation are different. It has also been shown that patients with cardiovascular symptoms are likely to react to stress with cardiovascular symptoms rather than muscle tension, whereas headache patients are more inclined to react with muscle tension rather than cardiovascular symptoms (Malmo and Shagass, 1949).

A major difficulty involving *personality-pattern theories* is that psychological assessment procedures are notably weak in appraising personality; certainly it is difficult to make meaningful predictions about behavior on the basis of standard psychological tests of personality as well as the other techniques of psychological evaluation. Again, it is possible that in the future, with the development of more sensitive assessment procedures, meaningful relationships will be ascertained.

Besides the five categories of theory indicated, there are a number of other kinds of theory that seem at present to be somewhat less useful. These include *symptom-symbol theories,* which maintain that the organ or system affected has symbolic meaning for the patient. For example, Felix Deutsch (1922) proposed that physical symptoms of organs innervated by the autonomic nervous system are symbolic representations of emotional arousal that is not expressed overtly. Karl Menninger (1938) has suggested that internalized hate is represented in diseases of internal organs as partial suicide. Garma (1950) maintains that peptic ulcer can be represented as a symbol of internalized aggression against the mother. Symptom-symbol ideas have often derived from earlier psychoanalytic conceptualizations or at least have been influenced by psychoanalysis. They seem not to be widely accepted currently.

However, the psychoanalysts have been actively interested in accounting for psychosomatic disorders and have provided a large number of

---

[1] Of course, it is possible that with more sensitive instruments and more subtle kinds of measurement—perhaps in terms of ratios of performance in dyads or groups of organs—differences will eventually be ascertained and related to particular stimulus situations or to self-reports of different emotional states.

theories—most of which are specific for each kind of disorder. Psychoanalytic theories of psychosomatic disorders generally have a developmental orientation. Below are a few representative psychoanalytic formulations.

1. *Gastrointestinal ulcer* has its origin at a time when the infant is confronted with resolving problems relating to eating. Rejecting behavior of the mother results in emotionality and hurt to the infant. The infant is motivated to be independent but is helpless and recognizes his utter dependence on the rejecting parent. This dependence-independence conflict, established so early in life, is likely to persist throughout life and manifests itself in the development of a gastrointestinal ulcer.

2. *Colitis* has its origin during very early toilet training as a consequence of excessive demands for bowel control made by the parent on the infant. The emotionality that results from such demands for control, which may be beyond the capacity of the infant, manifests itself in inclinations to punish the parent. Since, however, the parent is so much stronger, the punitive tendencies cannot be readily directed toward the parent and are directed internally. Punitive tendencies directed against the self—at least against the specific offending part of the body—result in destruction of the bowel. As an infant, hostility toward and punishment for the parent can be expressed in part by not acquiring bowel control; in effect the infant is expressing the idea: "If I cannot control it, you cannot either." A vicious circle of reciprocal punishment of each other by child and parent can be developed.

3. *Asthma* also has its origin in very early life. An infant recognizes his dependence on his parents—or at least on his mother—for his survival. However, the infant perceives his mother as cold and rejecting and as a consequence develops hostile tendencies toward her; yet, because of the possibility that his mother will respond to his hostile expressions by abandoning him, the infant is fearful about complaining directly or loudly, but does so indirectly in a more subdued way—in a wheezing or whining manner. Sounds accompanying the breathing difficulties of asthma resemble such wheezing or whining and presumably relate to similar lung activity. The asthmatic reaction may then be conceived as a partially suppressed plaintive cry.

Psychoanalytic theories concerning the genesis of psychosomatic disorders are highly complex and embedded within the larger framework of general psychoanalytic concepts. Although all such theories emphasize the idea that the origins or roots of the disorder stem from infancy, psychoanalytic theorists maintain that the development of various kinds of psychosomatic disorder are predicated on (1) the time in infancy of particular emotion-provoking events, that is, the age of the infant; (2) the nature of the general problem, that is, whether it involves feeding or bowel control or rejection or is in another area; (3) the nature of emotional reaction —whether it is rage or fear or dependence-independence conflict or some other emotional pattern; (4) the particular incident or emotional stimulus originally precipitating the reaction; (5) the particular tissue, organ, or system involved; and (6) other variables. Further, there are many variants of the psychoanalytic position. It is, therefore, not possible to do justice to psychoanalytic theories in the psychosomatic area when the presentation must of necessity be abbreviated. The factors indicated above, however, do reveal the scope and complexity of psychoanalytic theories regarding psychosomatic disorders.

At the present time, it is difficult to deal with these theories, since objective evidence concerning critical aspects of such theories is difficult to obtain and because the language in which the theories are expressed does not translate readily into terms of the mediating biological mechanisms.

AUTONOMIC LEARNING THEORY [2]

In this section I hope to provide a relatively new set of theoretical perspectives, based on empirical principles and anchored in observable events, capable of yielding hypotheses that are objectively testable. These speculations, collectively called an *autonomic learning theory* (Lachman, 1963), relate most closely to the organ response learning theories considered earlier. The rationale contains a series of related propositions, supported to a greater or lesser degree by empirical evidence. This rationale is not necessarily in conflict with other well-established theoretical views. In fact, at least some of the propositions specified may represent processes about which there is converging agreement in the different theories concerning the genesis of psychosomatic illness. What I hope to do in this presentation is to express overtly and objectively a set of harmonious propositions concerning the origin and development of psychosomatic phenomena, to relate these propositions to each other and present them in an organized way, and to provide thereby a propositional structure from which new hypotheses can be derived, checked, and further developed through methodical investigation.

My theory is stated strictly in behavioristic terms; it emphasizes the

[2] I acknowledge with thanks permission of The Journal Press to reproduce copyrighted material from my paper titled "A Behavioristic Rationale for the Development of Psychosomatic Phenomena," *Journal of Psychology*, 1963, **56**, 239–248. Much of the remainder of this chapter is reproduced from that article, with modifications.

role of learning in the development of psychosomatic aberrations without minimizing the role of genetic factors or of nongenetic predisposing factors. The essence of the theory proposed is that *psychosomatic manifestations result from frequent or prolonged or intense implicit reactions* [3] *elicited via stimulation of receptors.*

Definition of Emotion and Varieties of Psychosomatic Phenomena

Let me repeat my definition of emotion, slightly modified in form. *Emotional behavior refers to extensive and often pronounced patterns of reaction in structures innervated by the autonomic nervous system in response to stimulation of receptors.* Emotional reactions may be characterized as reactions that are not narrowly localized, reactions that are often intensive, reactions involving implicit structures, and reactions aroused originally by receptor stimulation.

Extensive implicit reaction to sensory stimulation, then, is the specifiable essence of the definition of emotional behavior; usually these physiological changes are in the direction of facilitating or preparing the organism for defense, that is, they are adaptive. If the physiological changes are of more than mild intensity or of more than brief duration, however, there may be further consequences relevant to the health of the organism. These are called *psychosomatic reactions*. At least three categories of psychosomatic phenomena can be distinguished.

1. Constructive psychosomatic reactions. These are physiological reactions to emotional stimulation that are of *special value to the organism in combatting illness or disease processes;* they *counteract* the effects of illness symptoms or disease or are otherwise adaptive for the organism. Examples would be reduction of internal hemorrhaging resulting from patterns of visceral vasoconstriction and peripheral dilation in response to emotional stimulation; increased cardiac activity in individuals with serious bradycardic symptoms; increased blood pressure in patients with very low blood pressure; and decreased digestive activity—perhaps even including regurgitation—as part of an emotional reaction by an individual who realizes he has inadvertently swallowed a poisonous substance.

Another interesting example of a constructive psychosomatic reaction

---

[3] The phrase "implicit reactions" refers to physiological reactions such as changes in heart rate, blood pressure, rate of stomach or duodenal movement, gastric gland or adrenal gland secretion, and similar activities. These are covert responses—responses that ordinarily are not directly apparent, but that may be detected by special procedures or instruments.

is the following (Collip, 1937). A diabetic using insulin in the treatment of his condition discovered, while walking on the street, that he was being overcome by the physical state that follows excessive reduction in amount of blood sugar. Having neglected to provide himself with sugar for such a circumstance, he staggered into a drug store and incoherently demanded a bar of chocolate. The druggist thought the man was drunk and threw him out. This enraged the diabetic, and with the physiological expression of his anger he suddenly recovered, for he was thereby able to acquire the sugar he needed to restore the equilibrium of his body fluids; the anger situation had so facilitated the output of his adrenal gland that, with its effect on his liver to release stored carbohydrates, his blood sugar content temporarily increased sufficiently to bring him through the crisis. He had then to ingest some sugar promptly, of course, or the beneficial effect would have dissipated.

2. *Destructive or pathological psychosomatic reactions.* Destructive or pathological psychosomatic reactions are physiological changes induced by repeated or persistent emotional stimulation that—because of intensity level—are disadvantageous to the organism and are of sufficient chronicity or duration to be considered aberrations or dysfunctions. In other words, these reactions, though they may sometimes be completely or partially reversible, are so unsuitable or unfavorable to the individual that they are regarded as significantly deviant or abnormal. To put it still differently, this category includes pathological functional alterations and is exemplified by certain varieties of hypertension, cardiac dysrhythmias, and asthmatic attacks.

3. *Psychosomatic diseases.* These are actual organic or physical pathologies resulting from sustained, repeated, or intense reactions to emotional stimulation. In other words, the psychosomatic diseases are conditions in which there is relatively permanent structural change of a maladaptive kind, that is, tissue damage and organ destruction. Duodenal ulcers, permanent cardiac dilation, or colonic abrasions resulting from physiological reactions to emotional stimulation are examples of psychosomatic diseases.

Objective Rationale for Psychosomatic Disorders

The proposed autonomic reaction learning theory of psychosomatic disorders may be clarified by a few assumptions regarding emotional behavior.

1. Regardless of the original or native stimuli that elicit emotional behavior, new cues may become conditioned or otherwise learned to serve as effective elicitors of intense internal behavior.

2. Intense implicit reactions to specific stimulus patterns, once aroused, tend to be extremely persistent; that is, recurrence of the specific eliciting stimulus pattern tends to produce particular implicit reactions repeatedly, with little tendency toward extinction.

3. Overt accompaniments of emotional behavior are more readily "controlled" and directed by the organism than are the internal reactions. They may be reduced, suppressed, or otherwise concealed in emotional situations; likewise, the overt behavior often associated with emotion may be displayed independently of emotion as earlier defined. The emotional behavior itself (the implicit reaction pattern) is not so readily modified.

The central thesis of our position is: Emotional behavior—intense internal reactions that initially in the history of the organism are aroused via receptor stimulation—may lead to conditions of chronic physiological activation or may produce more or less permanent structural changes—psychosomatic manifestations.

The anatomical-physiological response mechanism necessary for the development of psychosomatic phenomena in an individual must possess at least two characteristics, *reaction variation* and *response predilection to explicit stimuli*. (1) *Reaction variation* is the potential for or the capacity of an implicit response mechanism to vary its activity. This may be variation in rate or in amplitude of response from a typical "steady" or "constant" or "homeostatic" reactivity level. Essentially this refers to lability in physiological activity. (2) *Response predilection to explicit stimuli* is a characteristic of certain effectors; it means that response mechanisms that play a role in psychosomatic phenomena must have the capacity to respond to explicit stimuli (as well as to implicit stimuli) either natively or as a function of an associative process. (If there were no reaction variation and no response susceptibility to explicit stimuli, there would be no psychosomatic disorders.)

There is a necessary stimulus basis for psychosomatic phenomena as well as the necessary response basis outlined above. Pertinent to understanding this stimulus basis are the following concepts: *individual differences in thresholds of effective stimulation, emotional-stimulus learning, autonomic response learning and vicious circle effects*.

The concept of *individual differences in threshold* is the idea that the threshold of stimulation (i.e., the minimum stimulus intensity level) initially capable of provoking emotional reactions varies from one individual to another. It is possible that the *range* of native elicitors of emotional reaction also varies from one individual to another. Several general categories of effective stimulation were outlined in the chapter on emotion.

The concept of *emotional-stimulus learning* involves consideration of several supplementary ideas relating to learning, viz., stimulus substitution learning, emotional redintegration, stimulus generalization, symbolic stimuli, and ideation.

1. The role of stimulus-substitution learning. On an associative basis, new effective stimuli may be developed. In other words, stimuli originally incapable of eliciting a response but closely associated in time with effective emotion-provoking stimuli may themselves, sooner or later, come to be effective in producing emotional reactions. For example, a brown-colored toy rabbit that originally was very attractive to a youngster was viewed by the youngster immediately prior to each of his three violent falls from his swing; each time the youngster fell he hurt himself painfully and cried. Now mere sight of the toy rabbit elicits crying behavior and other autonomic reactions on the part of the youngster. The toy rabbit that originally did not elicit crying and allied reactions became effective in doing so on the basis of having been associated with an effective stimulus, namely, falling from the swing.

2. The role of emotional redintegration. A single component in the stimulus-situation earlier associated with a complex pattern of emotional reactions (i.e., physiological responses) may itself be effective in producing the total complex pattern of emotional reactions. A boy while fishing on a bridge over the Sagabaw River in Jackson Park near the town of Titusville fell 30 feet into the ice cold water, was swept down a rocky rapids, and almost was drowned. Now the sight of that bridge or river or of people fishing or of the rocky rapids serves to revive vividly all of the complex stimulus situation and emotional reactions associated with the earlier event.

3. The role of stimulus generalization. An internal response that has been associated with a particular stimulus may come to be elicited by a variety of somewhat similar stimuli, that is, stimuli somewhat like the originally learned stimulus but varying along one continuum or another. Such stimuli become capable of eliciting an internal response—an emotional reaction or aspect thereof—that they did not elicit prior to learning. To illustrate stimulus generalization, the youngster (earlier mentioned) cries and displays other autonomic reactions not merely to presentation of the brown-colored toy rabbit but also to any toy that is brown, or to any toy rabbit, or to any toy resembling a rabbit, or to any small furry object including a dog or cat. Thus the reaction extends from a single stimulus to many stimuli within a category, class, or type, such as "brown-colored toys," or "toy rabbits," or "objects which are small and furry."

4. The role of symbolic stimuli. Stimuli that in the personal history of the individual represent effective emotion-provoking stimuli, may themselves become emotion-provoking. At the human level, such symbolic stimuli (or stimulus symbols) are frequently but not always language stimuli. Symbolic stimuli are explicit stimuli that represent other overt stimuli. Using our earlier example to illustrate symbolic stimuli, later hearing or seeing the words "toy rabbit" may elicit the emotional reaction, or a shadow on the wall resembling a rabbit or a verbal description of a rabbit or someone holding up his right hand in the form of a fist with the first two figures erect may represent to the child a rabbit and elicit the emotional reaction. In the case of our second example, mere mention by spoken or written word of Titusville, of the Sagabaw River, or of Jackson Park may elicit a revival of the emotional reactions.

5. *The role of ideation.* Organismic effects of stimuli, probably largely in terms of central nervous manifestations, may persist in the form of "central percepts," "thoughts," or "ideas" (i.e., neural images or cognitive symbols) that can be revived in the absence of the originally relevant external stimulus situation, to produce a characteristic implicit emotional-reaction constellation. To illustrate ideation, again using our earlier example: In the course of his implicit associational processes—thinking—the youngster recalls in succession dominoes, checkers, a teddy bear, and a toy rabbit. The thought or idea of the "toy rabbit" in the absence of any obviously relevant overt stimulus elicits the emotional response pattern.

Autonomic response learning is another fundamental concept. Not only are autonomic responses learned on the basis of their being conditioned to new stimuli, but also particular autonomic responses are selectively learned on the basis of differential reward or reinforcement. A specific rewarded autonomic response tends to be differentiated out of the emotional response constellation and to be selectively strengthened. Thus, the individual who is rewarded for his expression of gastrointestinal pain by being permitted to stay home from school or from work and who is given special attention, consideration, and love under those circumstances is likely to have strengthened gastrointestinal reactions that led to the gastrointestinal pain, that is, increased gastric acid secretion. This is a statement of the idea that *rewarded autonomic responses may be selectively learned.*

The concept of *vicious-circle effects* is also necessary to understand certain psychosomatic phenomena. Once initiated, a psychosomatic event may produce stimuli that lead to implicit reactions, which rearouse or intensify the psychosomatic event, and so on. For example, the noxious stimulation from a gastric ulcer may elicit implicit reactions including facilitated stomach-acid secretion, which intensifies that ulcerous condition, which leads to further emotional reaction and further irritation of the

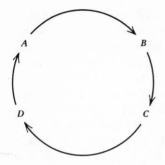

FIGURE 5-1. Vicious circle for ulcer development. *A* = noxious stimulation from area of ulcer; *B* = perceptual effect of noxious stimulation; *C* = Emotional reaction including gastric gland secretion; and *D* = further inflammation of ulcer.

ulcer. Theoretically, and perhaps in fact, an individual may worry himself to death in such a vicious circle. (See Figure 5.1.)

General Factors in the Genesis and Development of Psychosomatic Phenomena

In addition to the reaction basis and the stimulus basis outlined, it seems necessary to specify some principles regarding predisposing and precipitating determinants of psychosomatic phenomena. The predisposing factors are of two kinds, *predisposing genetic factors* and *predisposing environmental factors*.

1. Predisposing genetic factors. Physical structures of the organism are in the last analysis biologically transmitted—genetically inherited—structural characteristics of the organism. These include such characteristics as the quality of heart muscle, gastrointestinal tract, tracheal apparatus, endocrine glands, blood vessels, and the like. There may be many gradations of "strength" or durability of these structures as a function of genetic influence. Certain organic structures have a "low threshold" for or high susceptibility to harmful structural modifications. ·

Every structure has an "inherent level of resistance" to the field of forces that it encounters; there are vast individual differences. Some structures "break down" or "deteriorate" or "change" readily; others display greater resistance to change.

Differences in genetic predisposition are both interindividual and intersystemic.

2. Predisposing environmental factors. Acquired physical modifications are consequences of direct physical interaction of organismic structures with the environment, and include the effects of such phenomena as physical assault, parasitic infection, foreign toxic agents, nutritional deficits, and the like. These may alter inherited structure deleteriously or perhaps in some cases raise rather than lower the "resistance level" of these structures.

The "level of resistance," that is, the threshold of injury, of an organic structure may be altered as a consequence of direct and indirect physical interaction with the environment.

Precipitating factors of a phenomenon that is classifiable as a psychosomatic disorder, according to our rationale, must be provoked by internal behavior that in turn has been elicited by ordinary stimulation of receptor structures. These internal behavior patterns, that is, emotional reaction patterns, may vary in *extent, frequency, intensity,* or *duration* in producing such a phenomenon.

1. The extent of the emotional reaction pattern. There are wide individual differences in the number and variety of structures involved in an emotional reaction. Reacting structures may be few or many in number. There is variation from individual to individual and from time to time in the same individual. Such variations may depend on the biological makeup of the organism; they may also depend on earlier learning.

The structures involved in emotional reaction patterns are the structures that are primarily involved in the development of psychosomatic disorders.

2. The frequency of the emotional reaction pattern. There are wide individual differences in the frequency of occurrence of emotional reactions. The more frequently a given structure is involved in emotional reactions, the greater the likelihood of its being involved in a psychosomatic disorder, other things being equal.

3. The intensity of the emotional reaction pattern. There are wide individual differences in the "severity" of the changes in the functioning of a structure during an emotional reaction. The greater the deviation or variation in functioning of a structure from its "normal" resting or homeostatic level, the greater the likelihood of its being involved in a psychosomatic disorder, other things being equal. The intensity of reaction in a particular structure may depend on biological factors, such as heredity and earlier disease processes, and also on learning.

4. The duration of the emotional reaction pattern. There are wide individual differences in the duration of the emotional reaction pattern, although such reactions are typically of relatively short duration. Again, biological factors and learning have a role in determining duration, as does the pattern of emotion-provoking stimulation.

The longer a given structure is involved in an on-going emotional reaction pattern, the greater is the likelihood of its being involved in a psychosomatic disorder, other things being equal. (This implies that the factors specified as precipitating factors may also operate as predisposing influences).

The Genesis and Development of Psychosomatic Pathology

The basic notion of a psychosomatic disorder is that physical injuries or pronounced physiological dysfunctions may be elicited independently of externally induced physical agents. Such an injury or dysfunction, then, is a result of internal reactions elicited, at least initially, by means of sense-organ stimulation.

In order for emotional reactions to assume pathological significance, such reactions must be intense or chronic or both. Which structure will ultimately be affected depends on (1) genetic factors; (2) predisposing environmental influences; (3) the particular structures involved in emotional reactions; and (4) the magnitude—intensity, frequency, and duration—of their involvement.

A Few Details Concerning The Theory

What *structure* ultimately becomes involved in a psychosomatic reaction, then, depends on the biological condition of the structure (whether determined by innate or environmental factors), on the initial reactivity threshold of the organ, and on such learning factors as the development of stimulus-substitution reactions, generalization, symbolic stimuli, and ideation. The *magnitude* of the psychosomatic phenomenon is dependent on how frequently the structure is affected, how intensively it is affected, and how long it is affected. In this case, affect or influence is in terms of deviation of a structure from its optimal level of operation.

All internal response mechanisms are not activated to the same degree. Under various circumstances one group of structures, let us say peripheral blood vessels, the heart, or stomach muscles, may be intensely activated, while at other times different structures are maximally activated. As a consequence of such activation having occurred once, the immediate stimulus situation and other stimuli associated with it temporally are likely to be able to elicit similar reactions in the future. With frequent occurrence of the sequence (of stimulus situation and response), there is increasing likelihood of recurrence of the response to the stimulus situation, and an S-R pattern becomes firmly established. A small part of the total more complex stimulus situation may come to elicit the reaction—*redintegration*. Temporally associated stimuli may also do so—this is *stimulus substitution*. Stimuli similar in terms of stimulus dimensions may do so—this is *generalization*. Finally, *symbolic stimuli*—not similar in stimulus dimensions but similar in terms of meaning—may also do so, as may equivalent internal, that is, representative or ideational, stimuli. Essentially, these are learning factors.

Summary Statement on Autonomic Reaction Learning Theory of Psychosomatic Phenomena

No single autonomic reaction is emotional behavior; there are many possible autonomic patterns. With reference to the organs involved, the differences in pattern depend on different eliciting circumstances as well as on different genetic and nongenetic predisposing variables, and there are not merely intraindividual differences but also obviously interindividual differences in reaction patterns. New stimuli, through learning, may elicit emotional reaction patterns.

Much evidence at this time suggests the nature of the mechanisms involved in the development of psychosomatic phenomena, beginning with receptors and afferent structures and terminating with peripheral motor components of the autonomic nervous system, including also the structures influenced directly and indirectly by the autonomic nervous system. To elucidate these mechanisms is a major goal of investigators in the field of psychosomatic research. Pertinent to that objective, specific knowledge of value in understanding neural mechanisms in psychosomatic phenomena has emerged from many research studies.

A brief formalized framework such as the one herein proposed can provide (a) a means for encompassing in a general way much of what is now known and (b) the foundation for more systematic investigation of the proposed variables in the future.

Perhaps emotional reactions are basically constructive—defensive and adaptive. However, if emotional activity or reactivity is sufficiently frequent or prolonged or intense, it becomes maladaptive or destructive, leading to physiological aberration or structural damage to the organism and even to death. Thus, an organism may be injured or destroyed by its own defenses. The propositions outlined provide the framework of a rationale suggesting how this might occur psychologically and biologically.

Theoretically, any bodily structure or function can become the end focus of psychosomatic phenomena—but especially those directly innervated and regulated by the autonomic nervous system.

The magnitudes of particular frustrations, psychological traumata, conflicts, and other circumstances in terms of emotional reactivity provoked, must be individually assessed for each person—but first more general research is necessary to establish more specifically the major parameters of influence.

. . .

In the next several chapters a variety of psychosomatic disorders will be considered and samples of research evidence pertinent to them will be surveyed in terms of the major organ systems involved. It is difficult to classify psychosomatic disorders, and a classification in terms of major organ systems is arbitrary. Such a classification is also an oversimplification, since in each case of emotional reactivity, whether or not it is of clinical significance, changes in several systems occur simultaneously. In general, however, material for each chapter will be organized into the following sections:

1. General structure and function of a particular organ system.
2. Characteristic emotional responses involving the system.
3. Descriptions and discussions of representative psychosomatic disorders.
4. A general summary including consideration of the special significance, unusual problems, or physiological mechanisms associated with the particular organ system.

Discussions will cite research evidence concerning psychological factors in the genesis and development of psychosomatic disorders and for most part will be consistent with the theoretical rationale considered earlier in this chapter. Case histories are included for illustrative purposes.

CHAPTER SIX

PSYCHOSOMATIC
CARDIOVASCULAR DISORDERS

ANATOMY AND PHYSIOLOGY
OF THE CARDIOVASCULAR SYSTEM

The cardiovascular system is sometimes called the circulatory system and sometimes the vascular system. It consists of the heart—a complex muscle that functions as a pumping device—and a series of tubes leading away from and back to the heart. These tubes are called blood vessels. Those leading away from the heart are the arteries; the smaller arteries are arterioles. Those leading back to the heart are veins; the smaller veins that lead into the larger veins are venules. Interposed between the smallest arteries and veins are tiny complex networks of the very smallest blood vessels, called capillaries, with which the body is extensively supplied. A secondary set of arteries and veins leads to and from the lungs. (See Figure 6.1.)

Within the structure described is the blood. Blood has two major components, the formed elements and the plasma. The formed elements, sometimes called blood cells or corpuscles, are of three kinds: (1) red corpuscles or erythrocytes, (2) white corpuscles or leucocytes, and (3) platelets or thrombocytes. The plasma is the liquid part of the blood; it is a clear faintly yellow fluid composed mainly—more than 90 percent—of water, but in addition it has inorganic constituents, dissolved gases, and many biochemical substances including antibodies, enzymes, proteins, and a variety of other constituents.

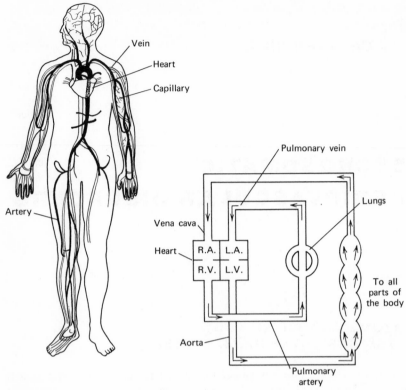

FIGURE 6-1. Circulatory system. R. A. = right auricle; R. V. = right ventricle; L. A. = left auricle; and L. V. = left ventricle.

Among the major functions of the cardiovascular system are the following.

1. Respiratory. The cardiovascular system serves to transport oxygen from air in the lungs to tissues that require it and to remove carbon dioxide from various tissues to the lungs for expiration.

2. Nutritive. It has a role in conveying food materials from the gastrointestinal tract to tissues.

3. Excretory. It has a role in transporting the waste products of metabolism including urea, uric acid, creatinine, and other substances, for elimination from the body.

4. Chemical regulation. It has a role in transporting chemical substances, particularly those of the endocrine glands, that have continuous effects on the functioning of various parts of the body.

5. Protective. By means of certain substances in the blood including the formed elements—especially leucocytes and antibodies—it has a role in protecting the body against disease organisms and injurious agents of various kinds.

In its ordinary operation, the periodic contraction of the heart serves to propel the blood through the arteries and other blood vessels to all systems of the body; blood is particularly well supplied to the capillary beds of the lungs.

A constant interchange of fluid, which in chemical composition closely resembles blood plasma, takes place through the walls of blood vessels. This substance, the tissue fluid, comes in contact with cells and it is via this means that passage of oxygen and food materials to cells and of waste products from cells is accomplished.

CHARACTERISTIC EMOTIONAL RESPONSES
INVOLVING THE CARDIOVASCULAR SYSTEM

There are many reactions within the cardiovascular system that normally occur after emotional stimulation. These include changes in cardiac rate, amplitude, and regularity; blood vessel dilation and constriction; blood pressure changes, changes in blood corpuscle content; and changes in the chemical composition of the blood (Lachman, 1969).

TYPICAL PSYCHOSOMATIC
CARDIOVASCULAR DISORDERS

A wide variety of cardiovascular conditions have been described as psychosomatic disorders. Among these are coronary disease, which includes heart attacks and cardiac occlusions due to embolisms and thromboses; irritable heart syndrome; functional dysrhythmias (including tachycardia, bradycardia, and arrhythmia); essential hypertension; vascular spasms; and anginal syndrome. Sometimes migraine is also considered within the province of cardiovascular disorders.

Case 6.1. *Hypertension.* A 39-year-old man with a long history of hypertension discovered that elevation of his blood pressure tended to occur when he was very dependent on the opinions of people in authority around him. When he could free himself of this dependence, his systolic blood pressure would drop as much as 50 points. By avoiding harassing situations and equipping himself emotionally to meet situations involving his acceptance by others, he was able to keep his blood pressure down "to reasonable limits" (English and Finch, 1964).

Case 6.2. *Hypertension.* A woman in her early 20s, self-sacrificing to care for her family, reacted to domination by her mother and to the arbitrary ways and inconsiderate behavior of her boss with constantly elevated blood pressure (White, 1964).

Case 6.3. *Hypertension.* A businessman who was constantly harrassed by business affairs and friction with his partners, and who carried his troubles home, lying awake many nights fretting about business problems and anticipating difficulties, eventually developed hypertension. Within six months following the initiation of psychotherapy that resulted in his (1) voluntary withdrawal from the work situation, (2) modification of his personal attitudes toward ordinary frustration, and (3) providing outlets for his energy in more congenial work, social activity, and recreation, his symptoms entirely disappeared (Kraines and Thetford, 1943).

Case 6.4. *Anginal Syndrome.* A businessman suffered his first anginal attack following announcement of his daughter's engagement to be married. His second attack occurred when he was threatened with a business reversal. Other later attacks could be related to stressful events in his life. During psychotherapy he began to perceive the significance of his attacks; thereafter the frequency and severity of his reports of chest pain began to diminish (Kisker, 1964).

Case 6.5. *Psychosomatic Hemorrhage.* A nationally prominent actor reported that while working under conditions of intense emotional arousal, he would occasionally suffer severe nosebleeds and sometimes his leg would break out in a rash.

Case 6.6. *Migraine.* The patient on leaving high school prepared to enter college but an accident to her father put the family in a poor financial situation; consequently she went to work to support the family. Since she was the only wage earner, she had to give up her own education, although part of her income went to support her brother through college. She felt that her family did not appreciate her and in fact abused her. When she discovered that her brother, who supposedly was using her money for his education, was really not even attending college but was spending the money for his own amusement, the patient had her first migraine attack. It involved vomiting among other symptoms, and lasted 2 days, during which time she was completely incapacitated. Thereafter headaches recurred at intervals of 4 to 6 weeks. The patient married at age 25. A child was born a year or so later. Her husband displayed fits of temper with minimal provocation and occasionally beat the patient and the child. Such situations sometimes precipitated headaches. At age 29, she sought clinical help (Grinker and Robbins, 1954).

Case 6.7. *Migraine.* The patient's first severe headache occurred at age 20, beginning in the midmorning on a day following an intensive argument with his parents concerning financial matters. It was accompanied by vomiting and required bed rest, after which it disappeared. A month later his second headache, much more severe than the first, occurred and from that time on he experienced an average of one such headache a month. The pain was usually confined to one side of the head and was invariably accompanied by nausea and vomiting and sometimes by other symptoms such as vertigo. Standard analgesic preparations were largely ineffective. He was drafted during World War II into the naval service (after deliberately concealing his history of headaches) and made a fair adjustment while assigned to the United States. However, he experienced intensive headaches during his period of sea service. At age 33 he was admitted to a neuropsychiatric ward of a large naval hospital with a tentative diagnosis of migraine. Interviewing disclosed that the patient's headaches frequently but not invariably were associated with an emotion-provoking incident of the previous day; sometimes they were related to occasions in which the patient experienced frustration (Lewinski, in Burton and Harris, 1947).

Neurocirculatory Asthenia

Neurocirculatory asthenia has also been called soldier's heart and effort syndrome. Sometimes the terms heart neurosis and cardiac neurosis are used as equivalents.[1] It refers to a condition in which cardiovascular symptoms are manifested in response to emotional stimulation. The major cardiovascular symptoms are palpitations and rapid and labile action of the heart. However, the condition is often also characterized by respiratory difficulty, fatigue, sweating, trembling, dizziness, and less frequently fainting; another prevalent symptom is aversion to physical effort, largely due to concern about the effects of work on one's physical condition. Exhaustion is reported by the patient after slight effort; it is often unrelieved by rest. The disorder occurs in both sexes, infrequently before age 20 or after age 40. Symptoms may be protracted unless the provoking psychological factors can be modified.

The beating heart is a delicate mechanism, highly sensitive to emotion-provoking situations. Therefore, it should not be surprising to find that organ implicated in several psychosomatic disorders. The disorder is regarded as psychosomatic to the extent that objectively verifiable physical symptoms are attributable to the physiological arousal of emotion. There is, of course, the possibility of simultaneously occurring symptoms based

---

[1] In the older literature, what are currently called psychophysiologic and visceral disorders, somatization reactions, or psychosomatic disorders, were called organ neuroses. As a consequence, there were cardiac neuroses, gastric neuroses, skin neuroses, and respiratory neuroses, among others. These terms are now less often used.

on other determinants. Unfortunately, in many cases diagnosed as neuro-circulatory asthenia (or its equivalent) the precipitant is not identified. However, the condition often appears to be initially precipitated by the kinds of stimulus situation that lead to fear or anxiety reactions; further recurrences or exacerbations of symptoms appear to be similarly provoked. Of course, infection, severe illness, and other physical variables can operate as predisposing factors in the development of the disorder.

Wittkower, Rodger, and Wilson (1941) consider emotional circumstances to be the most common precipitating factor. Friedman (1947) has suggested that sexual frustration plays a primary role in the genesis of the disorder, maintaining that ". . . the sexual act furnishes the greatest single outlet for emotional discharge and it is in people . . . deprived of this form of discharge that this form of acute functional cardiovascular disorder quite frequently occurs." That idea deserves further inquiry.

Cohen, White, and Johnson (1948) have suggested two kinds of "effort syndrome," chronic and acute. In the chronic type, symptoms were manifested throughout life and patients had never been able to engage in vigorous work or recreation. In the acute type, symptoms were not evident in the individual's more remote background, and the person was regarded as healthy prior to the first attack episodes in adulthood.

Psychosomatic Coronary Disease

One line of clinical evidence that serves to support the notion of emotional factors in coronary disease is the frequent observation that emotional stimulus situations immediately antedate the heart attack. The term coronary as used here refers essentially to the coronary arteries, which have the role of supplying blood to the heart.

It has been suggested that various stressful conditions, including time-pressure demands, lead to emotional reactions that provoke coronary disease. About one quarter of the deaths in physicians between ages 45 and 65 has been reported as due to coronary artery disease (Dublin & Spiegelman, 1947). Also, gross evidence of coronary disease has been found in autopsy studies of United States battle casualties in Korea in which the average age of the men was only 22 (Enos, 1953).

Often a heart attack is due to a blood clot that forms within a major blood vessel supplying the heart; this produces an occlusion or blocking of the artery. As a consequence, a portion of the heart muscle does not receive its appropriate blood supply, which results in an area of infarction. Clotting of the blood is a function of blood chemistry; in part it is regulated by functioning of the autonomic nervous system.

Cannon, many years ago, in describing the emergency reaction of the sympathetic nervous system, indicated as a major component of that reaction increased speed of blood coagulation. Macht (1952) reported an investigation consistent with Cannon's formulation, which lends demonstrative support to the idea that there is a direct relationship between intensity of emotion and speed of blood coagulation. Blood donors at a blood bank were classified into three groups: (1) those apparently calm, (2) those apparently apprehensive, and (3) those apparently frightened. Results indicated that the blood coagulation time for the apparently calm group was 8 to 12 minutes, for the apprehensive group 4 to 5 minutes, and for the frightened to very frightened group 1 to 3 minutes.

The major cause of the kind of occlusion that would engender a heart attack is a blood clot—a thrombus or an embolism. Clot formation is influenced by chemical factors in the blood that regulate rate of blood coagulation, and there is tentative evidence that such rates can be influenced by stimulus situations that provoke emotional reactions. It is possible that such clotting can produce a wide variety of further consequences, including even death.

Deleterious changes in heart structure may occur as a consequence of coronary occlusion or of other factors. One suggested mechanism of operation in psychogenic cardiac disorders is the following. A coronary circulation that to begin with is only marginally adequate to maintain normal myocardial activity in an individual may become inadequate when that person's reactions to emotional situations increase myocardial demands. These and other determinants of insufficient coronary circulation can result in the death of cardiac tissue. With such a condition repeatedly occurring and, therefore, with continued destruction of cardiac tissue, it is easy to understand why the heart in time would no longer be able to perform its basic function effectively.

Perhaps it is not inappropriate to draw an analogy between the contractile properties of a normal heart and the properties of an elastic band. The more fully the band is stretched, the more powerfully it rebounds—up to a point. Stretching it beyond that point, or replacing the elastic material with nonelastic or inert material, reduces its effective elasticity. In the case of the heart, death of tissue destroys effective cardiac contractile power, which is reflected in weakened action of the heart.

Essential or Cardiovascular Hypertension

There is extensive evidence to indicate that many normal individuals display sharply increased blood pressure in emotional situations. Probably the most frequently cited cardiovascular disorder is essential hypertension, a condition of intermittently or *chronically elevated* blood pressure. In this disorder, arterioles often exhibit abnormal resistance to the flow of blood;

such resistance is reflected in increased systolic, diastolic, and mean arterial pressure.

Essential or primary hypertension is so called to distinguish it from other forms of hypertension that are secondary to other disease—for example, hypertension due to kidney disease or to disease of the renal arteries. The term, "essential" has been used to indicate an absence of identifiable physical cause; the disorder is functional. In the early stages, it is likely that the condition is completely reversible—that the physiological pathology can be replaced with normal functioning. The consequences of an intense or well-established condition can be serious, however, since a diffuse thickening or hardening of the arteries may occur (arteriosclerosis), which in turn, by cutting off the supply of blood, may eventually lead to heart disease, kidney destruction, and cerebral hemorrhage.

Several independent studies relate emotional circumstances to physiological conditions effecting cardiovascular function as well as to the cardiovascular pathology.

1. Friedman and his associates (1958), in studying variations in work pressure on accountants, found that when work pressure was greatest, serum cholesterol rose and whole-blood clotting time was accelerated. Serum cholesterol fell and clotting time returned to normal under conditions of reduced work pressure. Further, these changes were found to be independent of variations in weight, diet, or physical activity.

2. Friedman and Rosenman (1959) also reported similar contrasts between men with intense and sustained achievement motives, who continually compete with others, and those less ambitious and in less exacting occupations.

3. Dreyfuss and Czaczkes (1959) reported an increase in serum cholesterol in male medical students during the week of their examinations. Serum cholesterol levels are believed to be related to the etiology of cardiovascular disease (Sim, 1963).

4. Russek and Zohman (1958) in studying 100 patients under age 40 who developed coronary heart disease, discovered that for 91 of them, severe emotional stress preceded the attack. They also suggested that certain personality characteristics such as intense recognition motives, compulsiveness, and scrupulosity were widely shared among the patients.

5. Chambers and Reiser (1953) related the onset of cardiac failure to emotional disturbance in 10 of 25 patients. They believe that a variety of stimulus conditions—those producing reactions likely to be termed rage, anxiety, depression or insecurity feelings—can be implicated as precipitants.

It is likely that the kidneys and the adrenal glands have a significant mediating responsibility in the case of hypertension. Apparently interference with kidney circulation, whether produced by constriction of the arterioles or in some other way, leads to release by the kidneys of a substance tending to raise blood pressure. Steroids secreted by the adrenal glands may influence kidney circulation. Relationships of emotional stimulus situations to excitation of the autonomic nervous system and relationships of the autonomic nervous system to the adrenal glands and the kidneys, both directly and indirectly, provide multiple mechanisms for explaining hypertension as a psychosomatic phenomenon. The indirect mechanisms include changes mediated by secretion of endocrine glands other than the adrenal.

Another mechanism is conceived in terms of chronic hyperactivity of the sympathetic division of the autonomic nervous system; this serves to accelerate cardiac activity and simultaneously functions to maintain certain blood vessels in a constricted state. Thus, more blood is directed through narrow blood vessels and blood pressure consequently is raised.

These are only a few of several plausible biological mechanisms that may be proposed to link emotional circumstances to hypertension. Presumably such mechanisms can operate separately or in combination.

A common theory concerning the genesis of hypertension is related to profound anger and rage reactions unaccompanied by explicit behavioral manifestations. In fact, the typical hypertensive patient has been described as being superficially calm, gentle, and affable, but "internally seething with anger." In the hypertensive patient, anger reactions apparently are not accompanied by much explicit activity; the physiological energies mobilized are not overtly discharged even indirectly. Explicit manifestations of anger, hostility, and rage are actively restrained or at least not expressed.

There are two implications of this conceptualization. One is that in the past the individual has been punished for overt expression of hostile or aggressive behavior and has learned to restrain such expression.[2] The second implication is that by engaging in hostile or aggressive behavior, the anger reactions, including heightened blood pressure, are reduced. The first implication has support in learning theory and in empirical evidence of learning. The legitimacy of the idea suggested by the second implication is subject to question and challenge, although there is some supporting evidence.

The idea of emotional situations as elicitors of hypertension is suggested by Binger, Ackerman, Cohn, Schroeder, and Steele (1945), who studied 24 patients with hypertension and reported that in 23 cases, the hypertension was discovered shortly after an acute emotional situation.

---

[2] It may be noted that such punishment though it may contribute to restraint of overt reaction, may simultaneously further augment its autonomic accompaniments, including elevated blood pressure.

Alexander (1939), with regard to a patient in the clinical situation, found that when the topic of conversation was emotionally disturbing, blood pressure rose, but when the topic of conversation was nonthreatening, blood pressure fell. Although Alexander interpreted this to mean that hypertension was due to the patient's inability to express hostility, it may be that a rise in this patient's blood pressure was a characteristic response of the patient to any kind of emotion-provoking circumstance.

An investigation by Wolf, Pfeiffer, Ripley, Winter, and Wolff (1948) provides some support for Alexander's general finding. These researchers reported marked rises in blood pressure when topics of strong personal emotional significance were discussed with patients during stress interviews. Control groups and control periods were used in assessing effects of interview content.

Wolf, Cardon, Shepard, and Wolff (1955) worked with 216 patients having circulatory disturbance histories and used records of circulatory functions during a period of relaxation for purposes of base-line control. During an interview with each patient, the interviewer in one phase attempted to decrease environmental stress and in another to increase it. Circulatory dysfunctions, including rise in blood pressure level, were found to be related to discussion of frustrating and threatening life experiences. Thus, circulatory functions could be modified by verbal interaction.

Two experiments (Hokanson and Shetler, 1961; Hokanson and Burgess, 1962) support the position that in anger situations in which blood pressure is raised, the blood pressure returns readily to normal when subjects are permitted to behave hostilely to the perceived source of anger, that is, to administer electric shock to the anger-instigating experimenter. Further, in subjects not given the opportunity to aggress against the experimenter, blood pressure remains high.

Experimental evidence demonstrates that blood-pressure increase occurs to "anger-instigating" situations. Clinical observation too indicates that in anger-producing situations or in the discussion of such situations, blood pressure rises in the hypertensive person. It also rises under similar circumstances in the normal person. Further, fear and other discretely named emotional reactions may also involve elevated blood pressure.

Saul (1939), on the basis of seven cases, reported that hypertensive patients characteristically had dominating mothers who had induced in the patients submissiveness and resentfulness. Other investigators have made similar reports. Whether the patients actually had such mothers is debatable because of problems of clinical method. Those problems include the possible unreliability of the clinical report, the role of interpretation of the therapist, and the lack of check on the actual situation, among other difficulties. However, even ignoring all of those shortcomings, there is the possibility that results were not representative in that they were founded only on a small population and a population selectively restricted on the basis of economic sufficiency for individual psychotherapy, as well as other variables. The question remains as to the backgrounds of other hypertensive persons, of persons with other psychosomatic disorders, and of the general population. A larger sample, appropriate control groups, and more direct evidence of dominance-submissiveness relationships between parent and offspring and its linkage to hypertension, would be of value in resolving this issue.

It has been suggested by Maher (1966) that two stages may be distinguished in the development of essential hypertension. In the early stage there are frequent intervals of high blood pressure typically of brief duration and presumably due to psychological determinants, that is, to stimulation by means of sense organs rather than by organic determinants. In time, however, a second stage is reached in which the condition of hypertension is chronic and persistent. This stage may be a function of learned autonomic reactions that have been generalized to a panorama of stimuli —and to symbolic representations of them—or they may be a consequence of organic modifications sustained during the earlier stage.

Schunk (1954) subjected cats to prolonged stress by exposing them to barking dogs for long periods of time over an interval of several months. About half of the cats developed hypertension, and some of them also developed cardiac anomalies. Further, the adrenal cortex was somewhat overdeveloped, suggesting overactivity of that gland. Other researches also sustain the idea that stressful and emotion-provoking situations may operate to produce hypertension, at least in certain individuals; differences in reaction among individuals may be a function of genetic factors; and earlier somatic problems and a variety of earlier experiences, including autonomic learning experiences, may also operate.

There is evidence that cardiovascular reactions, including elevated blood pressure, can be learned. Studies of Russian investigators reveal that elevated blood-pressure responses can be conditioned to words (Platonov, 1959) and that hypertension can be produced in monkeys via learned approach-avoidance conflicts (Miminoshvili, 1960). More recently, Miller (1969) and his associates have convincingly demonstrated that elevated and depressed blood-pressure responses can be instrumentally learned.

Basically, then, hypertension can be accounted for in terms of learning. Emotional situations produce constellations of reaction that frequently include elevated blood pressure. Originally neutral stimuli associated with such situations may in time also become effective in producing similar reactions. Eventually such a reaction may be produced by a wide variety of stimuli. If sufficiently repeated, prolonged, or continuous, and if augmented by circular feedback effects, the condition may become chronic and even result in physical damage to the heart, to blood vessels, and to other tissues.

Functional Dysrhythmias

Stressful situations produce a variety of changes in the activity of the heart. These include bradycardia, tachycardia, arrhythmia, and fibrillation, among other functional dysrhythmias. These conditions are defined and characterized briefly below.

Bradycardia refers to an abnormally slow rate of cardiac contraction —a heart rhythm of less than 60 beats per minute. In certain individuals and in certain emotion-provoking situations, the rate of cardiac contraction may be substantially depressed.

Tachycardia refers to an abnormally high rate of cardiac contraction —a heart rhythm of greater than 100 beats per minute. Normal heart rate is about 72 beats per minute. However, in emotion-provoking circumstances, heart rate may exceed 200 or rarely rise even to 300 beats per minute. Attacks are episodic and of varying duration, depending generally on the nature and duration of the emotion-provoking stimulus situation as well as on characteristics of the percipient.

Duncan, Stevenson, and Ripley (1950) investigated 15 patients with paroxysmal auricular tachycardia, and long-standing anxiety was found for 11 of them. It was also discovered that their cardiac irregularities were displayed under stressful circumstances. Patients were studied on a day-to-day basis for extended periods, varying from a few weeks to as many as 18 months; daily life events could therefore be correlated with other variables including emotional responsivity and cardiac symptoms. Cardiac attacks were actually engendered in two patients during stressful interviews while electrocardiographic recordings of the patient were being made.

Arrhythmia, which involves irregularity in heartbeat, and cardiac fibrillation, which consists of rapid irregular contractions of the muscular wall of the atria or ventricles of the heart, may also be regarded as a *psychosomatic* disorder under certain circumstances.

Anginal Syndrome (Angina Pectoris)

The anginal syndrome is characterized by brief episodes of pain or pain equivalents, often in the anterior chest alone or with various radiations. It is caused by a temporary inability of the coronary arteries to supply sufficient oxygenated blood to the heart muscle. The pain is believed by some to be due to stimulation of afferent nerve endings in the myocardium by accumulation of unoxidized metabolic products resulting from myocardial anoxia. That such a condition could be brought about through arteriosclerotic coronary narrowing, or through various conditions of physical exertion such as running, violent exercise, or normal coitus, is not questioned. However, the disorder as a psychosomatic phenomenon is brought about by stressful situations that result in emotional arousal. The emotional arousal may lead to the condition in question in a variety of ways, such as by chemical changes in the cardiovascular system, which produce clotting and occlusion, or through spasmodic contraction of the coronary arteries via neurological excitation.

Migraine

Migraine refers to a disorder characterized by recurrent headaches, usually restricted to one side of the head and sometimes associated with nausea, vomiting, or blurred vision. The headache is often intense, but it may be dull, throbbing, hammering, pressing, or viselike in its manifestation. Apparently migraine is a direct result of spasms of cranial arteries and of dilation of the blood vessels in the brain. Usually the attack endures for less than 24 hours. It is likely that other psychosomatic headaches have a similar physiological foundation, that is, they involve patterns of vasodilation. The association of negative emotion with headaches is so well established in the general population that the reaction to a stimulus presumed to induce such emotionality often is called colloquially a "headache."

In migraine patients, warning signals such as vertigo, visual problems, or paresthesias may precede an attack. For these and for other reasons, migraine is considered an epileptic equivalent by many clinicians.

Persons suffering from migraine have often been described as highly intelligent, very ambitious, and perfectionistic—in the sense of being meticulous, obsessional, scrupulous, and rigid—and as having strongly developed sets of ethical values (Marcussen and Wolff, 1949).

Migraine attacks generally appear to be precipitated by emotionality related to increased work pressure, interpersonal problems, ego-threatening situations, and problems involving financial or social position.

The disorder is found almost exclusively among females, and there are suggestions that genetic factors have a significant contributory role.

The mechanism for the dominant symptom of migraine—the headache —can be considered in three stages. (1) The initial symptoms are produced by spasms of certain cerebral arteries. (2) The second stage involves great distension of the arteries—branches of the external carotid artery— which activates the pain nerves of the blood-vessel wall to produce the headache. (3) The third stage consists of edematous swelling of the arterial walls, producing a condition in which blood vessels are maintained in a thick and rigid condition that serves to sustain the headache.

Miscellaneous Psychosomatically
Related Cardiovascular Conditions

A variety of other psychosomatically related cardiovascular conditions deserve special mention, including shock, aneurysm, and hemorrhage.

1. Shock. Shock refers to a condition of acute peripheral circulatory failure; although there may be many patterns, one possibility includes profound visceral vasodilation with a consequent diminution in the flow of blood. A dramatic manifestation of shock is syncope or fainting, a temporary loss of consciousness due to cerebral anemia. Profound emotional reactions may lead to either or both of these conditions.

2. Aneurysm. An aneurysm is a localized dilation or saclike enlargement of a blood vessel, particularly an artery. Effects of aneurysm depend on the pressure of the expanding mass upon nerves, respiratory structures, the esophagus, or bone. Another danger, of course, is hemorrhage.

3. Hemorrhage. Hemorrhage means bleeding; sometimes it refers to slight bleeding and at other times to a very profuse flow of blood. In any case, a blood vessel may rupture in any part of the body to produce a hemorrhage, which in turn may lead to other tissue damage. Cerebral hemorrhage is the rupturing of a cerebral blood vessel, in which case bleeding upon or into surrounding brain tissue may destroy such tissue and produce a variety of sensory, motor, and integrational effects, depending on the location and extent of the hemorrhage. Ecker (1954) discovered in investigating 20 cases of cerebral stroke that in 15 cases a specific emotional stress situation immediately preceded the stroke.

4. Other psychosomatically induced cardiovascular effects. Essential hypertension combined with weakened arteries—arteries with high vulnerability to rupturing—provides the mechanism whereby stressful situations may provoke emotional reactions leading to such phenomena as the rupturing of blood vessels in the nose with subsequent nosebleeds, unusual menorrhagias, rupturing of blood vessels within the kidneys, and breaking of vessels in close proximity to the retina, and their subsequent further pathological effects. It is possible that a formulation such as this can be used to explain the stigmata—the bleeding of some patients at the hands and feet or their vicinity in the manner said to resemble the wounds of Christ when crucified. Of the millions of people in the world, it should not be unexpected that some would display simultaneous blood-vessel weaknesses in the hands and feet.

SIGNIFICANCE OF PSYCHOSOMATIC CARDIOVASCULAR DISORDERS

The following statements indicate the significance of psychosomatic cardiovascular disorders.

1. The greatest number of deaths in the U.S. each year are attributed to cardiovascular disorders. In many cases the symptoms are determined or at least extensively influenced by emotional factors.

2. It has been estimated that nearly half the cardiac cases in army hospitals during World War II were of a psychosomatic variety (Lewis and Engle, 1954). Probably a similar proportion obtains also for nonmilitary hospitals.

3. Autopsy studies performed on United States soldiers who were killed in action in Korea revealed gross evidence of coronary disease in more than 75 percent of the hearts examined (Enos, 1953).

4. At least half of all people over 45 die of some form of cardiovascular-renal disease. Hypertension disorders are major contributors (Health, Education and Welfare Trends, 1962).

CHAPTER SEVEN

PSYCHOSOMATIC GASTROINTESTINAL DISORDERS

ANATOMY AND PHYSIOLOGY OF THE GASTROINTESTINAL SYSTEM

The gastrointestinal system is sometimes called the digestive system, and a major portion of it also is also called the alimentary tract. Structurally, it consists of a group of related cavities and tubes. These structures are the mouth, pharynx, esophagus, stomach, and intestines. Associated accessory organs include a number of glands. (See Figure 7.1.)

Basically, the functions of the gastrointestinal tract are ingesting and digesting food in order that it can be absorbed into the circulatory system for distribution throughout the body. The processes involved are both mechanical and chemical. Illustrative of the mechanical processes are the mastication of food, the swallowing of it, and the movement of it by the stomach and intestines. A wide variety of chemical processes are also involved in modifying the chemical and physical nature of the original food substances. For example, the secretion of the salivary glands contains ptyalin, the secretion of the gastric glands contains pepsin, and the secretion of the pancreas contains trypsin. These substances are enzymes, a word meaning biological catalyst. A catalyst is a substance that increases

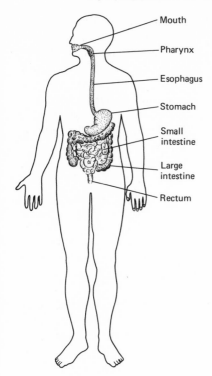

Mouth

Pharynx

Esophagus

Stomach

Small intestine

Large intestine

Rectum

FIGURE 7-1. Digestive system.

the velocity of a chemical reaction but is itself not chemically changed by that reaction.

Food taken into the mouth is masticated by movements of the tongue, lips, and teeth. It is mixed with secretions of the salivary glands. In addition to permitting the food to be rolled into a plastic mass called a bolus, this process moistens the food and gives it a lubricant coating. The bolus is drawn sharply backward by the tongue and passes into the pharynx, a tube in the region of the throat. It stays in the pharynx only briefly, muscles of the pharyngeal wall contracting and gripping or squeezing the food to force it into the esophagus. By peristaltic contractions of the muscular wall of the esophagus, food is moved to the stomach. Here the food is acted on mechanically by movements of the stomach and is also acted on chemically, primarily by secretions of the gastric glands. The gastric secretions contain many substances, including enzymes, mucin, and hydrochloric acid. Food is then passed into the intestinal tract, first into the small intestine and then into the large intestine. The first 10 inches or so of the small intestine are called the duodenum. Although of narrow diameter, the small intestine is about 21 feet long. The large intestine is of greater diameter, but only about 5 feet long.

The pancreas secretes substances having a digestive function into the small intestine. The liver manufactures and secretes bile, but instead of being passed directly into the intestine, the bile goes first into the gall bladder, from which it is discharged from time to time into the duodenum. In the small intestine, peristalsis—peristaltic movement—takes place. This movement characteristic of hollow muscular tubes generally, consists of a ringlike contraction of the muscular wall; as this contraction travels downward, it produces a certain degree of constriction in the intestine, which sweeps before it materials contained therein. Such peristaltic movements may follow each other at regular and frequent intervals, by that process moving food materials gradually but steadily. There are also rhythmical constrictions of the intestine that serve to break up and knead food and to mix it thoroughly with intestinal juices. It then passes into the large intestine, during which time water is absorbed to make the contents more plastic. Peristaltic movements occasionally also occur in the large intestine. Remains of the material acted on by the digestive system then pass into the lowest part of the digestive tube, the rectum, from which they are evacuated as feces.

The absorption of food materials is largely confined to the small intestine. Nutritive substances from there are taken into the circulatory fluid, from which they are distributed to tissues of the body requiring them.

A number of research observations have contributed to the development of knowledge concerning functions of the digestive tract and particularly its role in reaction to emotional stimulation. John Young in 1803 at the University of Pennsylvania demonstrated that the stomach secreted an acid fluid that played a significant role in the digestive process. He showed that the gastric fluid would digest or dissolve the flesh on the leg of a frog or the ear of a rabbit. A few years later another American physician, William Beaumont, had the opportunity to make further observations on stomach reactivity. His patient, Alexis St. Martin, on a hunting trip in the Northwest Michigan Territory suffered a partly destroyed stomach wall as a consequence of a gunshot wound; through this opening Beaumont was able to make observations on stomach activity over an eight-year period. He confirmed the acid content of the gastric juices and discovered that emotional stimulation seemed to directly influence digestive activities.

Much later Wolff and Wolf (1943) reported a case—the case of Tom —relating emotional stimulation to gastrointestinal activity. A 57-year-old workman almost a half century before (i.e., when about eight years of age) had swallowed some very hot soup, which resulted in the sealing of his esophagus. Unsuccessful attempts to repair the damage surgically resulted in the patient having a gaping hole into his stomach, and the patient fed himself first by chewing his food to satisfy taste needs and then by depositing the food into a funnel connected by a rubber tube to his stomach. The patient was secretive about his condition and apparently did not discuss it for many years. However, later in the hospital situation he did permit the repeated study of his stomach reactions, including reactions to a diversity of emotional stimuli.

CHARACTERISTIC EMOTIONAL REACTIONS INVOLVING THE GASTROINTESTINAL SYSTEM

There are a large number of reactions within the gastrointestinal system that normally occur in response to emotional stimulation. These reactions include changes in the rate of digestive canal contractions, changes in the rate and quantity and quality of gastrointestinal secretions, vomiting (which involves reversed peristalsis), and involuntary defecation, as well as others (Lachman, 1969).

TYPICAL PSYCHOSOMATIC DISORDERS INVOLVING THE GASTROINTESTINAL SYSTEM

A wide variety of conditions have been described as psychosomatic gastrointestinal disorders. Among these are gastrointestinal ulcer, colitis, gastritis, chronic constipation, and chronic diarrhea.

Gastrointestinal Ulcer

Perhaps the most frequently mentioned example of a gastrointestinal disorder believed to be of psychosomatic origin is gastrointestinal ulcer. This is sometimes called gastric or peptic ulcer because of the presumed role of the gastric juices, which contain pepsin; sometimes it is named in terms of its location and so it is called either stomach ulcer or duodenal ulcer, which refers to two major loci for the lesion. A gastrointestinal ulcer is a circumscribed erosion of the mucous membrane, typically of the stomach or the upper portion of the small intestine. Hypersecretion of the acid gastric juice plays a significant role in the production of such ulcers and in the reactivation of healed ulcers.

Ulcers are usually single, although multiple ulcers of the stomach or duodenum have been reported. The margins of an ulcer are sharp; the surrounding mucosal lining may be normal or inflamed. The floor of the crater may have layers of granulation of fibrous tissue. The report of pain is an outstanding symptom of peptic ulcer. In terms of self-report, the pain has four distinctive characteristics: a uniform quality and location, a tendency toward rhythmicity, periods of remission, and a tendency to become chronic. The pain varies from mild discomfort to an incisive, severe, and penetrating experience of extreme distress. It may have a steady aching or gnawing quality or it may be more acute—sharp and cramplike. The pain also tends to relate to the digestive cycle, usually being absent before breakfast and appearing during the day from one to four hours following meals. The pain is often relieved by bland foods and antacids; it may be intensified by spicy food and alcohol.

Case 7.1. *Psychosomatic dyspepsia.* A 27-year-old unmarried man complained of marked gastric distress following meals, although physical examination including x-ray study revealed no organ pathology. The patient was irritable and truculent. He had been married but quarreled with his wife and finally divorced her. He seemed unable to get along with his co-workers and quarreled with almost everyone in his life, casual contacts as well as those with whom he had repeated contact. In time he discovered how his own behavior interfered with his gaining basic satisfactions in life. Eventually, his behavior became more pleasant and friendly; he received more attention and more affectionate reactions from those around him and his symptoms subsided (English and Finch, 1964).

Case 7.2. *Psychosomatic ulcer.* Mr. R. M. lived at home until age 27. At that time he married; his marriage, a happy one, lasted 58 years until his wife's death. R. M., a retired mailman, then went to live with his son and daughter-in-law, but the situation in the son's home was not a happy one for the old man. Six weeks prior to hospital admission, conflict in the form of a quarrel with the daughter-in-law focused on the quality of meals, and prior to admission, the daughter-in-law had presented an ultimatum to R. M. to the effect that she would permit him to live at the house only on the condition that he prepare his own meals or get them in a restaurant. This corresponded with the onset of the 89-year-old patient's epigastric pains, which regularly followed eating by 15 to 30 minutes. It was those symptoms that led him to seek hospital treatment. R. M. was found on surgical examination to have a large but benign ulcer, apparently of recent origin (Hofling, 1968).

Case 7.3. *Psychosomatic ulcer.* A hardworking 35-year-old businessman reacted to the resignation of a close associate who left to establish a rival advertising agency by developing a peptic ulcer (Cameron, 1963).

Case 7.4. *Psychosomatic ulcer.* A man who grew up in an atmosphere of insecurity and who as a child was overdependent on his mother and as an adult overdependent on his wife, both of whom he hated, developed an ulcer. After a disagreement with his wife, in which she ordered him out of the house, he developed a severe hemorrhage of his ulcer (Kapp, Rosenbaum, and Romano, 1947).

Case 7.5. *Psychogenic vomiting.* A woman suffered from gastric spasms with severe heartburn followed by vomiting; this group of symptoms occurred whenever she encountered a serious frustrating situation within a short time after eating. As a youngster she had been forced by her mother to eat, even though she had little appetite. She frequently vomited the food a short time later, apparently not because the food was in any way unwholesome or poorly prepared, but because the mother subjected her to an emotional situation consisting of demands, nagging, insults, and incessant scolding during meals.

Case 7.6. *Ulcerative colitis.* A boy three and a half years of age had his first attack of ulcerative colitis the day summer school ended, when a nurse to whom he was devoted departed (Cameron, 1963).

Case 7.7. *Ulcerative colitis.* Gastrointestinal problems apparently began soon after birth. It was reported that at 10 days she became constipated and suppositories were administered almost every day until at 5 months of age she began to eat semisolid foods. From the time she was 18 months old her mother administered laxatives about once each week. Attacks of colitis began at age 12. At that age for the first time she visited a nearby metropolitan area, and although she was eager to explore everything there, she had to be restrained to suit the convenience of family and friends. Her first acute attack was characterized by loose stools that also contained blood, mucus, and water. Thereafter, similar attacks accompanied colds, and diarrhea was frequent between acute attacks. Emotional upsets sometimes precipitated attacks of diarrhea. A written autobiographical statement suggested feelings of isolation while growing up, feelings of being deprived of normal experiences, and feelings of being poorly equipped to meet competitive situations in school. Social relations, particularly those with boys, were evaluated by the clinician as impaired. A diagnostic evaluation was made at age 15 (Harris, in Burton and Harris, 1947).

Although occasionally ulcer symptoms have been present for 40 to 50 years before treatment is instituted and, therefore, ulcers are often not considered to be serious, conditions such as perforation of an ulcer constitute major health emergencies with the dangers of peritonitis and death, unless surgery is promptly performed.

The gastric secretions contain, as indicated earlier, three major components, mucus, pepsin, and hydrochloric acid. The mucus serves to protect the walls of the digestive tract from direct contact with noxious substances; pepsin has a role in the decomposition of protein; and hydrochloric acid also has a role in the breakdown of food substances and, although it is a powerful corrosive agent, it normally does not irritate the stomach or intestines, partly because their inner walls are covered with a mucinoid coat and partly because food absorbs much of the acid. An oversecretion of hydrochloric acid, however, may begin to attack the lining of the digestive tract where the mucinoid coat is absent or weakest; and, of course, acid secretion may occur in response to emotional situations whether or not there is food in the stomach.

In emotional situations, activation of the autonomic nervous system may include activation of the vagus nerve, which controls both secretion of gastric juice and movements of the stomach. This may be the major mechanism whereby emotional stimulation influences gastrointestinal activity. Perhaps movements of the gastrointestinal tract increase the probability of producing breaks in the mucinoid lining, which permits the corrosive action of hydrochloric acid to produce the lesions known as ulcers. In effect, an ulcer seems to be the consequence of the gastrointestinal tract's digesting itself.

Among the theories concerning psychological circumstances related to the development of gastrointestinal ulcer are the following.

1. An ulcer results from conflicts relating to dependence and independence (Alexander, 1934).

2. An ulcer results from resentment, hostility, and anger reactions (Wolf and Wolff, 1947).

3. An ulcer develops in an ambitious person who works under high pressure (Alvarez, 1941; Hartman, 1933; Dunbar, 1943).

For a number of reasons—and certainly because of much conflictful and unconvincing evidence—we will not consider theories concerning particular kinds of emotional situation or conflict or type of personality in relation to any specific psychosomatic disorder. At present it seems sufficient simply to indicate what there is least disagreement about, namely, that emotional stimulus situations produce physiological reactions leading to bodily malfunction and malstructure. Empirical findings in the future will establish whether particular situations, conflicts, or personality types relate to specific disorders. At our present state of knowledge, a firm answer to the question cannot be provided.

A number of research investigations—many of them experimental—pertinent to the role of emotional responses in gastrointestinal activation and in ulceration have been reported. The following studies are representative.

1. Mahl (1949), by subjecting seven dogs to strong electric shock preceded irregularly by a buzzer, not only developed chronic fear behavior but also developed an increased gastric acidity in six of the seven animals.

2. Mahl (1950) also found that, as compared with control periods, in a

stressful situation—immediately before an examination that would determine whether they would be admitted to medical school—premedical students had a general increase in quantity of hydrochloric acid in the stomach.

3. Hoelzel (1942) discovered an increase in acidity of a man—himself
—under actual conditions of life threat.

4. Sawrey and his associates (Sawrey and Weisz, 1956; Sawrey,
Conger, and Turrel, 1956; Conger, Sawrey, and Turrel, 1958) have reported on the effects of a chronic approach-avoidance conflict in the production of gastric ulcer in the rat. Animals lived for about two weeks in a
research apparatus; during this period shock was received whenever they
approached food or water. By the end of that time many of the subjects
had developed ulcers and some of them died from gastrointestinal hemorrhages. The control subjects deprived of food and water but not shocked
did not develop ulcers.

Another finding in this series of investigations was that when subjects
were placed in the conflict situation in groups of three at a time, the rate
of ulceration was substantially less than when subjects were used singly.
This seemed not to be an effect of earlier social experience.

5. One of the most frequently cited studies of experimental ulcer is
that of Brady and his associates (1958). In that investigation monkeys
were placed in restraining chairs and subjected to a series of shocks that
could be avoided by pressing a lever at least every 20 seconds. After a period of 20 seconds had elapsed without depressing the lever, shock was de-
livered to the feet. Ulcers were produced in monkeys by this technique;
however, left in doubt was the question of whether the psychological stress
involved timing the lever presses or whether the electric shock itself was
the major factor in the production of ulcers.

Brady (1958) developed a procedure to resolve the problem experimentally. He paired subjects in the apparatus and they sat in adjacent restraining chairs. One member of the pair served as the "executive" monkey. The executive monkey was able to avoid shocks to himself *and* to his
partner by pressing a lever. The control monkey also had a lever, but it
was functionless. Therefore, the executive monkey was responsible for preventing shock to both himself and to his control partner; both monkeys received the same number of shocks and at the same time, but only the executive monkey was confronted with the stressful situation, that is, the
decision-making opportunity to avoid the shock by pressing a lever. Under
these conditions the executive monkey developed ulcers, whereas the control monkey did not.

In order to avoid the possibility that social interaction between the monkeys contributed in some way to the stress situation, the approach was refined later by using soundproof isolation booths for each of the subjects, and it was found that ulcers still developed in the executives but not in the controls. Apparently, social variables were not of major significance. Further, the amount of work was unrelated to the development of the ulcer, since control monkeys did not develop ulcers even when working harder than monkeys with executive responsibilities.

Different schedules of shock avoidance and of test were employed during these experiments. A red light was turned on during the avoidance period and off during the rest periods. Executive monkeys quickly learned to press the lever many times during the avoidance period and to desist from pressing when the red light was off. Although the control monkeys also pressed their levers from time to time, the controls soon lost interest in pressing a nonfunctional lever.

A schedule of 30 minutes rest and 30 minutes of shock-avoidance session produced much activity but no ulcers. Likewise, a schedule of 18 hours of shock-avoidance session and 6 hours of rest also produced no ulcers. A schedule involving 6 hours of shock-avoidance behavior and 6 hours of rest proved to be most potent in the development of ulcers.

After 33 days of the 6-hour schedule, an executive monkey died suddenly during one of the shock-avoidance periods. No advance warning had occurred, nor had the animal lost weight during the research period. Autopsy disclosed a large perforation in the wall of the upper part of the small intestine; this is a region in which ulcers are frequently found in man. Autopsy of the control monkey who was sacrificed a few hours later disclosed no gastrointestinal pathology. An attempt was made to assess gastric activity throughout the six-hour cycle. A surgical incision in the abdomen and stomach permitted the sampling of stomach contents periodically. Measurements made of gastric activity under various periods of avoidance responding indicated that one-hour sessions had no effect on secretion, but that there was a considerable rise in the acidity *after a three-hour session had ended,* and even a more pronounced rise *after termination of a six-hour session.* The major aspect of these findings is that the gastric activity began *after* the session was over and did not occur during the actual shock-avoidance period at all.

Brady in attempting to answer questions raised by these experiments has suggested the hypothesis that emotional stress led to an ulcer when the stress was intermittent rather than continuous and when the period of emotional stress coincided with the natural periodicity of gastric secretions under normal conditions.

These last findings cited suggest several ideas relevant to temporal relationships concerning physiological reactions of emotion in the development of psychosomatic effects. Those ideas, which perhaps have broad and general applicability, may be formulated as principles in the following way.

A   PRINCIPLE NUMBER *1   Emotional Reaction Latency.* The autonomic patterns of reaction that are emotional behavior—or at least one or more components of such a pattern—may not be immediately operative; the response may be *initiated* only after a delay interval, attributable perhaps to certain idiosyncrasies within the central nervous system or to other idiosyncratic sequences of internal activities that intervene between the initial reaction to the emotion-provoking stimulus and the particular response in question.

B   PRINCIPLE NUMBER *2   Temporal Patterning of Stimulation.* The duration or repetition of an emotion-provoking stimulus situation influences the nature of an autonomic reaction—by modifying its duration, frequency, intensity, or quality, or in some other way.

C   PRINCIPLE NUMBER *3   Autonomic Reaction Maximum.* The maximal reaction—the highest magnitude or greatest intensity of arousal of an autonomic effector—may occur long after termination of the emotion-provoking stimulus situation, regardless of whether a less-intense reaction of that effector began at the time of stimulation or whether there was much latency in the initial arousal of the response mechanism.

D   PRINCIPLE NUMBER *4   Cumulative Effects of Response.* Response effects of a deleterious kind may be cumulative and eventually lead to pathology; fewer such responses (during the same period of time) produce less-pronounced effects. Changes in other dimensions of response, such as the magnitude of hydrochloric acid concentration in the gastric secretion, will produce other effects.

E   PRINCIPLE NUMBER *5   Temporal Patterning of Response.* The temporal patterning of responses may be of special significance in the elicitation of pathological effects. In part, this may result from the relationship of responses induced by emotion-provoking stimulations to random vacillations or to systematic variations (i.e., normal biological rhythms) in the occurrence or intensity of that response. Fortuitous coincidences or sequences of the response in question may facilitate or diminish pathological effects.

The value of the principles suggested above remains to be determined empirically; however, the work of Brady and of certain other investigators provide some support.

6. Mittelmann, Wolff, and Scharf (1942) interviewed 13 normal subjects and 13 patients suffering from ulcer or gastroduodenitis under control and emotion-provoking conditions. They found that an increase of free hy-

drochloric acid in the stomach occurred during the affective periods, along with a change in peristalsis from intermittent to continuous activity, in both groups, with greater intensity and duration of reaction in the patient population.

Among other research investigations elucidating factors in the development of ulcer are the following.

7. Dragstedt (1956) has reported that ulcer patients secrete 4 to 20 times as much acid at night as normal subjects do; this is at a time when the stomach is comparatively empty. The hyperactivity can be cut almost in half by severing the vagus nerve. In fact, such surgery has led to the disappearance of ulcers in many patients subjected to surgical treatment.

8. Wolff and Wolf (1943), in their work with Tom, reported that when their patient was anxious, angry, or resentful, stomach movements and stomach secretion increased and the stomach lining became engorged with blood; on the other hand, when he was fearful or sad, stomach motility and secretions and vascularity all declined.

9. Mirsky and his associates (1952) discovered a relationship between peptic ulcer and the excretion of pepsinogen in the urine and the level of pepsinogen in the blood; the excretion of pepsinogen was much greater in patients with peptic ulcer than in normal persons.

In connection with the Wolff and Wolf (1943) study already cited, the investigators found that a collar of gastric mucosa had grown out to surround the fistula, permitting access to the stomach. A small erosion induced on this exposed gastric mucosa where the supply of mucus was inadequate was artificially kept moist with gastric juice for four days; the erosion increased in size, resembling in every way a chronic ulcer, and was painful when touched. When the wound was protected from gastric juice by a dressing, the area healed completely in about three days without even leaving a scar. This finding and others support the contention that prolonged acid secretion of the stomach has a significant role in producing ulceration.

10. Neural structures implicated as mechanisms that intervene between emotional stimulation and the physiological responses involved in the genesis of ulcers include particularly the hypothalamus and various other central and peripheral structures of the autonomic nervous system. Folkow and von Euler (1954) have demonstrated that stimulation of specific hypothalamic areas promotes selective liberation of adrenalin and noradrenalin. Hillarp (1953) has presented evidence indicating that cells of the adrenal medulla may release adrenalin or noradrenalin independently; he further suggests that such cells are controlled by different hypothalamic areas.

French, Porter, Cavanaugh, and Longmire (1957) reported the development of ulcerlike lesions in monkeys exposed to long-time electrical excitation of structures in a low midline region of the hypothalamus. Much earlier, Harvey Cushing, a pioneer American brain surgeon (1932), observed that when surgery involved this region, his patients sometimes developed ulcers; they were believed to be caused by stimulation or injury to a part of the hypothalamus.

Glaser and Wolf (1960) related gastrointestinal activities—both secretory and motor—to excessive vagal discharge. Waddell (1956) demonstrated that differences in urinary levels of catecholamines in ulcer and nonulcer patients were related to sympathetic nervous system and adrenal gland reactivity.

To review, the lining of the stomach and the upper part of the duodenum are protected from the digestive action of an acid solution by means of a mucinoid coating. The precursor of an ulcer involves some break or other impairment in the mucinoid coat. In the course of normal digestive activity, it is probable that the thin mucous lining is transiently abraded or worn off. If this occurs in the absence of a hypersecretion of gastric juice, no further changes occur and the lining is quickly replaced. However, if there is heightened gastric secretion, the probability is raised that in one or another of the abraded areas, the mucosa itself will be destroyed by digestive juices. Once begun, the lesion is likely to be durable, since the protective mucinoid coating cannot be readily reformed under those conditions.

Colitis

Another major disorder of the gastrointestinal system frequently regarded as psychosomatic in origin is colitis, which is an inflammation of the colon. Two forms are often distinguished. One of these is chronic ulcerative colitis, a persistent nonspecific inflammatory and ulcerative condition of the colon; the second is mucous colitis, a less-serious condition characterized by derangement of the motor activity and mucus-secreting activities of the colon.

That the lower as well as the upper part of the gastrointestinal tract is quite responsive to emotional stimulation is evident from the often-reported observation that bowel movements may increase in frequency during conditions of stress; or alternatively that under such conditions there may be a decrease in frequency of bowel movements, which can result in a condition of constipation. Likewise, the physical quality of defecated material may also change. The passing of mucus in the stools often indicates the beginnings of a psychosomatic disorder of the colon.

That a psychogenic disorder can involve the colon may be understood in terms of several mechanisms. For example, for a particular person, stressful stimuli may induce spasms of the colon that damage colonic tissue and that permit bacterial invasion to produce further damage; or alternatively, minor damage via physical agents including allergens, to the internal surface of the colon may be further irritated by more profound changes in bowel activity caused by emotionality, thus producing lesions, including abcesses and hemorrhages.

As the mucosa becomes progressively involved, inflammatory and hemorrhagic processes may also extend into and destroy muscular structures of the bowel. Arrest or healing may occur in any stage, but even in mild cases, the structure of the mucosa often does not return to normal. Residual scar tissue that develops gives the area a granular or pockmarked appearance and renders it so friable that hemorrhaging may readily occur.

Ulcerative colitis is a serious psychosomatic condition in which an ulcer may develop in the wall of the colon in a manner similar to that in which the peptic ulcer develops in upper portions of the gastrointestinal tract; such a condition is dangerous in that hemorrhaging or perforation may occur. In certain advanced cases, the entire mucous lining of the colon may so disintegrate as to make partial removal of the colon necessary.

Implicated in this disorder is the parasympathetic nervous system, which facilitates activities of the intestinal canal, promoting blood flow, mucous secretion, peristalsis, and other activities of relevance to the digestive process.

1. Lium and Porter (1939) demonstrated that activation of parasympathetic fibers produces colonic spasms and congestion of blood in the colon. Pronounced and prolonged spasms could produce swelling and edema of the mucous membrane and proximal tissue and even bleeding. Such a condition makes the colon readily vulnerable to abrasion. The ulcers in ulcerative colitis are typically restricted to areas in which muscular spasms are most pronounced.

2. In healthy volunteers, Almy, Kern, and Tulin (1949) found a relationship between the magnitude of stress perceived as personally threatening and the magnitude of colonic reaction.

3. It has been reported (Grace, Wolf, and Wolff, 1950a) that direct observation of the mucous membrane of the colon in a colitis patient disclosed that during emotionally stressful situations the colon became congested and hyperactive. Under such conditions the colon becomes fragile, so that even minor psychological or physical irritants could produce hemorrhages and ulceration.

4. On the basis of an investigation of four patients suffering from ulcerative colitis, all of whom had been colostomized, thus rendering the

colon easily accessible to observation, Grace, Wolf, and Wolff (1950b) reported that emotional conditions were associated with hypermotility of the colon, increased engorgement with blood, increased mucous secretion, and increased secretion of lysozyme. Fragility of the mucous membrane was also increased, and sustained emotionality led to submucosal loci of bleeding and ulceration.

5. Lysozyme, an enzyme discovered by Fleming, is normally present in tears, nasal secretions, and gastrointestinal secretions. Its function relates to its capacity for breaking up and dissolving bacteria as well as its capacity for dissolving mucus. Research by Meyer, Gellhorn, Prudden, Lehman, and Steinberg (1947) disclosed that stools from patients with chronic ulcerative colitis had 56.0 lysozyme units per gram weight, whereas the rate was 2.7 for normal stools; these researchers also demonstrated that the lysozyme came from the colon rather than the small intestine.

6. Grace, Seton, Wolf, and Wolff (1949) found that the quantity of feces lysozyme varies and is related to the emotional state of the subject. Even in a nonpathological population, emotionality produces a transient increase in fecal lysozyme. In patients with ulcerative colitis, symptoms and concentration of lysozyme increased after conditions of emotionality. On the other hand, with the decline in symptoms during remission periods, lysozyme concentration was also low.

7. Prugh (1950) has suggested that a "conditioned hypermobile response of the rectosigmoid region of the large bowel to emotional stimuli of a specific type" is a potent factor operative in the etiology of ulcerative colitis. Several alternative mechanisms—in the form of hypotheses parallel to that of Prugh and in harmony with the proposed *autonomic learning theory* of psychosomatic disorders—operating independently of or in combination with each other, may also be suggested.

(a.) Conditioned vascular responses in the colon to a wide variety of emotional stimulus-situations have a role in the development of ulcerative colitis. Engel has emphasized the significance of impaired vascularity of the colon—of both the mucosa and the submucosa—in ulcerative colitis. His point that bleeding rather than diarrhea or constipation is usually the first symptom in the illness can be related to this hypothesis (Engel, 1954a; Engel, 1954b). A critical intermediate link is provided by the *autonomic learning theory,* viz., that the conditioned vascular responses be sufficiently chronic, frequent, or intense to produce bleeding.

(b.) Conditioned responses relating to decreased or deficient formation of intestinal mucus established to a variety of emotional stimulus situations have a role in the development of ulcerative colitis.

(c.) Conditioned responses relating to the excessive formation of intestinal lysozyme established to a variety of emotional stimulus-situations have a role in the development of ulcerative colitis.

These hypotheses need to be more definitely particularized as empirical results are accumulated. Attempts to identify precisely the neural and hormonal mediators of the involved behaviors—the chain of events—is also essential in the acquisition of more solid knowledge in the genesis of psychosomatic disorders of the intestinal tract. At present, however, at least two mechanisms may be proposed by which the parasympathetic nervous system may act on the colon to give rise to ulceration: (1) Augmented vascular congestion may increase the vulnerability of the colon. (2) Augmented lysozyme secretion may increase vulnerability of the colon. Attempts to relate a unique and specific personality pattern to colitis susceptibility have not yet been fruitful, although a number of suggestions have been proposed.

That psychogenic factors are closely related to the disorder is supported by the fact that separation from or death of a person with whom the individual has had close and affectionate affiliation; loss of a job; divorce; and similar emotionally stressful circumstances of major significance have precipitated attacks of ulcerative colitis. Such situations, however, may also precipitate other psychosomatic symptoms as well.

Among the other disorders of the gastrointestinal tract regarded as psychosomatic are gastritis, chronic constipation, and chronic diarrhea.

Gastritis

Gastritis refers to an inflammation of the stomach. Obviously such a condition could occur in particular situations involving psychological stress; however, as a consequence of repeated exposure to such emotional situations, the digestive changes relating to gastritis become chronic. A variety of symptoms may accompany this disorder, including indigestion, hyperacidity, eructation, flatulence, and nausea. The disorder may vary in degree from a relatively mild condition to one of great severity.

The nature of the symptoms varies with the severity of the disorder. In chronic superficial gastritis, however, the majority of patients report sensations of epigastric burning—sometimes called heartburn. Fullness of the stomach or pressure within the stomach and sometimes nausea and vomiting may also occur.

Acute gastritis may be a direct consequence of the potent activation of the sympathetic nervous system. Among other effects, the autonomic responses to stress may include disorganization of digestive functions; components of such disorganization include disturbance of acidity-alkalinity balance and interruptions of peristalsis, among other changes. Obviously, if such reactions occur frequently enough to particular stressful situations, they may come to be persistently associated with those particular stimulus situations, or such reactions may even occur in response to symbolic representations of such situations. It is also obvious that these reactions, if they are reinforced by valued attentions from members of the family and by other advantages accruing from the symptoms, tend to become strengthened and made permanent.

The background and personality profile proposed for the gastritis patient includes a domineering parent, sibling rivalry, and resentment toward authority. Until more evidence is acquired, such suggested correlations are to be regarded with skepticism.

Chronic Psychogenic Constipation

Chronic psychogenic constipation is a condition of infrequent or difficult evacuation of feces, primarily due to emotionality. In patients suffering from spastic constipation, Almy, Hinkle, Berle, and Kern (1949), using an interview procedure combined with observation of colon reactions, found an increase in symptom magnitude under emotional conditions; the most obvious changes occurred in response to discussion of their personal emotional problems and life difficulties.

Chronic Psychogenic Diarrhea

Chronic psychogenic diarrhea is a condition of abnormal frequency and fluidity of fecal discharges, primarily due to emotionality. Patients with this disorder are reluctant to be more than a short distance away from a lavatory or similar facility. In some cases there are as many as 40 or 50 bowel movements each day.

Psychogenic diarrhea may occur in persons with unusually sensitive gastrocolic reflexes as part of the total physiological reaction to emotional stimulation (Aldrich, 1966; Daniels, et al., 1962; Engel, 1955; Grace and Wolff, 1951).

Psychogenic Cholecystic Disease—Gallstones

Bile—at one time called gall—a fluid manufactured and secreted by the liver, passes first into the gall bladder and from it is discharged intermittently into the duodenum to aid in the digestive process. Gallstones are concretions formed usually in the gallbladder; apparently the concentration of various chemicals in the bile reaches a level that produces precipitation and the formation of such concretions. Undoubtedly, there are many determinants for that end result. It has been suggested, however, that at least in some cases, the major determinant of such cholecystic disease is psychogenic. The essential rationale is that the secretion of bile is sometimes one reaction in an emotional constellation. In particular individuals, there may be an aberration in the secretion of bile, facilitating the genesis of gall-stones. Goldman and Ulett (1968), on the basis of clinical observation of cholecystic disease, support this position. They cite as an "observation" in commenting on the psychogenic hypothesis concerning cholecystic disease that over a period of many years, three female office employees of one physician required cholecystectomies as did the maid who served his household, and the authors refer to that particular doctor—who apparently was a domineering, controlling, sharp-tempered person—as a "chole-lithogenic individual." As with other uncontrolled observations and case-history studies, such inferences, though interesting, are subject to formidable challenge.

SIGNIFICANCE OF PSYCHOSOMATIC GASTROINTESTINAL DISORDERS

A number of facts testify to the significance of gastrointestinal disorders, many instances of which appear to be fundamentally psychogenic. The following statements—restricted to ulcer—are representative. (1) It has been reported that as many as three million persons in the United States have a peptic ulcer. Although ulcers may be discussed facetiously, they are nevertheless a potentially serious disorder with the possibility of perforation and peritonitis. (2) About 10,000 persons in the United States die of peptic ulcer annually. (3) The economic cost of peptic ulcer in terms of lost income due to disability, of expected income unfulfilled due to premature death, and of medical expenses may be as much as a billion dollars each year.

CHAPTER EIGHT

PSYCHOSOMATIC
RESPIRATORY DISORDERS

ANATOMY AND PHYSIOLOGY
OF THE RESPIRATORY SYSTEM

Structurally, the respiratory system includes the nasal cavities, the pharynx, the larynx, the trachea, the bronchi, the bronchioles, and the air sacs of the lung. (See Figure 8.1.)

Air passes through the nostrils into the nasal cavities, which open posteriorly into the pharynx and past the larynx (which is situated in the neck anterior to the lower part of the pharynx) through the trachea, or windpipe (a tube about one half inch in diameter and four and a half inches long), and into two branches, the right and left bronchi. The air sac from within each bronchus enters the lung as the bronchi progressively divide into smaller branches, the final twigs being referred to as bronchioles. The bronchioles enter into the air spaces of the lung. Blood flowing through the lung is separated from air in the air spaces by two membranes, the alveolar and the capillary walls, so extremely thin that little resistance is offered to the free exchange of respiratory gases.

The fundamental function of the respiratory system is gaseous exchange with the atmosphere; essentially this involves inspiring oxygen—or at least inspiring air that contains oxygen—and expiring carbon dioxide. These processes are essential to life. The mechanism for respiration operates automatically for most part. It is regulated by control centers in the medulla.

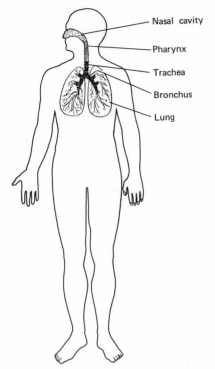

Nasal cavity

Pharynx

Trachea

Bronchus

Lung

FIGURE 8-1. Respiratory system.

CHARACTERISTIC EMOTIONAL REACTIONS INVOLVING THE RESPIRATORY SYSTEM

Common respiratory reactions to emotional stimulation include changes in the pattern of inspiration and expiration, such as sudden cessation of breathing, sighing, gasping, a sudden inspiration and gradual expiration pattern—as in crying or weeping—a gradual inspiration and sudden, sometimes explosive, expiration pattern—as in laughing—and a variety of other characteristic reactions (Lachman, 1969).

TYPICAL PSYCHOSOMATIC DISORDERS INVOLVING THE RESPIRATORY SYSTEM

A wide variety of conditions have been described as psychosomatic respiratory disturbances. Among these are bronchial asthma, hyperventilation syndrome, vasomotor rhinitis, chronic bronchitis, sinusitis, and laryngitis. It is also possible that emotional reactions involving the respiratory mechanism influence the course of disorders for which the primary determining agent is physical, as in pulmonary tuberculosis and pulmonary pneumonia.

Bronchial Asthma

Bronchial asthma is a condition manifested by recurrent paroxysms of dyspnea of a characteristic wheezing type caused by narrowing of passages of the bronchi and the bronchioles. In other words, it is a condition marked by breathing difficulties caused by spasms of bronchial muscles. There may also be inflammations of or swellings of the bronchial mucosa. Overtly, however, the major symptoms are shortness of breath, gasping, coughing, wheezing, and reports of thoracic constriction.

During an asthmatic attack, the mucosa of the bronchi are thickened and the epithelial cells are distended; this results in a narrowing of the lumen, which is further obstructed by excessive secretion of thick tenacious mucus. Both inspiration and expiration are hampered by this narrowing of the air passages, but the greater interference is with expiration. Expiration, the passive phase of respiration, is prolonged and often incomplete because air is trapped within the lung. Inspiration, which involves dilation of the narrowed air passages, is accomplished more readily. The major problem is to get rid of chest air in order to continue breathing. As a result of incomplete expirations, the lungs become distended with air during the acute attack, and repeated attacks may produce chronic emphysema with its consequences—prominent reduction of lung vital capacity, loss of lung elasticity, and perhaps eventually chest deformity.

The breathing problem is complicated by the thick, sticky mucinoid substance secreted. It is a further obstruction to breathing, produces lung congestion, and can be expelled only slowly and with difficulty.

The bronchial spasm, such as that which occurs in asthma, may be the direct result of a physicochemical reaction to an allergic substance or it may be a component in the reaction-complex to emotional stimulation. Asthmatic attacks may, therefore, have a strictly physical origin as a reaction to particular chemical substances. Only with physical determinants eliminated and with substantial evidence—including a well-defined linkage of attacks to specific emotional situations combined with the absence of such attacks in the absence of such situations—should asthma be considered psychogenic.

Case 8.1. *Asthma.* A patient who had asthmatic attacks regularly when brought into contact with roses, also displayed such an asthmatic attack when confronted with an artificial rose (Mackenzie, 1886).

Case 8.2. *Asthma.* The patient's mother was described as lacking in basic warmth and as a child the patient had not known mothering in the usual sense of that word. She suffered from asthma and eczema since childhood. The eczema reached its apex during adolescence and thereafter became less noticeable, but the asthma attacks became more frequent. The patient married and had children, but her marriage was not a happy one and motherhood was not satisfying to her. At the time of initiating therapy at age 38, the patient complained of intense personal unhappiness. During the course of prolonged treatment, the patient gradually became a much more relaxed person and established a more comfortable relationship with both herself and others. During the course of a two-year follow-up, she was free of asthma and had only occasional mild symptoms of eczema. The personality changes achieved through psychotherapy helped her reduce tension to the point where her psychophysiological symptoms were rare (English and Finch, 1964).

Case 8.3. *Asthma.* At age 16, Mr. X had his first asthmatic attack while at a summer camp where he had been sent while his parents were traveling in Europe. Another attack occurred while he was a freshman at a college in another part of the country. After his marriage his attacks increased in frequency and severity to the point where he consulted a medical specialist. With psychotherapy, he began to recognize some of the circumstances leading to his symptoms and the functions they served. His symptoms gradually disappeared (Kisker, 1964).

Case 8.4. *Asthma.* A 32-year-old man who was advancing steadily in a highly competitive academic situation developed attacks of asthma and episodes of dermatitis in response to perceived neglect by his wife (Cameron, 1963).

Case 8.5. *Hyperventilation syndrome.* Mrs. R married her husband suddenly after having been jilted by another man. At that time she also gave up an excellent job. A daughter was born to the marriage. Mrs. R regarded her husband as self-centered, buried in his work, disinterested in social life, and disparaging of his wife and her activities. At the age of 50, she received medical care for her menopausal symptoms which included headaches, nausea, tremulousness, and cold sweats. After five years, during which the patient did well, the physician treating her was abruptly dismissed by the patient's husband. The husband's behavior toward her, including particularly his termination of the physician who had helped her through the menopause, repeatedly produced anger reactions in Mrs. R. During the next two years, her husband took Mrs. R to several other physicians because of her increasingly frequent and severe attacks of apparent shortness of breath. These occurred early in the morning upon waking; besides seeming to be short of breath she also reported becoming dizzy and weak. The symptoms prevented her husband and daughter from going to work and prevented Mrs. R from doing her housework. At about that time she was referred by her husband for psychiatric treatment; he stated in her presence that he could no longer stand her "huffing and puffing." A physical examination revealed only a slight elevation in blood pressure. Mrs. R was requested to hyperventilate and it was demonstrated to her that her symptoms could be reproduced by that procedure (Kolb, 1968).

Case 8.6. *Asthma.* A 22-year-old male suffering constantly from asthma with little relief became slowly but progressively worse while hospitalized on a general medical ward for several months, during which time medication—sometimes large quantities of adrenalin compounds and derivatives—was ineffective. After transfer to the psychiatric unit, he improved rapidly and soon was free of major asthmatic attacks. After he left the hospital, psychotherapy continued. Relapses occurred when problem situations developed, but psychotherapy apparently led to steady improvement (Grinker and Robbins, 1954).

Several lines of evidence associate asthmalike reactions with emotional stimulation and lend support to the significance of psychological determinants in asthma. The following are representative.

1. Stevenson and Ripley (1952) discovered a prolonged expiration characteristic of asthmatic breathing in response to emotional stimulation that was more frequent in asthmatics than in anxious subjects.
2. Faulkner (1941) investigated bronchial reactions to emotional stimulation via a bronchoscope in a 75-year-old patient. Frustration (or ideational equivalents) produced spasmodic narrowing of the lumen—constriction; suggestion relating to pleasant conditions produced dilations of the bronchial lumen.
3. Tuft (1959) reported cures in 90 percent of children with intractable asthma by a single transfer from their homes to a national center for asthmatic children. Since 10 youngsters who lived in the same city as that of the institution were among the cures, the results are not attributable to change in climate or pollen level; rather, they are better explained in terms of a change in emotional atmosphere.

The role of suggestibility in the symptoms of asthmatics has been demonstrated recently by Philipp (1970). By presenting his subjects with a neutral substance—physiological saline—as an inhalant and informing them that they would experience breathing difficulties, Philipp obtained asthmatic responses. His subjects also reacted less intensively to mecholyl—a bronchospasm-inducing drug—when told that the inhalant was a neutral substance and would not lead to any changes in breathing reactions than when they were informed of its actual breathing-interference properties.

A dramatic demonstration of the psychological nature of at least some asthmatic reactions is provided by the observation of Dekker and Groen (1956) on two patients who exhibited asthmatic paroxysms simply on viewing a toy goldfish.

There is much experimental evidence that modifications in breathing pattern, particularly in the direction of asthmatic reactions, can be learned. Such modifications have been observed in an experimentally neurotic dog (Gantt, 1947), in farm animals—goats and sheep (Liddell, 1951)—in monkeys (Masserman and Pechtel, 1953), and in experimentally conflicted cats (Seitz, 1959). These alterations in breathing accompanied other behavioral changes deliberately induced in the research situation.

Turnbull (1962) demonstrated that an asthmalike reaction can be acquired in animals via conditioning procedures. Ottenberg and associates (1958) administered egg white by aerosol spray to produce asthmalike attacks in guinea pigs; later, animals responded asthmatically to an associated stimulus, namely, mere sight of the aerosol device, and to other concomitant stimuli, even the experimental pen.

Herxheimer (1953) and others have observed that when asthmatic subjects were merely placed in a situation in which on earlier occasions they had been exposed to allergens, they would develop asthmatic reactions *without exposure* to the allergen.

Dekker and Groen (1956), by presenting idiosyncratic emotionally charged stimuli based on particular life histories of patients or by presenting replicas of situations that earlier provoked an attack, discovered that many patients reacted with asthmalike attacks.

Dekker, Pelser, and Groen (1957) found that two patients with severe bronchial asthma reacted with an asthmatic attack when they inhaled an aerosol presentation of substances to which they were reaction-sensitive. Subsequently however, they displayed the asthmatic reaction to inhalation of neutral substances and even to pure oxygen. Eventually an attack could be redintegrated, that is, produced by a part of the originally effective stimulus situation; for example, mere presentation of the mouthpiece earlier used in the inhalation of the reaction-sensitive substances was effective in evoking the attack.

There is, therefore, much evidence that asthmalike patterns may be learned in a variety of situations by experimental animals and by humans.

Breathing patterns may be altered by modifications in autonomic nervous system functioning that influence respiration; respiratory changes may be conditioned to stimuli associated with the original effective elicitor. Breathing patterns—even though nondeliberate—are also under direct immediate control of the organism (via the somatic nervous system) and therefore readily changed. Probably both these mechanisms—autonomic and somatic—operate together. Differential reinforcement of breathing patterns may lead to the acquisition of an asthmalike respiratory pattern. Consider a child whose remaining silent or whose crying and screaming reactions elicit no parental response, but whose sighing, wheezing, and gasping reactions invariably lead to special attention from the parents. Those respiratory patterns are promoted by their repeated reinforcement; they can be enhanced in definiteness and amplitude, and they can be developed and well established by such reinforcement. Later in life, in stressful situations, the individual may revert to those strong earlier-established and frequently practiced habits.

Many suggestions have been made concerning the relationship of particular personality patterns or particular kinds of emotional situations to the development of bronchial asthma. To date research evidence in support of those contentions has been neither conclusive nor impressive.

There are many degrees of severity in bronchial asthma. It may vary from rare occasional attacks to conditions in which individuals are continually ill to the point of being chronically disabled. Varying degrees of symptom intensity in terms of wheezing, choking sensations, and gasping for breath may occur, from the very rare and mild to the very frequent and severe; in some cases a bronchial spasm may be of such intensity and duration as to cause death.

Hyperventilation Syndrome

Hyperventilation syndrome is a condition characterized by hyperpnea or overbreathing, which leads to alkalosis and symptoms related to it. Typically, the hyperventilation syndrome consists of episodes of deep breathing with the mouth open or of rapid shallow breathing. Such reactions are part of a sympathetic pattern and may occur in response to many emotion-provoking situations. Accompanying symptoms include reports of blurred vision, dizziness, thoracic pressure or pain, numbness, and tingling of the extremities. The condition may be evoked by situations that instigate general and intense emotional arousal and in some cases may be precipitated even by nightmares. The excessive exhalation of carbon dioxide produces vasoconstriction and an estimated 30 percent reduction in cerebral blood flow (Sim, 1963), which may account for most of the symptoms. It certainly helps to explain some of the complaints such as tingling in the fingers and loss of power in the limbs and jaws. The washing out of carbon dioxide deranges the acid-base balance by removing an important buffering agent—carbonic acid; if extreme enough, it can result in fainting or convulsions, accentuate allergies, and produce changes in gastrointestinal and genitourinary activity.

Vasomotor Rhinitis

Vasomotor rhinitis (rhinorrhea) is characterized by a swelling of the nasal mucous membrane, profuse nasal fluid discharge, itching, and sneezing. Other frequent symptoms include nasal congestion, watering of the eyes, and conjunctivitis, a form of eye inflammation. Although often a function of an infection or an allergen, apparently the symptoms may also be produced psychologically as reactions to emotional circumstances. When the condition is due to botanical vegetation, particularly pollen of trees, grasses, or flowering shrubs, it is called hay fever and occurs annually at about the same time each year—during a particular season.

Rhinitis and asthmatic reactions have been reported clinically not only to real flowers but also to artificial ones (Mackenzie, 1886) and to pictures of flowers. The latter reactions have encouraged a psychological—rather than a biochemical—explanation for such disorders. The psychogenic position is further supported by more systematic research investigation. For example, Metzger (1947) produced attacks of vasomotor rhinitis in hayfever patients by exposing them to artificial flowers. He also reported success in relieving symptoms of allergic patients with placebos.

An abundant supply of autonomic fibers to the nasal mucosa provides a peripheral mechanism for mediation of emotional-stimulus effects and for the development of vasomotor rhinitis. More systematic study is needed to identify characteristics of susceptible individuals and the nature of emotional circumstances including the syndrome.

Other inflammations of the respiratory system include bronchitis, sinusitis, and laryngitis.

Bronchitis

Bronchitis is an inflammation of the bronchial tree. The disorder may be acute or chronic, localized or diffuse, and while typically due to infection and other physical agents, in some individuals it is instigated by emotional circumstances. Frequent symptoms include sore throat, chilliness, fever, malaise, and muscle pain. That psychological factors may function to elicit the disorder is suggested by the fact that bronchial irritation can be induced by a variety of physical and chemical irritants including mineral and vegetable dusts, strong acid fumes, volatile organic solvents, ammonia, hydrogen sulfide, sulfur dioxide, and tobacco smoke, among many others; stimuli repeatedly associated with the effective irritants may eventually themselves come to elicit the reaction. Inflammation of the bronchial tree in response to emotional stimulation achieved through pronounced dilation of blood vessels associated with the respiratory system may also produce symptoms of bronchitis and represents an alternative kind of psychological basis. Probably, the bronchitis reaction can also be acquired instrumentally, that is, via selection and connection learning. If in early life the bronchitis reaction (whether or not at first psychologically engendered as part of a more complex response constellation) is frequently, differentially, and intensely reinforced, the reaction may become more highly specific and of greater amplitude, that is, may become more pronounced and more sharply defined. Once the reaction is sufficiently strengthened, it may be used automatically by the individual in the service of his life situation.

Sinusitis

Sinusitis is an inflammation of the nasal sinuses. While often produced by respiratory-tract infections, respiratory obstructions, and allergens, apparently such changes may be elicited by emotional stimulation.

Laryngitis

Laryngitis, a condition of inflammation of the larynx, may be established as a psychosomatic disorder either as a function of conditioning of the symptom to new stimuli or as a function of differentiation of this particular response from a constellation of physically induced cold symptoms through a process of differential reinforcement.

The Common Cold

It is possible that coryza, the so called "common cold," is frequently the result of psychological conditions, that is, it is the effect of frustration, conflict, unpleasant circumstances, and other emotion-provoking situations. Further, it has been suggested that persons subjected to continuous or severe pathological stress are more likely to develop colds than individuals not so subjected.

The autonomic nervous pathways to the nose, mouth, throat, and sinus cavities provide mechanisms for the development of cold symptoms. During emotional states, especially those accompanied by weeping, the nasal mucosa swells. Such tissue changes increase the vulnerability of the individual and in fact are themselves very similar to the symptoms of the common cold.

That one may learn to develop such symptoms should not be excluded as a possibility. The very fact that a common cold may occur in early life (or later) regardless of what the original physical determinants may have been, provides an experiential background of responses in a given stimulus situation. If the consequence of such a response is of a rewarding kind— that is, if the individual is permitted to escape from a difficult task at school or from the work situation or from some other unpleasant obligation—there is thereby some strengthening of that response. And perhaps there is some tendency to repeat the response that has been followed by favorable circumstances. This simply relates to the basic principle of learning that rewarded or reinforced behavior tends to be replicated.

Further, Cappon (1955) has empirically associated the cold with persons having emotional problems. He found that in a sample of about 400 patients, psychiatric patients had twice as many colds as the nonpsychiatric and their colds tended also to be of longer duration. Since the actual basis of a cold is not known and since a number of characteristics of a cold, such as rise in temperature, suggest that the basis is an infection, the following speculation may not be out of order. *Marked functional changes in the respiratory system as part of an emotional reaction pattern, reduce the threshold level of resistance to infection; under such conditions the likelihood is increased that ubiquitously present microbes, viral agents, or inanimate substances will exert deleterious effects on the body.*

At this point, while the major determinants of a cold have not yet been clearly identified and the tendency is to think of the primary determinants as infectious rather than psychological, the issue is not yet clearly settled and psychological factors have been implicated. The likelihood is that the role of psychological factors in the development of the common cold varies from insignificant to highly significant in different people.

GENERAL SUMMARY STATEMENTS CONCERNING PSYCHOSOMATIC RESPIRATORY DISORDERS

1. Many respiratory responses are involved in emotional reaction constellations. The nose and lungs are among the major respiratory structures implicated.

2. Two general patterns of nasal reaction have been distinguished. (a) Vasoconstriction with drying and shrinking of nasal membranes, which serves to dilate air passages and which may provide part of the mechanism for hyperventilation syndrome. (b) Vasodilation of the nasal mucous membrane accompanied by turgescence of erectile tissue in the nasal turbinates and nasal septum and by increased secretion, which serves to interfere with respiration and to provide part of the mechanism for vasomotor rhinitis.

3. That emotional factors and other psychological influences affect the respiratory system is supported by many lines of evidence. (a) Certain respiratory disturbances occur only in emotion-provoking situations; they disappear when the individual is removed from such situations. (b) Aberrant respiratory patterns including asthmalike reactions have been conditioned and otherwise learned. (c) Respiratory disturbances have been en-

gendered by therapists who introduced for consideration patterns of emotional stimulation relating to sensitive areas in the patient's background; reduction and disappearance of respiratory symptoms have also been achieved after the patient has had opportunity to examine and discuss such stimulation in the secure atmosphere of the psychotherapeutic situation. (d) Asthmatic reactions can often be temporarily relieved by suggestion. (e) Under certain kinds of emotion-provoking circumstance there may be a reduction rather than an exacerbation of symptoms. For example, Hajos (1948) found in persons undergoing deportation, military seizure, confinement to a labor camp or ghetto, and similar stressful situations, a tendency toward *reduction* and *disappearance* of asthmatic attacks.

4. At least three general theories obtain with regard to respiratory disorders such as those discussed—particularly asthma and vasomotor rhinitis. (a) Respiratory disorders are due to allergens. (b) Respiratory disorders are due to emotional factors. (c) Respiratory disorders are due to a combination of allergens and emotional factors.

Perhaps some disorders are due primarily to allergens and some primarily to emotional factors. The combinatorial approach suggests that emotional factors may reduce the threshold of susceptibility to a respiratory disturbance, which is then precipitated by an allergen, or that the allergen modifies somatic reaction sensitivity so that emotional factors precipitate a respiratory disturbance. All three viewpoints may be of value and perhaps obtain for different disorders or situations.

5. Infection in early life may render the respiratory system hypersensitive or vulnerable; conflict, frustration, and other kinds of emotional situations can then interact with those earlier effects to produce a respiratory disturbance, for example an asthmatic attack. A study by Rees (1964) supports the idea of such predisposing factors in the genesis of asthma. He found a history of previous respiratory infection in 80 percent of a sample of asthmatics, in contrast to 30 percent in nonasthmatic controls.

6. Respiratory disorders may be incapacitating or fatal. Leigh (1955), on the basis of observations of sudden death from asthma, suggests that *status asthmaticus* may be due to extensive vagal discharge, which in turn engenders bronchial constriction and increased bronchial secretion.

CHAPTER NINE

PSYCHOSOMATIC
SKIN DISORDERS

ANATOMY AND PHYSIOLOGY OF THE SKIN

From one perspective, the skin is the largest organ system of the body. It provides a mechanism that separates the relatively stable internal environment of the organism from the relatively unstable external environment. It is the only organ system that is completely visible to direct observation, that is, to observation without special instrumentation. (See Figure 9.1.)

Sometimes the skin, hair, and nails are grouped together as the integumentary system. These structures serve a function as a covering of the body. In so doing, they protect internal structures of the organism; they serve as a mechanism of respiration; and they serve a function in heat insulation and temperature regulation. Although the skin is often thought of merely as an inert outer coating of the body, actually it contains a wide variety of cells, including sense organs, that are constantly reacting to pressure, temperature, and noxious stimulation of the outer world; it may, therefore, not only constitute a wall between the internal self and the outside world, but also, obviously, be a means of detecting changes in and communicating with the outside world. The skin contains numerous glands, blood vessels, and many smooth muscle elements that serve to relate its characteristics directly to the viscera. Many of these characteristics are regulated by the autonomic nervous system.

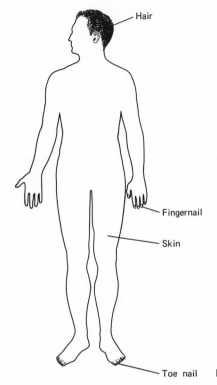

Hair

Fingernail

Skin

Toe nail   **FIGURE 9-1. Integumentary system.**

CHARACTERISTIC EMOTIONAL REACTIONS INVOLVING THE SKIN

A number of common reactions of the skin to emotional stimulus situations have been specified. These include blushing, a reddening or flushing of the skin surface, particularly of the face, which is produced by dilation of cutaneous blood vessels; pallor, a paling or whitening of the skin surface, particularly of the face, which is a function of constriction of cutaneous blood vessels; cutis anserina, a pattern of roughness in the skin consisting of multiple swellings or protuberances—sometimes called goose flesh—which is a function of constriction of the nonstriated muscular fibers of the skin at the bases of hair follicles; horripilation, a frequent accompaniment of the previously mentioned reaction, which involves erection of the hair; and sweating, the deposition of moisture on the skin, which is essentially the excretion of fluid by the sweat glands (Lachman, 1969). The electrodermal response—a change in resistance of the skin to passage of an electric charge—is often utilized as a single general indicator of emotional activity.

TYPICAL PSYCHOSOMATIC DISORDERS INVOLVING THE SKIN

Before discussing psychosomatic skin disorders, it may be worthwhile to consider the general nature of allergy. This is a condition of unusual or exaggerated susceptibility to a substance—because of its chemical composition—that is harmless in similar amounts for most other members of the species. Liberation of histamine from affected cells is believed to play a role in producing and maintaining allergic reactions. The major manifestations of allergy are urticaria, asthma, rhinitis, gastrointestinal disturbances, angioneurotic edema, and fever, although a great many other pathological symptoms may also occur. Actually, any structure of the body may be involved in an allergic reaction.

Allergic symptoms are often due to the inhalation of pollens, and so in certain instances pollinosis may be a more accurate term than allergy. Among the *inhalants,* beside pollens that function as allergens are fungi, epithelial emanations of animals or vegetables, vapors, tobacco smoke, and perfumes. Although allergic symptoms may be developed in response to almost any *food,* those most frequently implicated are milk, eggs, fish, nuts, chocolate, and strawberries. Any *drug,* including aspirin, may function as an allergen. *Contractants*—substances that act on the skin or mucous membrance—may produce a dermatitis as well as other symptoms; insecticides, furs, jewelry, cosmetics, flameproofing chemicals, dyestuffs, and plants are among the most common ones. Allergic reactions may occur in response to *physical agents* such as temperature, light, and pressure. *Vaccines and serums* injected in medical treatment may also produce allergic reactions.

Allergic shock—inappropriately called anaphylactic shock—is a dramatic and extreme form of allergic reaction that is usually fatal but fortunately rare. In susceptible persons, almost immediately following injection—whether of medical serums or by such means as a bee sting—symptoms begin, including itching, generalized urticaria, sneezing, coughing, and asthma. A state of physiological shock ensues, which may be followed by convulsions and death within a very brief period—sometimes 15 minutes or less.

Although a variety of symptoms may be considered allergic reactions, and practically any bodily structure can be implicated, the skin changes elicited have been given particular attention. Various effects of poison ivy, poison oak, and poison sumac on normal persons are similar to the reactions evoked by certain allergens in reaction-sensitive persons.

Bronchial asthma, eczema, and hives frequently occur in the same person. Generally, eczema is the earliest appearing. These disorders tend to be associated in people within a family. Often they are based on allergic reactions to certain substances, usually proteins, that enter the organism by being swallowed (foods and beverages) or inhaled (dust, pollen, and various vapors). They may, however, also have a psychological basis.

Although symptoms may be similar, we are not basically concerned with skin reactions to allergens, to infection, to changes in temperature, or to other such direct physical influences. There is no doubt that most skin disorders are of that type. However, our major focus is on psychogenic reactions—disturbances mediated via emotional stimulus situations, the nervous system, and the appropriate response mechanisms.

The psychogenic nature of various skin disorders is attested to by the following facts.

1. Rashes may break out in emotional situations or in response to frustration.

2. Skin eruptions may occur to conditioned stimuli. For example, (a) In one case, a young woman displayed an inflammatory skin reaction to the presence of flowers. It appeared to be an allergic kind of reaction and would have passed as a kind of pollinosis or another type of allergy, but for the fact that the attending physician found that the same dramatic reaction was induced also by an artificial flower. (b) Shoemaker (1963) has suggested on the basis of observing 40 patients displaying a nonallergic urticaria that emotional reactions associated with conflict are related to that disorder. Fear of abandonment and rage engendered by a state of helplessness were suggested as critical factors.

3. Apparently, skin disorders have been cured by suggestion, occasionally merely by authority figures indicating that changes of a recuperative sort will take place within a given period of time, sometimes with the aid of a placebo.

4. Of 13 subjects studied by Ikemi and Nakagawa (1963) whose skin was reaction-sensitive to specific leaves but not to chestnut leaves, the following occurred. (a) Under hypnosis, 5 subjects were told that they were being touched with chestnut leaves while actually allergenic leaves were used. On the other arm, chestnut leaves were applied with the suggestion that they were the allergenic leaves. (b) Eight subjects were given the same set of suggestions with the same kinds of leaves while blindfolded and without hypnosis. All 13 subjects showed a skin response—flushing, erythema, or papules—when given the suggestion that chestnut leaves were

allergenic. Four of the 5 hypnotized subjects and 7 of the 8 nonhypnotized ones displayed no observable response to the allergenic leaves when they were represented as chestnut leaves. The role of psychogenic factors—particularly the effectiveness of suggestion with or without hypnosis—in inducing and diminishing allergic skin responses is apparent in the results.

5. Certain researches on blisters and warts—both studies subject to some criticism—may be cited to support the position that skin disorders may have prominent psychological components. (a) Subjects under deep hypnotic trance have developed blisters in response to suggestion. The subject's skin was touched by an object—for example, a pencil—with the suggestion that it was a red-hot iron. Vascular changes began immediately, and some hours later a blister developed at the locus of the suggested burn. Histologically, it was similar to a blister caused by a burn. The healing of blisters via suggestion during the hypnotic state has also been reported (Doswald and Kreibich, 1906). (b) Sulzberger and Wolf (1934) reported disappearance of warts as a result of suggestion in about 78 percent of 179 cases investigated. Many of the patients had suffered from warts for months or even years; the warts disappeared within 2 to 12 weeks following initiation of psychological treatment.

6. A person may show a reaction—let us say a skin disturbance—to a food he has eaten when he knows that he has eaten it, but does not display that reaction to the same food when it is disguised among other ingredients and he does not recognize that he has eaten it.

Case 9.1. *Neurodermatitis.* An apparent inconsistency was a prominent feature in parental treatment of the patient during her development. The patient at age 4 developed an eczematous eruption on both arms and hands. After about 2 years the condition cleared. When she was 9, her mother was pregnant and the patient, perhaps interpreting the pregnancy as a threat to the mother-daughter relationship, developed a skin reaction. At age 13 with onset of menarche, her hands, wrists, and arms broke out; the outbreak disappeared in about 8 weeks. When she was about 20, after having been married for 2 years, her husband discussed leaving her to take a trip. Concurrent with discussion of his plans for going away, the patient's skin broke out. As the day for departure neared, her symptoms increasingly worsened. Eventually, she had to be hospitalized for 17 days with severe dermatitis and its complications. She was discharged from the hospital somewhat improved. A number of problems were considered during outpatient psychotherapy, and at the conclusion of therapy the patient's skin had been completely clear for about a year (Grinker and Robbins, 1954).

Case 9.2. *Neurodermatitis.* A youngster "allergic" to milk at home, while at camp drank a quart of milk every day with no skin eruption (Sadler, 1953).

Case 9.3. *Raynaud's Disease.* The patient's mother and all siblings were described as emotionally volatile persons who passed in and out of deep grief, sudden intense rages, and other affective reactions to only minor stresses. His sister appeared to be particularly labile and vulnerable to emotional reactivity; often she suffered eczematous skin reactions that persisted for weeks following an emotional arousal. When the patient was 17 his father died; the patient remained grief-stricken for two years. He married at age 24; sexual relations with his wife were unsatisfactory. Eventually his wife began having extramarital affairs, and after 5 years of marriage she left him. He considered himself disgraced, gave up his job, and moved to another city. He had difficulty finding steady work there. During one winter there, his major symptoms appeared. One day he left home to avoid an imminent quarrel with the cousin with whom he was living. He noted that although the day was mild, his hands quickly became blanched, numb, and cold, and could be restored to a normal condition only by much rubbing, warmth, and rest. Such episodes, precipitated by emotional circumstances, increased in frequency and intensity throughout the winter. Subsequent observation in a hospital ward confirmed the role of affective factors in precipitating the patient's vasospastic attacks. His condition was identified by two internists as symptomatic of early Raynaud's disease (Masserman, 1955).

Case 9.4. *Urticaria.* An 11-year-old child broke out with a severe case of urticaria after eating chocolate or eggs, after playing with animals, and after walking through a wheat patch. Under hypnosis he was told that he could eat chocolate and eggs and play with animals without breaking out in hives. He was then given a chocolate bar, which he ate without breaking out. When he was under hypnosis about 9 months later, one of the physicians present questioned whether the therapist "could make the hives return." Appropriate suggestions were made. The child was given a chocolate bar, which he ate, and he was told that in exactly 15 minutes he would break out in hives. He broke out into generalized hives 15 minutes later. A doctor then inquired whether it would be possible to remove a particular wheal from the child's cheek, and a particular wheal was indicated. The subject was told that in 15 minutes a particular hive would disappear; it did (Erickson, Hershman, and Secter, 1961).

A wide variety of conditions have been described as psychosomatic skin disturbances. Among these are neurodermatitis, alopecia, Raynaud's disease, and urticaria (hives). Brief discussions of some of the more common kinds of psychosomatic skin disorder are provided below.

Neurodermatitis

Neurodermatitis is an inflammation of the skin of emotional origin. It may be acute, subacute, or chronic, and although it is characterized by erythema or redness of the skin, there may also be small circumscribed solid elevations in the skin (papules) or small circumscribed elevations in the skin containing serum (vesicles). At times there may be oozing of serous substances and also encrusting, scaling, and thickening of the skin. A variety of skin conditions, sometimes originating or developing on the basis of emotional arousal, are eczema, acne, and psoriasis.

1. Eczema. Eczema is an inflammatory condition of the skin characterized by redness, itching, and oozing vesicular lesions that become scaly, encrusted, or hardened. Sometimes there may be accompanying burning sensations and various paresthesias. Wittkower and Edgel (1951) found that onset or exacerbation of eczema was preceded by emotional situations in 77 of 90 patients studied.

2. Acne. Acne is an eruption on the face; it is an inflammatory disease involving the oil glands and hair follicles of the skin, and it is most frequently found in adolescents.

A research paper by Wittkower and MacKenna (1947) on seborrheic dermatitis concluded that emotional disturbances preceding the onset of seborrheic dermatitis were "severe, uniform and specific, i.e., of such a nature as to reactivate conflicts to which the patients had been previously sensitized." They believe that relationships between the emotional event and the onset of the skin disorder are so close as to preclude the possibility of mere coincidence.

3. Psoriasis. Psoriasis is a chronic skin disease that is characterized by circumscribed red patches covered by white scales. Poussaint (1963) reported a patient with a five-year history of chronic psoriasis; he noted that the illness was precipitated by emotional factors and later exacerbated by them. Although there is some evidence concerning psoriasis as a psychosomatic disorder, the evidence is weak.

Alopecia

Alopecia is a sudden loss of hair. As a psychosomatic manifestation it may be due to problems mediated by the vascular system as well as the nervous system.

Raynaud's Disease

Raynaud's disease is a condition characterized by an abnormal degree of vascular spasm in superficial blood vessels, especially those in the digits; blanching and numbness of the fingers occur and the hands are typically cold and moist. Pronounced reaction of the sympathetic nervous system produces the marked vasospasms, which are sufficient to produce cyanosis and lead to trophic changes in skin and nails of the periphery. Although the changes are not often sufficiently severe to destroy tissue, on rare occasions deficient circulation and the resulting low temperature may foster gangrene.

By means of a radiometer, Mittelmann and Wolf (1943) measured skin temperature, which is a function of the extent of dilation of blood vessels in the skin. They ascertained certain consistent relationships between emotional circumstances and skin temperature. Vasoconstriction tended to be associated with increases in conflict; vasodilation was associated with emotional security. A fall in skin temperature accompanied a wide variety of emotional situations. The researchers demonstrated that blood vessels of the skin, even at the fingertips, are highly sensitive and responsive to a variety of emotional situations. The degree and speed of temperature decrease were determined by the intensity of the emotional reaction.

Urticaria

Urticaria or hives is a disorder marked by raised edematous patches of skin or mucous membrane, usually with intense itching. Stimuli initially adequate to produce urticaria include (1) emotional situations that produce profound physiological changes; (2) foods, particularly fruits, vegetables, and nuts, and also eggs, milk, wheat, and pork; (3) drugs, including aspirin, barbiturates, and bromides; (4) injection of foreign serum, hormones, and insect bites; (5) allergic inhalants such as dust and pollens; and (6) bacterial antigens. Any of these can serve in susceptible individuals as the initial basis for a skin reaction, which then can be conditioned to new stimuli.

Urticaria is characterized by local wheals arising in the dermis. The wheal is a swelling made up of an exuded serum together with a variety of white blood corpuscles. Local blood vessels and lymphatic vessels are distended. It is possible that histamine or a histaminelike substance liberated by cells in the vicinity serves to produce the dilation and consequent edema. One of the first symptoms of urticaria is pruritis, an itching in the area, which is followed shortly by urticarial lesions that vary considerably in appearance from tiny pinhead spots to areas as large as eight inches in diameter. Typically, the crop of hives appears and disappears, the lesions remaining in one site perhaps for several hours, then disappearing only to appear again somewhere else.

It is, of course, known that urticaria often occurs in response to non-nutritive allergins. But food seems to be a more important specific factor. However, for some persons, stressful or high-tension stimulus situations serve as elicitors. It is possible that a particular food fortuitously associated in time with emotional factors inducing urticarial-like conditions, itself then becomes effective in producing similar conditions. The reverse is also potentially effective, namely that an emotional stimulus situation fortuitously associated in time with food allergens eliciting urticaria, may itself later serve to induce urticaria.

Graham and Wolf (1950) investigated the nature of psychological precipitants in urticaria and reported that urticarial attacks were not correlated with exposure to allergens. They further disclosed that stimulus situations associated with patient reports of intense feelings of resentment produced urticaria, whereas a variety of other stimulus situations leading to emotional reactions to which respondents gave different names such as anxiety or grief were not directly associated with urticarial attacks.

The literature on urticaria documents vicissitudes of emotionality in the onset and disappearance of urticaria. The following are representative reports.

1. Kreibich and Sobotka (1909) reported a patient who displayed urticarial attacks when emotionally aroused. This was demonstrated in the hospital situation on two occasions when he was wrongfully accused by a nurse of a minor transgression. In both instances, he was emotionally aroused, and within a few minutes an urticarial rash developed.

2. Hansen (1927) reported a woman who while dining on lobster with her lover was discovered by her husband. Within a few minutes she displayed a general urticaria and thereafter suffered an urticarial attack whenever she ate lobster.

3. Stokes, Kulchar, and Pillsbury (1935) reported evidence suggestive of psychogenic stress in 83 of 100 patients. However, they concluded that personality type rather than the nature of the emotional situation was of the greater importance in the development of urticaria.

4. Kaneko and Takaishi (1963) produced urticarial eruptions in urticarial patients by suggesting under hypnosis feelings of aggression that could not be expressed.

With regard to psychosomatic disorders, Grace and Graham (1952) have suggested a conceptual variant relating to the stimulus-situation theories and the emotional reaction-pattern theories (as outlined in Chapter 5). According to it, the specific attitude associated with a conflict situation is critical in the elicitation of a psychosomatic symptom; specific attitudes, according to the Grace-Graham theory, determine the kinds of psychosomatic symptoms that develop. Grace and Graham attempted to distill in language form the essential attitudes of patients affected by particular diseases, and they carefully specified the attitude they believed to be associated with each of several disorders.

Later, Graham and his associates (1958) hypnotized a group of normal young male subjects and gave them suggestions intended to produce the attitudes specific either to (1) urticaria (hives) or (2) Raynaud's disease. Among the obvious differences between these two disorders is skin temperatures. Urticaria patients have elevated skin temperatures, while patient's with Raynaud's disease have subnormal skin temperatures. The subjects, of course, were given no information concerning to what the suggested attitudes were supposed to be related. Each subject was exposed to each "attitude condition," half the subjects in one sequence, the other half in the opposite sequence. In that way, the reaction engendered could be ascribed to the attitude and not to individual differences in the subjects; furthermore, the effects of one attitude served as a kind of control for the effects of the other attitude. Results indicated clearly differences in skin temperature. The hives attitude produced an elevation in skin temperature, while the Raynaud's-disease attitude produced a decline in skin temperature. These results, then appear to lend support to the specific attitude theory of Grace and Graham (1952).

Hyperhidrosis

There seems to be little doubt but that sweating is a general index of sympathetic nervous system arousal. Further, stimulus situations frequently described as fear-inducing, rage-inducing, or anxiety-inducing have often been associated with sweating. Cuno et al. and Herrmann, Prose, and Sulzberger (1951) indicate two distinct forms of perspiration, thermal and emotional. Thermal sweating is most evident on the forehead, neck, trunk, and dorsum of the hand and forearm. Emotional sweating appears primarily on the palms, soles, and axillae. Hyperhidrosis is a condition of the skin in which the sweat glands are overactive. Such excessive sweating may be a link in the development of rashes and blisters and in the facilitation of infection.

Other Considerations Regarding
Psychosomatic Skin Disorders

With regard to various skin eruptions, such as acne, a boy or girl who accepts the traditional idea that masturbation is an evil or immoral act that may lead to psychosis, mental deficiency, or skin blemishes may likewise believe that his (or her) bodily blemishes reveal to other people that the individual has masturbated. Although the skin disturbances may actually be a function of *emotional arousal* of a different sort, this belief exacerbates concern about both masturbation and the skin blemishes and may lead to a "vicious-circle" effect. Thus, concern about either the masturbatory activity or the skin blemishes provokes physiological arousal, including extensive and intensive circulatory changes that serve to maintain the skin eruptions.

Psychoanalytic theories concerning skin eruptions have taken several forms. Two representative formulations suggest the patient is using his skin symbolically and may be termed the exhibitionistic theory and the self-hostility theory.

1. The *exhibitionistic theory* holds that skin eruptions in certain cases represent exhibitionism. One variant of this theory maintains that the individual is motivated to display his genital organs but restrains that tendency, displaying skin blemishes instead.

2. The *self-hostility* or *masochistic theory* holds that repulsive skin eruptions represent internally directed hostile tendencies, that is, masochistic tendencies. By directing his hostility inwardly, the individual is hurting himself physically; simultaneously, he is punishing himself socially by being repulsive to other people.

These two kinds of explanation are less than parsimonious and complicate rather than simplify the problem of elucidating relevant biological mechanisms.

With specific regard to the development of acne vulgaris, often considered a form of psychosomatic acne, the following theoretical conception —perhaps a variant of the two cited above—has been suggested. In the adolescent, an inclination to rebel against parents—as a consequence of frustration—is in conflict with learned inclinations to be dutiful and compliant. Tendencies to display overt behavior concomitant with the physiological arousal engendered by the conflict situation are restrained or suppressed and come to be manifested in skin eruptions. Confirming evidence is insufficient.

BIOLOGICAL MECHANISMS IN SKIN DISORDERS

Independently or in combination, a variety of mechanisms probably operate between emotional stimulation and the development of psychosomatic skin disorders.

1. By means of the autonomic nervous system, pronounced and sustained vasodilation or vasoconstriction may occur in the superficial vessels serving the skin. Such conditions can lead to a local or general hyperemia and its accompanying flushing of the skin or to a local or general stasis and its accompanying blanching of the skin. Various exudations may occur as a consequence of accumulation of large amounts of fluid in the intercellular tissue space, which sometimes results in the formation of blisters. Some blisters may contain blood or (under various conditions) they contain only certain components of the blood; for example, pus blisters, which are composed mainly of leucocytes.

The latter condition, stasis, sustained over time can result in trophic changes in hair, skin, and nails, and necrosis of such tissue.

2. By means of the autonomic nervous system, modifications in the rate of secretion of sweat glands may be accomplished. This can influence the moisture level of the skin surface—its degree of dryness or wetness.

3. Although the sebaceous glands apparently are not directly influenced by the autonomic nervous system, they may be influenced by it indirectly. For example, secretions of sebaceous glands are responsive to changes in skin temperature. Skin-temperature changes may be accomplished by vasomotor activity, which is regulated by the autonomic nervous system. Sebaceous glands may also be influenced by secretions of the endocrine glands, which in turn are regulated to some extent by the autonomic nervous system as well as the circulatory system.

The mechanisms mentioned are suggested tentatively. Verification of their operation depends on further research, and it is more than likely that other mechanisms also operate in the development of psychosomatic skin disorders. However, those above suggest means by which a number of changes are accomplished that are eventually of significance in pathogenesis, including skin-temperature modifications, wetness, dryness, various degrees of oiliness, skin cracking, and stimulation of various sense organs serving to produce a variety of subjectively reportable sensations including itching and burning, as well as many other changes occurring via operation of these mechanisms as a consequence of emotional stimulation.

SOME PERTINENT CONSIDERATIONS REGARDING PSYCHOSOMATIC SKIN DISORDERS

The following statements serve to summarize certain pertinent considerations regarding psychosomatic skin disorders.

1. In considering the development of psychosomatic skin disorders, emphasis may be focused on various parameters. Psychosomatic disorders

of the skin depend on (a) the nature of the personality from a physiological perspective; attention is focused on persons whose emotional reactions are intense as far as peripheral blood vessel and other superficial structures are concerned, (b) the basic type of skin of the person affected, (c) the nature of the predisposing and precipitating circumstances, and (d) the characteristics of the emotional situation.

2. In the attempt to understand how psychological factors operate, it may be suggested that psychological factors serve to lower the threshold of a normally physically engendered condition—allergy or otherwise—or that psychological factors aggravate or intensify a physically-engendered reaction.

3. A circular reaction relating to a psychosomatic skin disorder may be of significance in exacerbation of the disorder. Let us say that a skin disorder is engendered by emotional stimulation via one of the mechanisms proposed. Suppose that among the other accompaniments of the skin lesion, there is itching. (a) In the attempt to relieve the discomfort, itching leads to rubbing or scratching the area. (b) Scratching leads to changes in the condition of the skin. (c) Such changes promote increased damage and increased stimulation; perhaps they also increase sensitivity of sensory endings there. (d) Such damage, stimulation, and augmented sensitivity are manifested in increased itching. And the circle may then be repeated with increasing bodily damage.

4. With regard to skin disorders, as a consequence of changes in outward appearance due to discolorations and textural anomalies, secondary psychological effects often occur. These may result from (a) direct self-evaluation or (b) indirect self-reactions—the influence of other people's behavior on the self-reaction.

CHAPTER TEN

PSYCHOSOMATIC
GENITOURINARY DISORDERS

ANATOMY AND PHYSIOLOGY
OF THE GENITOURINARY SYSTEM

The genitourinary system consists of those structures that have roles in reproduction and micturition. Reproduction refers to the creation and development of new members of the species; micturition refers to the elimination of liquid wastes. (See Figure 10.1 and 10.2.)

The structures concerned with reproduction include the sex glands or gonads; these are the ovaries in the female and the testes in the male. There are also accessory structures of great significance for reproduction in both sexes.

The female sex glands or ovaries are oval bodies lying near the side walls of the pelvic girdle; they manufacture ova (female reproduction cells) and by means of slender channels, the Fallopian tubes or oviducts, communicate with the uterus. The uterus terminates at the vagina, a passage that leads to the exterior.

Within the ovaries are the Graafian follicles, which contain the ova or egg cells. One maturing Graafian follicle is liberated each month as part of the physiological cycle in the female. Each month a ripened follicle advances toward the surface of the ovary, ruptures, and ejects its ovum into the mouth of the Fallopian tube. After the mature follicle is ruptured, cells lining it multiply and form large yellow groups; these collections of cells in

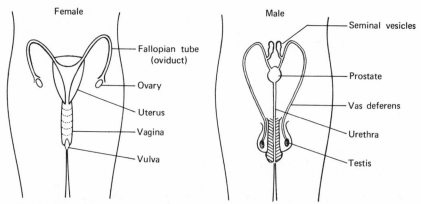

FIGURE 10-1. Reproductive system.

the ovary are called the corpora lutea. If pregnancy occurs, the corpus lu-
teum of that month increases in size and produces an internal secretion
that facilitates the development of the uterus during pregnancy.

The time of discharge of the ovum from the follicle is usually the mid-
period between two successive menstruations, and therefore at that time a
woman is most fertile.

The uterus is a hollow pear-shaped and highly muscular organ. The
lowest part of it projects into the upper part of the vagina—the female
genital passage—and is called the cervix. The uterus is lined with cells,
many of which have glandular functions; the lining is called the endometrium. In the nonpregnant uterus, the endometrium undergoes a complex
series of changes each month in preparation for possible pregnancy. During the constructive stage of this cycle, the endometrium becomes much
thickened, partly by cell division and partly by engorgement of its glands
with blood; the period of thickening is followed by a destructive stage during which blood is liberated into the uterine tissues. Within a few days the
blood, with the sloughed-off epithelium, appears as a discharge—
menstruation. Then the repair and constructive stage occurs again in replication of the cycle. This complicated cycle is regulated primarily by internal secretions of the ovary and the pituitary gland. If a male reproductive
cell unites with the ovum, however—that is, if conception occurs—
degeneration of the endometrium is averted and the fertilized ovum becomes imbedded in it. Pregnancy is, therefore, accompanied by a cessation
of menstruation.

The male reproductive structures consist of the testes, which produce
male reproductive cells or spermatozoa; the accessory sexual apparatus
(the epididymis, prostate and the seminal vesicles); and the various chan-

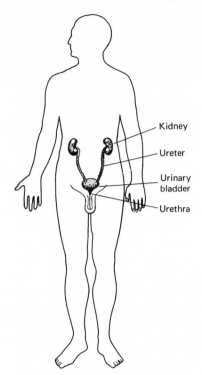

FIGURE 10-2. Excretory system.

nels and tubes along which the spermatozoa pass (the epididymal canal and vas deferens). The interior of the testes is a mass of convoluted tubules, the seminiferous tubules, where the male germinal cells are manufactured. These tubules lead into a large convoluted duct on each side known as the epididymis, and then to the vas deferens on that side, which communicates with the seminal vesicles. The ejaculatory ducts are short tubes, one on each side, formed by the union of the duct of the seminal vesicle with the vas deferens; they open into the urethra, a tube that traverses the penis or phallus, which contains erectile tissue and many vascular spaces that enable the organ to become turgid when engorged with blood. The erectile tissue is spongelike and erection is accomplished by the filling of its spaces with blood, whereby the organ becomes larger, warmer, and more rigid. These results are produced both by an increase in the amount of arterial blood reaching the penis and by a reduction in outflow from it, which results from compression of its veins. It is by means of this structure, the penis, that semen is deposited into the female genital passage. Erection and ejaculation are controlled by centers in the spinal cord. The terminal act of coitus is, therefore, essentially a reflexive act.

It is convenient to consider the normal sexual act in three successive stages—tumescence, orgasm, and detumescence.

In the male: (1) *Tumescence* is critical; heterosexual intercourse cannot occur without it, regardless of the willingness of the participants. (2) As a consequence of friction applied to the glans of the penis and the penis shaft during intercourse, *orgasm or ejaculation* occurs, which involves rhythmical expansions and contractions of the penis and simultaneous discharge of the seminal fluid, which contains spermatozoa. (3) This is followed—usually immediately—by *detumescence,* in which the blood flows out of the veins and capillaries and the penis resumes its typically flaccid condition.

In the female: (1) *Tumescence* is characterized by expansion of the clitoris and secretion of a lubricating fluid from glands near the genital opening. (2) *Orgasm* produced by mechanical stimulation of the clitoris and female genital tube, due to a pistonlike action of the penis and other stimulation, is characterized by rhythmical dilation and constriction of the vagina and related activities. (3) *Detumescence* involves a return of the genital system to its customary physiological condition.

The kidneys are the critically important organs in micturition. Waste products generally diffuse out of the cells in which they are produced into the tissue fluid and eventually into the bloodstream. Waste products pass from the bloodstream into the kidney where, after mechanical and chemical action of this structure, these products are transported in solution by means of a duct, the ureter, into the urinary bladder. The waste products are then passed through the urethra and expelled as urine.

CHARACTERISTIC EMOTIONAL REACTIONS INVOLVING THE GENITOURINARY SYSTEM

There are a variety of reactions of the genitourinary system that occur in response to emotional stimulation. These include enuresis, involuntary micturition, erection, priapism, penis flaccidity, many menstrual disturbances (amenorrhea, hypermennorrhea, and dysmenorrhea), and ejaculatio praecox (Lachman, 1969).

TYPICAL PSYCHOSOMATIC DISORDERS INVOLVING THE GENITOURINARY SYSTEM

Many conditions associated with the genitourinary system have been considered psychosomatic disturbances. It is convenient to consider them in three major groups: (1) disorders of sexual function, (2) disorders of reproductive function, and (3) disorders of urinary function.

Among the disorders of sexual function are impotence, frigidity, and vaginismus. The disorders of reproductive function include disturbances in the menstrual cycle, spontaneous abortion (miscarriage), and pseudocyesis. Disturbances in urinary function include involuntary micturition and inhibition of micturition.

Disorders of Sexual Function

Let us consider first sexual dysfunctions. These may be due to organic determinants, and are also often found associated with a wide variety of psychological disturbances, including the neuroses, the psychoses, and personality disorders. However, sexual dysfunctions such as impotence and frigidity in almost all cases are believed to involve affective factors and to be mediated via autonomic mechanisms; they are, therefore, generally within the realm of psychosomatic disorders. Among the most frequent forms of sexual dysfunction in the male are impotence, premature ejaculation, and retarded ejaculation. Emotional reactions of the sort frequently termed anxiety, guilt, or fear apparently interfere with male sex activities.

Case 10.1. *Psychosomatic impotence.* A man who was continually nagged and berated by his wife almost invariably failed, despite his efforts, to maintain an appropriate physiological state of his penis sufficient to permit coitus or even penetration. However, the patient had had regular coital relations with her prior to marriage, and concurrent with and subsequent to his marital failures in this regard did have occasional and invariably successful sexual relations with his secretary, who expressed admiration for the patient's business skills and personal characteristics.

Case 10.2. *Psychogenic hypermenorrhea* (*menorrhagia*). The patient had married in her early 20s, apparently in part to escape from her family; she had two miscarriages and one child after a normal pregnancy. At age 32 she quarreled with her husband over the question of another woman with whom the patient's husband was having an affair. As a consequence, the marital situation became more and more discordant. Although her menstrual periods had been regular, she now developed irregular bleeding —often amounting to flooding—in addition to other symptoms. After therapy involving the husband, who promised there would be no further cause for suspicion on the part of his wife, she reported that marital relations were perfectly satisfactory and that a normal menstrual cycle had resumed (Ambrose and Newbold, 1968).

Case 10.3. *Pseudocyesis.* A 21-year-old girl insisted that she was pregnant and displayed certain symptoms of pregnancy including abdominal enlargement, vomiting, and amenorrhea. There were, however, no conclusive signs of pregnancy, and all clinical tests of pregnancy were negative; she was in fact not pregnant. Rejection by her husband and jealousy of her pregnant younger sister were cited as background circumstances relevant to the condition displayed (Masserman, 1955).

Case 10.4. *Infertility.* As a youngster the patient had been ignored, exploited, and mistreated by her mother, while her father had been gentle, kind, devoted, and particularly fond of his daughter. At the age of 32, after 8 years of marriage, she sought help for a number of complaints, including "constant anxiety." She also disclosed that although since marriage she had never used a contraceptive and strongly desired to become pregnant, she had never been able to. She entered psychotherapy for other reasons with no assumption that it would enhance her procreative ability. It was suggested that she had made an inadequate feminine identification and regarded mothers as hostile, exploitative, and cruel. Her desire for children may have been ambivalent, based on the fear that she might become that sort of person. As therapy proceeded she gained more understanding of herself and of children and presumably achieved better adjustment in terms of emotional reactivity. At that point she became pregnant (English and Finch, 1964).

Case 10.5. *Urinary urgency.* The patient's childhood was spent in a strict and rigid environment created by a meticulous mother and grandmother who domineered her, placed emphasis on her performance (rather than her feelings), and developed little in the way of genuine affectional relations with the youngster. As a 35-year-old married woman, she reported urinary urgency, particularly when she was in crowds or traveling. She was concerned about being very far away from a lavatory and fearful that "I may have to go and there won't be an opportunity and I won't be able to hold it." During treatment she revealed that she considered all people unfriendly and unbending about matters of urination as had been her mother and grandmother. Eventually her level of self-confidence increased and she achieved greater urinary control (English and Finch, 1964).

Case 10.6. *Psychogenic amenorrhea.* A 21-year-old girl had sexual relations with her fiance. She then became very much concerned about pregnancy. This cognitive concern was simultaneously manifested in extensive autonomic symptoms including amenorrhea. She visited her physician who assured her she was not pregnant. Under hypnosis a posthypnotic suggestion was made that she would begin to menstruate at a particular time the next day; the suggestion was effective (Ambrose and Newbold, 1968).

Psychosomatic impotence may be either absolute or relative. Evidence of relative or selective impotence is significant evidence for the psychological basis of the disturbance. For example, a man may be impotent with his wife but not with his mistress, or he may be impotent with prostitutes or receptive females of his acquaintance but not with his wife, or he may be impotent with women generally while awake but potent during sexual dreams, that is, dreams that are accompanied by actual orgasm.

Emotional reactions relating to guilt due to extramarital relations may lead to impotence involving the wife. Worry reactions relating to economic, social, health, or political problems may influence sex activity. Regarding sex as evil or sinful may also have a role in inadequate sex functioning.

Related to impotence, at least in part, are ejaculatio praecox and retarded ejaculation. In ejaculatio praecox, discharge may occur immediately after beginning intercourse or in some cases even prior to intromission (ejaculatio ante portas). In part, the mechanism involved is overactivity of the parasympathetic system. Ejaculation may also occur as part of an emotional reaction constellation to apparently nonsexual emotional situations. Feldman (1951) has reported ejaculation in several situations not directly concerned with sexual stimulation.

Prolonged delay in ejaculation or inability to ejaculate may also be psychosomatic, a function perhaps of heightened parasympathetic activity or heightened activity of both the sympathetic and parasympathetic systems, which leads to conditions of reciprocating counteraction and therefore of stability.

The sexual dysfunction most frequently recorded for the female that may have a psychosomatic origin is frigidity, the absence of involuntary contractions of pelvic and perineal muscles during or at the conclusion of coitus. A second criterion is the absence of glandular lubricating secretion at the vaginal entrance, although *presence* of such secretion is not a critical diagnostic indicator.

On the other hand, it has been pointed out that while a certain degree of physiological change in the genital organs of the male is necessary in order for the sex act to be performed, an equivalent condition does not obtain for the female; she may play a relatively passive and receptive role in intercourse. Thus, frigidity may be defined as the partial or complete inability of the female to be aroused sexually or to achieve orgasm. It is also a condition often characterized by relative unresponsiveness and lack of cordial participation in intergenital activity on the part of the female.

Although there are certain parallels, the absence of absolutely equivalent physiological changes in the female makes it difficult to equate frigidity with impotence. Frigidity, like impotence, may occur in varying degrees. While there may or may not be substantial physiological changes in the female genital apparatus, in actual practice what are typically accepted as more diagnostic are the severe lack of pleasurable affect or sexual feeling, diminished desire, and the lack of warmth and receptivity in genital interaction.

An extreme and rare symptom of frigidity is vaginismus, a spasm of the vagina that makes penetration by the penis virtually impossible, thereby effectively preventing coitus. Although this condition may result from rupture of the hymen or lacerations or bruises of the urethral canal, it is discussed here as psychogenic. Vaginismus is reported frequently during the honeymoon, perhaps as a function of painful or difficult coitus and perhaps as a function of fear or other emotional determinants.

Among the emotional factors that may have a role in the frigidity are guilt feelings, concern about capacity to receive the penis or about competence to perform, fear of injury or of disease, and hostility toward males in general or at least toward the male partner in particular. Also, of course, frigidity may be related to fear of pregnancy.

Disorders of Reproductive Function

Among the disorders of the genitourinary system concerned with reproduction are those relating to menstruation. That emotionality occurs with and sometimes precedes the menstrual period has frequently been reported. Among the symptoms noted have been increasing restlessness, emotional outbursts, inability to concentrate, crying spells without provocation, and general irritability. So dependable has this condition been that in France the premenstrual week has been officially recognized in legal terms as a form of temporary insanity or mental incompetence.

In psychogenic amenorrhea, there is a decrease or complete cessation of menstruation in the absence of appropriate organic determinants. A variety of emotional conditions probably lead to psychogenic amenorrhea.

Loeser (1943) reported cessation of menstruation in four women after their being exposed to traumatic emotional circumstances during the bombing of London in World War II. Microscopic examination disclosed that the uterine mucosa did not undergo continued normal periodic development but rather remained unchanged from the time of the emotional situation.

Menorrhagia (hypermenorrhea), a condition in which menstrual flow is of excessive quantity or duration, may also be a reaction to emotional situations. Blaikley (1949) found that menorrhagia appeared, disappeared, and reappeared depending on the occurrence, cessation, and reoccurrence of emotional difficulties.

A variety of other kinds of psychosomatic menstrual disturbance occur. For example, O'Neill (1952) reported concomitance between emotional circumstances and the onset of menstruation in a dozen patients. In some of the patients menstrual attacks regularly followed emotional stressful circumstances, while reduction of emotional problems or environmental change brought about return of the normal menstrual cycle.

Pseudocyesis (false pregnancy) has been suggested as a psychosomatic phenomenon. The patient develops the classical signs of pregnancy including the swollen abdomen, amenorrhea, weight increase, and such mammary changes as enlargement of the breasts and darkening of the nipple; there may even be labor pains and a trip to the hospital. Psychogenic explanations with a psychoanalytic inclination have typically involved the idea of a potent wish for pregnancy. Others hold that the symptoms of emotionally engendered pseudocyesis are strictly fortuitous.

It has been suggested that emotionality may interfere with the manufacture of sperm cells or maturation of ova—psychosomatic infertility.

Spontaneous abortion (miscarriage), it has been suggested, is often emotionally based. Persistent dramatic or intense emotionality may be effective in precipitating an abortion, which can occur in women whose uterus is hyperresponsive to emotional stimulation. Tupper (1963) has reported pathological changes in placentas resembling those found in collagen diseases—which are recognized as due at least in part to stressful stimulation—in women who habitually abort.

It is possible that women who display extreme emotional reactivity (i.e., extreme physiological deviations from their normal levels of function) immediately prior to, during, or immediately subsequent to sexual intercourse, reduce their chances to conceive. Various kinds of emotionality may be involved—positive, negative, or not clearly either—for example, emotionality related to an overenthusiastic desire for pregnancy, a profound fear of pregnancy, or a generally high level of excitement, expectation, sexual interaction, or other stimulation. It is suggested that several mechanisms may operate. Here are a few general formulations.

1. Emotional stimulation produces patterns of endocrine and autonomic activity that interfere with the normal process of ovulation; for example, sterility may be due to spasm and closure of the Fallopian tubes, which prevents the ovum from reaching the uterus where conception normally occurs.

2. Emotional stimulation produces patterns of endocrine and autonomic activity that provide a vaginal medium incompatible with survival of spermatozoa; for example, oversecretion or aberrant secretion of glands in the cervix or changes otherwise related to the female reproductive tube may destroy spermatozoa.

3. Emotionality may influence metabolic processes sufficiently to inter-

fere with the manufacture of sperm cells. Several studies (Kroger, 1952; Marchbach and Schinfeld, 1953; Blum, 1959) offering some support to the notion of sterility as a psychosomatic condition are based on often-reported observations that after repeated efforts and failures to conceive and shortly following adoption of a child, pregnancy occurs. Supposedly with the adoption of a child, a problem is solved, level of emotionality is reduced for one or both prospective parents, and the conditions fostering sterility are removed or at least reduced.

Disorders of Urinary Function

Urinary disturbances may include inability to urinate as well as frequent urination or involuntary urination. Enuresis or bed-wetting is often a disturbance of childhood. However, it may also occur later in life during periods of great stress among those who have acquired urinary control. Involuntary micturition is not an uncommon emotional reaction among front-line troops or in the imminence of danger.

It is likely that emotional conditions also influence the chemical composition and physical nature of urine, including sugar level, presence of ketone bodies, color, volume, specific gravity, and other characteristics. To date, psychosomatic factors in this area have not been extensively investigated.

SIGNIFICANCE OF GENITOURINARY DYSFUNCTION

1. Since heterosexual coitus is a normal, regular, highly satisfying state of affairs in most marriages, inability to perform adequately in a fundamental sex role, whether a psychosomatic condition or otherwise, is likely to produce a state of dissatisfaction for one or both partners in the marriage. Thus, the importance of such conditions as frigidity, impotence, and ejaculatio praecox is obvious.

2. The personal satisfaction and the social values placed on creating children make it apparent that whether as a result of psychosomatic sterility or other causes, failure to produce children is likely to be a major source of frustration to many people. (Under certain conditions, of course, frequently producing children may be a source of frustration.)

3. Since menstruation is considered a distinctive characteristic of the female, obviously aberrations in menstrual function, whether psychosomatic in origin or not, can lead to distorted images of the sexual self and of disturbances in self-evaluation.

CHAPTER ELEVEN

PSYCHOSOMATIC MUSCULOSKELETAL DISORDERS

ANATOMY AND PHYSIOLOGY OF THE MUSCULOSKELETAL SYSTEM

The musculoskeletal system consists of all the muscles and all the bones of the body. Muscles are contractile organs. Contraction refers to the phenomenon of becoming shorter in the long dimension and thicker in the short dimension. By means of contraction, movements of various organs and parts are effected. Typically, the muscle is attached at each extremity by means of a tendon to a bone or other bodily organ. The points of attachment of a muscle are called its origin and insertion. The attachment to the more fixed structure is the origin; the attachment to the more movable part of the skeleton, or to the part that is moved by contraction of the muscle, is the insertion. Three kinds of muscle cell may be distinguished.

1. Striated muscle—sometimes called striped or skeletal or voluntary muscle—is so called because under microscopic examination it appears to have alternate transverse bands of dark and light. Such muscle is typically attached to the boney skeleton, which accounts for its being called skeletal muscle; such structures are under the direct immediate control of the organism, and therefore this muscle is sometimes termed voluntary muscle.

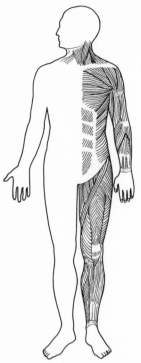

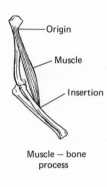

Muscle — bone
process

FIGURE 11-1. Muscular system.

2. A second kind of muscle lacking these alternate bands of dark and light is sometimes called unstriped or unstriated muscle but more usually smooth or visceral muscle. It is called visceral because it is often associated with the soft internal organs of the body, which collectively are termed the viscera; ordinarily, movements of these structures are not much under the direct immediate control of the organism.

3. The third variety of muscle is cardiac muscle, a complex striated muscle, which is unique to the heart.

Muscles are responsible for bodily movement, including movement of internal organs, and also for locomotion and manipulation. Muscle cells produce movement by contracting; when striated muscle contracts, it pulls the boney part of the skeleton to which it is attached to a new position. Smooth muscle, which is not attached to bone but is located in such structures as the walls of the digestive tract, may contract or relax, and those activities serve to constrict or to dilate passageways. (See Figures 11.1 and 11.2.)

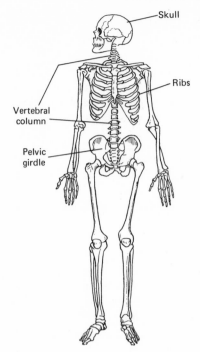

FIGURE 11-2. Skeletal system.

Bones are organs consisting of a matrix of cells and fibers impregnated with mineral matter, primarily calcium phosphate and calcium carbonate. There are about 200 distinct bones in the body, each of which has a fairly definite size and shape. Most of them make up the skeleton. A bone consists of an outer layer of dense compact tissue and an inner looser spongy tissue; the central portion of long bones is filled with marrow, a soft fatty substance believed to have a role in blood formation.

The skeletal system is responsible for support of the rest of the organism. General body shape and size is largely determined by bones. Bones making up the skeleton serve to protect many of the softer organs of the body and also serve as points of origin and insertion of muscles.

CHARACTERISTIC MUSCULOSKELETAL REACTIONS TO EMOTIONAL STIMULATION

Common musculoskeletal reactions to emotional stimulation include changes in muscle tone, twitching, tremor, convulsions, muscle spasms, immobilization or freezing, shivering, and muscle cramps (Lachman, 1969).

COMMON PSYCHOSOMATIC DISORDERS INVOLVING THE MUSCULOSKELETAL SYSTEM

A wide variety of pathological conditions—muscular, joint, and postural disorders—have been described as psychosomatic musculoskeletal disorders. These include rheumatoid arthritis, chronic destructive skeletal disorders, low back pain, and torticollis. Perhaps three general kinds of disorder can be distinguished.

1. Rheumatism: Disorders marked by inflammation of various structures, particularly muscles, with pain stimulation from those structures.
2. Arthritis: Disorders marked by inflammation of one or more joints.
3. Osteopathology: Disorders involving bone.

Rheumatism and Arthritis

Research studies—including tambour situations, Luria techniques, and other methods—indicate that under conditions of emotional stimulation, there may be an increased expenditure of energy via muscles that are not immediately involved in actively and directly coping with the situation. Emotional stimulation may produce a variety of neurological and other changes. For example, emotional stimulation may promote heightened muscle tonus. To some extent the conditions of excessive muscular tonicity generated and energies mobilized by such emotional stimulation may be relieved by means of muscular activity. When such emotional-stimulus situations are prolonged or intense and when use of the muscles involved is minimal, more persistent muscular strain may lead to sustained aches and pains.

Case 11.1. *Rheumatoid arthritis.* A 23-year-old girl who on admission to the clinic, among other things, complained of pains in her arms and legs and who earlier had reported pains in her shoulders, elbows, knees, wrists, and fingers, displayed symptoms "consistent with an early rheumatoid arthritis" that was, after extensive consideration, evaluated as a psychosomatic illness. A temporal relationship between symptoms and situations was observed: ". . . it was in situations where she felt rejected and angry that her joint pains occurred" (Miles, Cobb, and Shands, 1952).

1. *Rheumatoid arthritis* is a chronic systemic disease, its major manifestations involving the joints with morphological changes in the synovial membrane, periarticular structures, cartilage, skeletal muscle, and perineural sheaths.

It is a condition of inflammation and stiffness of the joints and often leads to their destruction. Joints may lose their lubricant fluids and become sore and swollen.

The disease, which results in marked tissue damage, may begin insidiously or there may be a sudden acute onset. There are wide variations between extremes of severity. Also there are variations in extensity—from involvement of one or a few joints to involvement of a large number. Joint lesions are generally symmetical and accompanied by muscle atrophy.

Typical of the case studies reported suggesting a psychogenic basis for symptoms of rheumatoid arthritis are the following (Ludwig, 1967). (a) One patient reacted with flare-up of joint symptoms on the anniversaries of deaths of close relatives. (b) After her husband forgot her birthday, a patient wept and then displayed anger and painfully swollen joints. A few weeks later in reaction to a mildly critical letter from her mother, she experienced swelling of midphalangeal joints. (c) Another patient displayed marked swelling of the knees within 24 hours of an altercation with her mother. (d) Still another patient displayed joint swelling—in addition to emotional arousal—after she interpreted a remark of her therapist as meaning her mother had rejected her. These case-history incidents are, of course, subject to the limitations of all case-history data and to the same criticisms.

Possible circumstances predisposing to initial or recurrent attacks are emotional situations including loss of support or separation from a significant person. The physical symptoms ascribed to this condition are pain, swelling of the joints, and limitations of movement. Studies disclose that there are about four times as many women affected as men.

Selye (1956), by injecting an irritating substance such as croton oil or formalin under the skin of the sole of the rat's hind paw, produced a "local experimental arthritis." The fact that an exogenous substance can produce such a condition suggests the possibility that an endogenous substance—particularly an endocrine secretion—or circulatory aberration may also have a role in the development of psychogenic arthritis. Unfortunately, experimental research in this area is meager. Successful use of cortisone in the relief of symptoms, however, may lead to suggestions for the identification of the mediating mechanisms.

2. *Low back pain (lumbago)* is a backache that commonly involves the lumbar and sacral vertebral areas; often it is accompanied by pain radiating throughout the regions supplied by the sciatic nerve. It may vary from soreness or a dull ache to sharp intermittent pain or constant agony. It has been suggested that this condition may be due to faulty postures adopted and sustained, increased muscular stress and effort, and muscular tonus insufficiency. If it is essentially due to the adoption of faulty posture, the disorder can be considered psychologically effected, but it would not

be considered psychosomatic. A condition is psychosomatic from the point of view that has been stressed only to the extent that it is the direct result of emotional reactions mediated by autonomic mechanisms.

3. *Torticollis* (*wryneck*) is a constant or transient spasm of muscles of the neck resulting in a rotated and extended attitude of the head.

One of the psychoanalytic formulations for "psychosomatic" musculo-skeletal disorder can be paraphrased as follows: *Leg and arm symptoms, including pain, result from active restraint of tendencies to attack.* In other words, active impulses toward destruction are countered by active resistance to such behavior; a balance is achieved between aggressive impulses and control, which is accompanied by reports of discomfort.

This may be reformulated in a more general, more objective, and more readily testable way as follows. *Tendencies to action—possibly but not necessarily hostile action—can produce conditions in which increased barrages of neural impulses are directed toward sets of antagonistic muscles raising intramuscular tension levels (and producing rigidity) without accomplishing any effective movement. If sufficiently intense and sustained, such intramuscular tension conditions can lead to structural changes and unusual sensory patterns including the activation of pain receptors.* Thus, a stiff back, stiff neck, bent posture, and locomotor difficulties may develop.

It should be pointed out, however, that while both of these formulations are consistent with a *psychological* point of view, neither is a *psychosomatic* point of view. They represent models that involve *soma-modifying behavior.* A psychosomatic point of view requires reaction to emotional stimulation *via the autonomic nervous system,* which leads to pathological conditions.

If, however, the symptoms for a musculoskeletal disorder—whether lumbago or pleurodynia or torticollis or whatever—are mediated via autonomic nervous or endocrinological mechanisms—for example, pronounced blood-vessel constriction with accompanying ischemia—then the disorder can be considered psychosomatic (in a manner consistent with the way in which that term has been used in this book).

Certain secondary conditions of a physical nature can also be induced on the basis of a psychosomatic disorder. For example, as a consequence of pain, an unusual position may be adopted for a part of the body that may lead to unusual tendon and ligament effects—effects of a deleterious nature. But it should be noted that this, too, is soma-modifying rather than psychosomatic behavior.

Osteopathology

Bone disorders themselves may be psychosomatic. Chronic destructive skeletal disorders are pathological degenerations of bone, particularly skeletal structures of the lower back, and it has been suggested that they may sometimes have a psychosomatic origin.

The following is one of several possible formulations for the mechanisms that operate. *Emotional situations produce physiological reactions, one component of which by influencing calcium metabolism can regulate the brittleness and other characteristics of bone.* Another formulation may implicate the circulatory system as a mechanism for bone pathology, stressing deficiencies in transporting oxygen, waste products, or nutritive substances.

Changes in the structural characteristics of teeth—for example, their calcium content—may also be psychosomatic and may involve mechanisms similar to those proposed for bone.

SIGNIFICANCE OF PSYCHOSOMATIC MUSCULOSKELETAL DISORDERS

Following are a few general statements concerning psychosomatic musculoskeletal relationships.

1. *Predisposition.* Emotional reactions, particularly those involving marked vascular changes at or in the vicinity of muscles and joints, may not only produce psychosomatic pathology but, under conditions in which reactions are less intense, may also increase susceptibility of musculoskeletal structures to pathology induced by barometric changes, toxic conditions, infections, fatigue, and mechanical effects. In other words, emotional reactions may lower bodily resistance.

2. *Circular reaction.* Localized pain produced by vasomotor changes in a muscle may be interpreted by the recipient as an emotional stimulus leading to physiological reactions including further vasomotor changes and further pain, which is again interpreted as an emotional stimulus, and so forth. In this way, a psychosomatic symptom can be perpetuated and exacerbated in a circular or spiral fashion.

3. *Bodily resistance.* Physiological changes induced by emotional situations and influencing musculoskeletal structures may sometimes be of a constructive and health-promoting sort; they are not always destructive.

CHAPTER TWELVE

PSYCHOSOMATIC ENDOCRINE DISORDERS

ANATOMY AND PHYSIOLOGY OF THE ENDOCRINE SYSTEM

While the nervous system controls and correlates manifold activities of the body, there is also a chemical method of bodily integration accomplished through various biological substances, including hormones. The system responsible for such organization is the endocrine gland system.

Glands are structures that are specialized for manufacturing chemical substances. Some glands have tubes or ducts and secrete the substances that they manufacture by means of these tubes either into body cavities or onto the surface of the organism; such glands are called exocrine glands. The salivary glands that pour their secretions into the mouth and aid in digestion, the gastric glands that pour their secretions into the stomach and also aid in digestion, the lacrimal or tear glands that pass their secretions onto the surface of the eyes, and the sweat glands that pass their secretions onto the surface of the body, are all examples of exocrine glands.

Endocrine glands, sometimes called ductless glands because they lack a tube or duct, manufacture specific chemical substances called hormones that are capable of evoking functional changes in other organs. Hormones are secreted directly into the bloodstream, which distributes them to var-

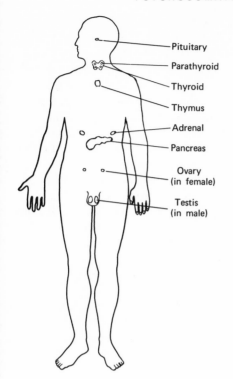

Pituitary
Parathyroid
Thyroid
Thymus
Adrenal
Pancreas
Ovary
(in female)
Testis
(in male)

FIGURE 12-1. Endocrine system.

ious parts of the body; they may therefore exert a regulatory influence on various structures and on bodily activity. Since an endocrine gland may secrete more than a single hormone and since the hormones of one gland may influence the secretions of another, the effects of the endocrines are interrelated and complex and their influences are extensive. (See Figure 12.1.)

To be more specific about their general functions, secretions of endocrine glands control maturational rates of bodily structures and processes. They regulate metabolism, the complex series of chemical changes constantly in progress in living tissues. They also promote homeostasis—the maintenance of an internal physiological equilibrium.

Endocrine glands include the thyroid, parathyroid, adrenal, gonads, and pituitary.

The thyroid gland is a bilobed structure located in the neck on either side of the trachea, and it secretes a hormone called thyroxin. The parathyroid glands in which are very small organs found in the vicinity of the thyroid gland, secrete parathormone. The adrenal gland is located on the kidney and has two parts, an external part called the adrenal cortex and an internal core called the adrenal medulla. The adrenal cortex secretes cortin, which contains a number of active biochemical agents. The adrenal medulla secretes two hormones closely related chemically and called epinephrine and norepinephrine (sometimes termed adrenalin and noradrenalin, respectively). The gonads or sex glands secrete a variety of hormones. Principal hormones secreted by the testes of the male are testosterone and androsterone. A number of hormones, one of which is estrone, are also secreted by the female gonads or ovaries and related structures.

The pituitary gland is located at the base of the brain with certain direct neural connections to the brain and has two portions, an anterior portion that secretes a number of trophic hormones (chemical substances that rather directly influence the activities of other specific endocrine glands) and a posterior part that secretes pituitrin, a substance that contains more than one hormone. The pancreas, which lies below the stomach, is both an exocrine gland and an endocrine gland. In its role as an endocrine gland, it secretes two hormones, the best known of which is insulin.

The endocrine glands have an intimate association with the autonomic nervous system. Activity of the endocrines resulting from emotional stimulation can produce profound changes in the blood chemistry and thereby of metabolic functions and general bodily chemistry.

CHARACTERISTIC EMOTIONAL REACTIONS INVOLVING THE ENDOCRINE SYSTEM

It is believed that among the more frequent reactions of the endocrine glands to emotional stimulation are changes in the pattern of thyroid gland secretion and adrenal gland secretion; however, activity of the pituitary, the pancreas, the gonads, and the parathyroids may also be involved (Lachman, 1969).

Although all of the endocrine glands influence each other, perhaps activation of the pituitary is particularly important, since the anterior portion contains trophic hormones that may directly activate the gonads, the thyroid, or the adrenal glands, each of which in turn has multiple effects.

Emotional situations may lead to an increase or decrease in secretion of an endocrine gland, either through direct autonomic innervation of the specific gland through changes in functioning of the pituitary, or through indirect means such as vascular changes.

REPRESENTATIVE PSYCHOSOMATIC ENDOCRINE DISORDERS

A variety of endocrine disorders have been described as psychosomatic. These include hyperthyroidism, goiter, diabetes mellitus, and hyperinsulinism. Many other endocrine conditions may also be of emotional origin.

Case 12.1. *Hyperthyroidism (thyrotoxicosis).* Miss J was the oldest of four children. Her father, a house painter who became an alcoholic, was divorced by her mother when the patient was 8 years old. Her mother by working and with help from relatives was barely able to support the family, and the patient often took care of the younger children. The patient was hardworking and conscientious and a good student; however, she quit school at age 16 to work and supplement the family income. A half year prior to her admission to the hospital, the patient's mother had abdominal symptoms that interfered with her working regularly and that sometimes required nursing. At age 19 the patient was admitted to the hospital for medical observation and was found to have a fever and leucocytosis as well as other symptoms. The patient's mother had entered the hospital on the preceding day for abdominal surgery. On the seventh day of the patient's hospitalization it was inadvertently revealed to her by a visitor that her mother had died of postoperative complications. On the eighth day of her hospitalization the patient developed a tachycardia (without corresponding temperature elevation or leucocytosis). The thyroid was enlarged and the basal metabollic rate was found to be +52 and a diagnosis of hyperthyroidism was made (Hofling, 1968).

Case 12.2. *Psychosomatic goiter.* A married woman saw her husband kill his two brothers. The husband bitterly reproached her for not coming to his defense at the trial. A week after the trial a goiter became obvious in the woman and it enlarged further within the next week. Within a few months it became huge; when the wife came to the hospital it pulsated visibly and was causing a condition of suffocation. Exophthalmos was pronounced, and tremor was conspicuous; basal metabolism varied from + 40 to +117 percent (Cannon, 1928).

Case 12.3. *Diabetes (hypoinsulinism).* A 25-year-old woman expressed her first diabetic symptoms under the following circumstances. She suspected that her husband was in love with his secretary. One day she came into his office unexpectedly and found them in a compromising situation. She experienced intense autonomic reactions and 3 days later was taken to a hospital in a diabetic coma. For the next 15 years she was well maintained via insulin injections. Then there was a revival of resentful attitudes toward her husband and concomitant physiological reactions that led to another diabetic coma that required a month's hospitalization (Ambrose and Newbold, 1968).

Case 12.4. *Glycosuria.* A 65-year-old man in a hospital on insulin was passing sugar-free urine. Suddenly one day he secreted 43 grams of sugar and on another day he secreted 76 grams and developed a mild acidosis, without any change in the hospital regimen. Later it was discovered that the patient had received information that led him to fear that the corporation in which he had been an officer for many years had initiated steps to retire him; that was the occasion for his sugar-metabolism disturbance (Cannon, 1928).

Case 12.5. *Psychosomatic adrenal-cortical disturbance.* Laboratory evidence of hyperactivity of the adrenal cortex occurred in a 24-year-old girl. One possible explanation was that continuous stimulation of the adrenal cortex resulted from a stressful series of life situations. The mother had encouraged her daughter to be a pianist, dancer, and actress, in each of which roles the daughter felt she had failed. There was much strife in the family situation: an older brother had had a behavioral breakdown; the patient's love affairs were generally unsuccessful; she seemed to be very lonely. Urinary secretion of 17-ketosteroids was 17.7 mg, significantly above the normal of 6 to 12 mg. Examination demonstrated no tumor of the adrenal gland (Grinker and Robbins, 1954).

Hyperthyroidism

Hyperthyroidism, sometimes called Basedow's disease, Graves' disease, or thyrotoxicosis, is characterized by excessive secretion of the thyroid. It has long been suggested that emotional stimulus situations can induce hyperthyroidism and that among that disorder's most prominent symptoms are overactivity and alterations in mood. Excessive secretion of the thyroid produces changes detectable by means of internal receptors that may lead to further concern on the part of the patient, which in turn increases thyroid secretion; in this way a destructive cycle can operate.

Hyperthyroidism ordinarily leads to accelerated metabolism with increased muscular tension, increased restlessness, and increased activity. Loss of body weight may also occur, as well as inability to sleep and a state of general excitability.

The significance of emotional factors in precipitating thyrotoxicosis was reported as early as 1803 by Caleb Parry, who reported its acute onset in a 21-year-old girl following intense fear arousal. The idea that such a condition could be induced by acute emotional arousal became so firmly established in the course of time that it was given a separate name —Shock Basedow.

Kracht and Kracht (1952) have reported a thyrotoxicosis in wild rabbits who were exposed to a fear situation—a barking dog. In fact, the hyperthyroid response was so severe that some animals died and others required special treatment for continued survival.

Goiter

Goiter is a chronic enlargement of the thyroid gland that is not due to a neoplasm. It may or may not be accompanied by a hyperthyroid condition.

Diabetes Mellitus

Diabetes mellitus is a metabolic disorder ascribed to inadequate production of insulin by the pancreas—hypoinsulinism—which results in high blood sugar level and increased excretion of urine, with elevated urine sugar levels.

Von Mering and Minkowski demonstrated in 1889 that diabetes developed following removal of the pancreas in dogs. Earlier Langerhans (in 1869) had identified certain structures in the pancreas—now called the islets of Langerhans—believed to carry a substance that controlled sugar consumption and that was therefore believed to be related to diabetes. In 1922 Banting and Best isolated that substance, insulin. The discovery of insulin quickly revolutionized treatment of diabetes, which in extreme form until that time had doomed its victims to an early death.

Insulin promotes the permeability of cells to sugar, which passes into them from the bloodstream. Insulin acts particularly on the liver, leading to the storage there of sugar in the form of a complex carbohydrate (glycogen), which is released into the bloodstream on demand—the demand typically being the action of epinephrine.

In the diabetic, the carbohydrate supply of the liver is low, due to deficient storage primarily as a consequence of insulin lack. Because of that lack, sugar cannot pass from the blood into the liver and other cells that require it; thus blood sugar level is high and excessive quantities of sugar are excreted in the urine.

The body normally uses sugar in its activity, but since (as a consequence of insufficient insulin) there is less than a normal supply available to the cells that require it, the diabetic burns body protein and fat. This involves an unusual kind of metabolism resulting in the formation of certain poisonous by-products known as ketones. Accumulation of ketones in sufficient concentration leads first to acidosis, later to coma, and eventually to death.

Insulin can counteract this process by acting on the liver and other cells, permitting them to obtain the sugar required for fundamental metabolic activities. Injection of insulin by accomplishing that end has been an important aspect of treatment in diabetes.

In emotional situations, blood sugar level is often affected. Excessive secretion of epinephrine tends to raise it. Action of the thyroid and pituitary glands may also influence blood sugar level and the utilization of sugar by the body.

An extensive review of the literature from as far back as the seventeenth century by Slawson, Flynn, and Kollar (1963) in a search for psychological antecedents and concomitants in the development of diabetes led to the suggestion that object loss, grief, and depression were of major significance in the precipitation of diabetes.

It was demonstrated about half a century ago (Cannon, 1920) that emotional situations—fear and anxiety—can provoke glycosuria in normal humans.

Perhaps one mechanism in the development of diabetes is repeated exposure to emotional situations with emotional response that includes autonomic activation of the adrenal gland with liberation of epinephrine and its consequent action on the liver to break down the glycogen and deplete the carbohydrate supply normally stored therein. Hinkle and Wolf and their associates (Hinkle and Wolf, 1949, 1952; and Hinkle, Conger, and Wolf, 1949) have reported that stress interviews could rapidly produce ketosis in severe diabetics. It has also been determined that emotional stress conditions produce a rise in concentration of blood ketones in normal subjects.

Whether or not emotional factors are major determinants of diabetes, there is no question but that emotional conditions can effect biopathological processes in diabetes. Personal variations in emotional reactivity appear to be of great importance in understanding and treating the diabetic patient.

It is known that normal persons exposed to emotional situations do experience changes in blood-sugar level. Such changes are transient, however.

Addison's Disease

Addison's disease is a condition of hypofunction of the adrenal cortex (adrenocortical insufficiency), characterized by a bronzelike pigmentation of the skin, extreme exhaustion, progressive anemia, low blood pressure, and digestive disturbances, which is usually fatal. Although the major causal determinant is unknown, Marañon (1924) suggested many years ago that it may be the resultant of a prolonged emotionally depressed state. Wallerstein and his associates (1954) have also suggested on the basis of a case study that an extended period of psychological disturbance preceded the development of physiological symptoms. While the evidence at this time is far from convincing concerning the psychogenesis of Addison's disease, there is some suggestive evidence.

Other Psychosomatic Endocrine Disturbances

Fatigue states based on changes in endocrine gland structure and function as a consequence of emotional stimulation may also be considered psychosomatic disorders. These may be functions of low blood sugar due to an overactive pancreas or they may involve lowered basal metabolic rate due to underactivity of the thyroid. Likewise, it is conceivable that states of heightened activity, including even convulsive attacks, may derive from emotional stimulation.

Perhaps *hyperinsulinism,* at least some forms of it, may also be psychosomatic. The accompanying symptoms may include fatigue, hunger, perspiration, tremor, difficulty in concentration, abulia, and depression or anxiety. It is possible that the fatigue, sometimes cited as an outstanding symptom, results from a condition of hypoglycemia (deficient blood sugar level)—which is a direct result of hyperinsulinism.

Many disorders—cretinism, myxedema, acromegaly, and the like—are known to be consequences of long sustained overactivity (hyperfunctioning) or underactivity (hypofunctioning) of particular endocrine glands. To what extent emotionality influences such chronic glandular conditions and their consequences remains to be ascertained.

Eosinophils are particular kinds of white blood cells. Eosinopenia—a reduced eosinophil count—has been found in persons exposed to emotion-provoking situations (McDonald and Yagi, 1960). Basowitz, Persky, Korchin, and Grinker (1955) discovered that paratroopers in training have below-normal eosinophil counts following their first jump and that a low eosinophil count is found even among those who refused to jump. These and other researches raise the question of whether disorders such as leukemia can be emotionally induced via endocrinological mechanisms.

Further, while it is probable that most cases of *obesity* are a function of overeating, there are occasions when endocrine imbalance, for example, thyroid insufficiency, is a primary determinant. It is possible that some cases involving aberrant endocrine functioning in obesity are fostered by emotional stimulation and therefore may be considered psychosomatic. In fact, Gilbert-Dreyfus has described a type of obesity that reportedly relates to emotional circumstances significant to the patient. The condition develops rapidly and the accumulated fat is very spongy due to a high degree of water retention. It is not due to overeating and in fact may occur even in the undernourished.

GENERAL SUMMARY

The following statements serve to summarize certain fundamental ideas concerning the endocrine system that are pertinent to psychosomatic disorders.

1. Endocrine glands, although spatially separated from each other, do influence each other and are functionally interdependent and interlocked. Thus, disturbed functioning of one gland may initiate a chain reaction leading to malfunctioning of other glands.

2. In general, secretions of endocrine glands influence activity level, although this effect appears most obvious for thyroid functioning.

3. Continued stressful circumstances—physical or psychological— tend to enlarge many endocrine glands as well as other structures.

4. *Mechanisms of psychosomatic endocrine disorders.* The endocrine glands are rather directly influenced by the autonomic nervous system. Since the chemical secretions of these glands are mediated by the circulatory system throughout the entire body, it is not difficult to understand how emotional stimulation can come to influence a wide variety of disorders; to the extent that emotional stimulation does so, these disorders may be considered psychosomatic.

SIGNIFICANCE OF THE ENDOCRINE SYSTEM

Endocrine glands may be activated in response to a wide variety of emotional stimulus situations. Selye in his elaboration of the general adaptation syndrome has theorized about (and during a period of more than 30 years has obtained evidence implicating) the endocrine glands, particularly emphasizing the role of the pituitary and adrenal glands in reaction to emotional stimulation as well as in reaction to other stressors.

Various metabolic processes are often delicate and may operate within only quite narrow limits. For example, certain enzymes may function effectively only within restricted temperature limits or only under conditions providing a narrow range of acidity-alkalinity ratios. Alteration in endocrine functions can substantially alter the conditions necessary for effective operation of many vital biochemical processes.

Effects of endocrine activation as part of the emotional reaction constellation may be constructive as well as destructive. For example, increased epinephrine secretion as part of an emotional reaction could save the life of a person undergoing a severe asthmatic attack, since epinephrine causes dilation of air passages and reduces constrictive spasms of the bronchioles.

CHAPTER THIRTEEN

PSYCHOSOMATIC
SENSORY DISORDERS

ANATOMY AND PHYSIOLOGY OF THE
SENSORY SYSTEM

The so-called sensory system is really a collection of sensory subsystems. It includes all those organs, tissues, or cells of the body that are specialized for reception of stimulation and their accessory structures. The special senses include the eyes, the ears, taste cells in the tongue, odor receptors in the olfactory mucous membrane, and structures in the semicircular canals (labyrinthine mechanism). Kinesthetic sense organs are found in muscles, tendons, and joints. The general senses are located in the skin and in a variety of internal organs. (See Figure 13.1.)

Psychosomatic reactions of the senses can be distinguished from conversion reactions involving sensory structures. Conversion symptoms are mediated by means of the somatic nervous system; psychosomatic reactions are mediated through the autonomic nervous system.

Conversion blindness, deafness, and anosmia are characterized by an apparent absence of sensitivity in the various modalities—visual, auditory, and olfactory—but without any pathological changes in the biological nature of the receptor apparatus. Disturbances in vision, audition, or olfaction, in order to be considered psychosomatic, must be mediated via autonomic mechanisms and involve detectable physiological or anatomical changes in the sense organs themselves or in closely related structures.

155

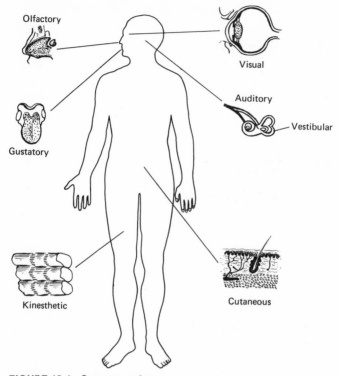

FIGURE 13-1. Sensory system.

CHARACTERISTIC REACTIONS OF SENSORY SUBSYSTEMS TO EMOTIONAL STIMULATION

Theoretically, a wide variety of reactions to emotional stimulation involving the special sense is possible. For example, conjunctival hyperemia (bloodshot eyes) could result from dilation of blood vessels within the eye as a response to sustained emotional stimulation. Certainly similar conditions are observed in individuals who in response to emotional stimulation are on the threshold of crying. Nasal membranes that are swollen in response to emotional stimulation may also interfere with olfaction (Lachman, 1969).

ON PSYCHOSOMATIC SENSORY DISORDERS

Relatively little research has been accomplished regarding psychosomatic sensory disturbances. Nevertheless, mechanisms for the development of psychosomatic disturbances in any sensory modality can be elaborated in theory. Three sensory disorders implicated as psychosomatic are angiospastic retinopathy, glaucoma, and Ménière's disease.

Case History 13.1. *Psychosomatic glaucoma.* At age 37 the patient married. On the third day of the honeymoon, following an argument with his wife, he had a sudden and severe attack of pain in both eyes. Examination shortly thereafter disclosed glaucoma. An earlier—premarital—examination had indicated that he *did not have the disorder at that time.* (Grinker and Robbins, 1954).

Psychosomatic Visual Disorders

Probably a number of disorders involving visual difficulty are related to excessive activity of autonomic fibers of the eye, particularly those associated with pupillary, accommodation, vasomotor, and lacrimal responses.

Theoretically, unusual and sustained tension in extraocular muscles as a direct consequence of emotional stimulation can lead to elongation or shortening of the eyeball to produce conditions of visual difficulty including psychogenic myopia (nearsightedness) or hyperopia (farsightedness). Other refractive errors and psychogenic conjunctivitis are also theoretically plausible.

Harrington (1948) has suggested that physiological changes in the eye aroused psychologically, while normally reversible, if sufficiently prolonged and intense can result in an irreversible organic disorder of the eye. *Angiospastic retinopathy,* which begins as an edema of the macula, producing a pronounced visual disturbance that may be followed later by complete or partial restoration of vision, is considered such a condition. Zeligs (1947), on the basis of his observations of the disorder, concluded that it is due to *emotionally induced* spasms of retinal blood vessels.

Glaucoma is a condition marked by high intraocular pressure. In part, this condition is due to restricted outflow of the aqueous humor through veins of the eye; theoretically, this condition could be influenced by the autonomic nervous system. Clinical evidence also supports the contention that emotionality influences glaucoma (Schlaegel, 1957).

Schoenberg (1945) has cited cases of attacks of primary glaucoma that suggest precipitation by emotional circumstances such as an accident, the death of a close relative, or a personal worry. He indicates that clinical reports of emotional arousal concerned with acts such as infidelity or arguments involving matters of deep concern have been related to subsequent increases in intraocular pressure and attacks of glaucoma.

Ripley and Wolff (1950) suggested the operation of neurotic tendencies and emotional instability in the sample of glaucoma patients they studied.

Berger and Simel (1958) found that direct waking suggestion could produce symptom relief in glaucoma patients; reduced intraocular pressures were found in response to suggestions in all patients. In some patients, symptoms could be reduced by means of posthypnotic suggestion.

Psychosomatic Auditory Disorders

Although there is little or no evidence, the following are theoretical possibilities of psychosomatic disturbances involving structures of the auditory system. (1) An emotionally engendered increase in cerumen can produce an impacted condition to occlude the auditory canal and impair hearing. (2) Profound vasoconstriction of the outer ear to emotional stimulation may produce a condition similar to "frostbite." (3) Tinnitus may be developed through a psychosomatic cardiovascular hypertension.

Psychosomatic Olfactory Disorders

Theoretically, swelling of the turbinates and septum via psychogenically evoked vasomotor reactions can interfere with olfactory efficiency, as can hypersecretion of mucus or other nasal fluid.

Psychosomatic Gustatory Disorders

Theoretically, certain gustatory disturbances may be psychogenic. Among other mechanisms, it is suggested that pronounced hyposecretion or pronounced hypersecretion of the salivary glands may play a prominent role in such disorders.

Psychosomatic Labyrinthine Disorders

The best known of these is Ménière's disease, which is characterized by vertigo, nausea, vomiting, and progressive deafness. It is apparently due to hemorrhaging into the semicircular canals and possibly other structures.

It has been suggested by Fowler and Zeckel (1953) that such reactions may be precipitated by emotional situations. They concluded that emotional factors have a role in development of the disorder. Their data suggested that the first acute attack of vertigo and most subsequent attacks were related to emotion-provoking situations. They discovered circulatory changes in the labyrinthine vessels of their patients. Clumps of blood occluding tiny vessels of the labyrinth produce local anomalies that eventually lead to the structural pathology characteristic of the disorder.

Psychosomatic Cutaneous Sensory Disorders

To some extent these have been suggested in the chapter on psychosomatic skin reactions. However, psychologically induced hyposecretion or hypersecretion of the sweat glands may modify receptor function in deleterious ways. Perhaps they also provide conditions of maceration or dryness of the skin that promote the activities of various microbes.

Pain receptors may be excited as a consequence of the development of various psychosomatic conditions such as peptic ulcer, colitis, anginal syndrome, asthma, or psychogenic menorrhagia. Presumably, also, general or localized emotionally induced physiological changes—perhaps involving histamines—could produce general or localized pain on a psychogenic basis.

CONCLUSION

Although not yet firmly demonstrated, it is clearly within the realm of probability that emotional situations do provoke changes in the circulatory fluid, both chemical and mechanical, of such magnitude as to affect the operation of various sensory subsystems to produce tinnitus or other noises, flashes of light, or vertigo by influencing receptors or other structures involved in audition, vision, or balance, respectively. Numbness in an appendage, a deficiency in cutaneous sensory experience, may also be a function of circulatory aberrations induced by emotional excitants.

On the whole, psychosomatic sensory disorders have been investigated much less extensively and less intensively than psychosomatic disorders involving other organ systems. However, it is presumed that the same kinds of peripheral mechanism, namely glandular secretions, blood-chemistry changes, and vasomotor reactions, mediated via the autonomic nervous system are operative in the genesis and development of such disorders and that no special kinds of mechanism need be proposed to account for psychosomatic sensory disorders.

CHAPTER FOURTEEN

PSYCHOLOGICALLY INFLUENCED SOMATIC DISORDERS

A distinction may be drawn between somatic disorders in which the *major* determinants are psychological and somatic disorders in which psychological determinants play only a *minor* role in the genesis and development of the pathological condition. The first group are the psychosomatic disorders; the second group are the psychologically influenced disorders. These may also be called *primary* and *secondary* psychosomatic disorders, respectively. We are, of course, using the term "psychological" in the restricted sense of "engendered by emotional stimuli via activation of the autonomic nervous system."

There are a wide variety of conditions that, while they are not primarily due to psychological variables, are nevertheless believed to be psychologically influenced, that is, influenced by physiological arousal mediated via emotional stimulation and autonomic nervous mechanisms. We will consider briefly three of these: (1) cancer, (2) pulmonary tuberculosis, and (3) the common cold—coryza.

CANCER

Cancer or carcinoma is a malignant growth; the terms neoplasm and tumor are approximate synonyms. A cancer is a morbid swelling or enlargement

—a mass of new tissue biologically detrimental to the organism (or at least of no physical value) that persists and grows independently of surrounding structures. The term includes a wide variety of pathological types.

With increasing mean ages in the general population, carcinoma has become increasingly important as a major disease producing incapacity and death. A number of questions may be raised concerning emotion and cancer: (1) To what extent is the origin and development of cancer related to emotional reactions? (2) Are specific types of emotional reaction related to particular kinds of cancer or to particular structures in which cancer develops? (3) Are particular personality characteristics associated with particular varieties of cancer? To date only minimal empirical evidence is available bearing on the answers to such questions.

Although the determinants of carcinoma have not been clearly and unequivocally identified, mechanical trauma, abrasion, irritants, various chemicals, viruses, and a variety of other factors have been implicated and probably have roles in the genesis of the diverse forms of cancer. It is not inconceivable that at least certain cancers develop as a consequence of failure of homeostatic mechanisms. Alteration in metabolic activities as a consequence of hormonal or enzyme system anomalies may result from or contribute to such homeostatic failures. Further, it is plausible that such alteration in function, that is, homeostatic failure, may be mediated via the nervous system in response to emotional stimulation.

While the rationale indicated above has not been clearly established for the development of carcinoma, certainly it is not outside the realm of feasibility.

An individual is likely to react to diagnosis of any physical pathology with fear or another emotional pattern. The seriousness of carcinoma is widely known, and mortality statements involving that disorder have been widely disseminated. Thus, diagnosis of cancer may result in pronounced emotional arousal. The individual's life is threatened under conditions of uncertainty in the psychological world of the patient, and in fact, the precise origin of his condition is unknown and the likelihood of successful treatment may not be good. It is an occasion for a variety of reactions—anxiety, fear, and depression, among others. There may be persistent symptoms in terms of pressure, pain, or other sensations. Further, one type of treatment for carcinoma is surgery which, in its own right, is threatening and emotion-provoking. Other treatment techniques, such as radiation or chemotherapy, often involve risk of destroying healthy tissue as well as pathological tissue.

As far back as the ancient Greeks, relationships between affect and illness were noted. Galen suggested that cancer was more frequent in women of melancholic disposition than in women of sanguine disposition. Physicians in the eighteenth and nineteenth centuries, on the basis of observations of cancer patients, inferred that negative emotional reactions—variously termed melancholia, depression, grief, disappointment, despair, or hopelessness—were carcinogenic. Early in the present century, Freund (1905) reported similar observations. Evans (1926) suggested on the basis of examining 100 cancer patients that cancer may often have been precipitated by loss of hope following loss of an important relationship. More recently, Greene, Young, and Swisher (1956) suggested that loss of emotional support or separation from a key goal or object may generate depression, which in turn has a role in the carcinogenesis of lymphomas and leukemias.

Support for the notion of a relationship between emotionality and the development of internal cancer is also obtained from research studies in Russia (Kazansky, 1955), which indicated that cancers developed "spontaneously" in dogs subjected to prolonged stress. They also indicated that carcinogenic substances produced skin cancer in dogs and mice when these animals were subjected to experimental stress.

LeShan and his associates have published several reports concerning the relationship of psychological variables to cancer in humans. The following are representative.

1. On the basis of a projective inventory—the Worthington Personal History—LeShan and Worthington (1955) studied 152 patients with cancer and 125 patients with other illness or no known disease. The investigators discovered that the cancer group as compared with controls (prior to diagnosis of tumor) often (a) experienced loss of an important interpersonal relationship, (b) had difficulty in expressing hostility, and (c) had experienced persistent tension concerning the death of a parent. These investigators also made "blind" analyses of another set of records that had been completed by patients with malignant tumors and by cancer-free persons. On the basis of 28 records, they made correct diagnoses in 89 percent of the cases, that is, they were correct in 25 out of 28 records.

2. LeShan (1961) also reported that in more than 60 percent of 300 cancer patients and about 10 percent of controls whose emotional life histories were investigated, early-life interpersonal relationships were perceived to be so dangerous that close interpersonal relationships could be established only at a cost of "much pain." Typically, according to LeShan, cancer patients develop an emotional attitude of despair after a major traumatic event occurring *before* the first tumors are noted. This despair involves the conviction that the individual can no longer find satisfactions or meaning in life; it is compounded of expressions of hopelessness and a sense of futility regarding life.

3. A study by LeShan and Reznikoff (1960) indicated that psychological factors may be of significance in the development of malignant disease. More specifically, the investigators provided data that suggested that early emotional trauma may interact with other factors and thereby play a role in the etiology of a later malignancy.

A study by Kissen (1962) disclosed that of 212 males with lung cancer, there was a significantly higher frequency of peptic ulcer than in a control group. Lung-cancer patients also had histories of more frequent psychosomatic complaints than did controls.

Up to the present time, substantial evidence has been accumulated linking smoking—especially cigarette smoking—to cancer of the lung. Theoretically, however, there also may be psychological factors involved in the genesis of lung cancer. Several formulations can be suggested.

1. Hypothesis 1: *Lung cancer is the outcome of emotionality and smoking.* According to this viewpoint, people with tendencies toward emotionality are also those most likely to smoke, and lung cancer is a function of both smoking consequences and emotionality. Thus, lung carcinogenesis is a conjoint function of smoking and emotionality.

2. HYPOTHESIS 2: *Lung cancer is precipitated in smokers by later emotional reactivity.* Smoking habits are learned by all kinds of personalities, just as eating habits are; however, in persons who *later* display pronounced and prolonged emotionality, lung cancer is most likely to develop. Here there is the idea that physical disposition via smoking is potentiated into pathological process by emotionality. Thus, smoking plus *later* superimposed emotionality leads to lung cancer.

3. HYPOTHESIS 3: *Lung cancer in the emotionally predisposed is precipitated by later smoking.* People with habits of emotionality that predispose and make vulnerable certain tissues of the body—in this case the lungs—when they later take up smoking further contribute to the development of pathological conditions in the lung. According to this formulation, lung carcinogenesis results from predisposition developed via emotionality plus a later smoking effect.

There is little evidence to support any of these hypotheses regarding a psychological factor in the development of lung cancer. The evidence that smoking itself is carcinogenic does nothing to promote the idea of a potent psychological factor.

In fact, the methodological weaknesses in all investigations of psychological factors in the development of cancer in the human are so substantial as to make the acquired data of little value. Definitions of emotional situations have been vague; control groups have rarely been employed;

quantification procedures regarding the psychological variables are seldom used; types and sites of cancer are often not specified; distinction between premorbid personality traits and postdiagnosis personality characteristics are often ignored or unspecified by researchers—to mention only some of the major problems.

PULMONARY TUBERCULOSIS

Tuberculosis is an acute or chronic communicable disease with extensive effects, and until recently it was characterized by a relatively high mortality rate. Although the microbe involved may affect the gastrointestinal and genitourinary tracts, the bones and joints, the nervous system, the skin, and the lymphatics, it usually affects the respiratory system. Pulmonary tuberculosis is the result of an infection of the lungs by the tubercle bacillus. Generally, inhalation is the method by which the germ enters the body. It is readily spread by coughing, sneezing, or the expectoration of tubercular patients.

The microorganism for tuberculosis is widespread in our society; nearly all people are exposed to it at some time in their lives and yet relatively few develop the disease. This suggests one or both of two influences that operate in determining whether a particular individual develops tuberculosis—a constitutional predisposition or a somatic change that in part may be mediated via emotional stimulation. It is possible that physiological reactions to emotional stimulation serve to increase or decrease disease susceptibility.

Creative writers have suggested relationships between emotions and tuberculosis. One of the characters, Mimi, in Puccini's *LaBoheme,* is precipitated by unrequited love into an episode of tuberculosis that proves fatal. The relationship of emotion to tuberculosis is also suggested for major characters in Alexandre Dumas' *Camille,* Thomas Mann's *The Magic Mountain,* and W. Somerset Maugham's short story, *The Sanatorium.*

Berg (Grinker and Robbins, 1954), on the basis of about three years' study of patients in Winfield Tuberculosis Sanatorium, concluded that many of his patients were precipitated into their initial attacks of pulmonary tuberculosis by an intensification of sexual conflict.

Case 14.1. *Tuberculosis.* The patient was hospitalized first at age 13 for about 4 years. Six months after being released from the hospital, she became ill again and remained in the hospital for 5 years. After a release of less than 6 months she was again hospitalized until the time of commencing therapy at age 27. Between her second and third periods of hospitalization she married a man several years older, also a patient, whom she had met at the hospital during her second hospitalization. Her husband later divorced her. The patient was highly reactive emotionally not only to new frustrating situations but also to dreams, to fantasied situations, and to recalled stressful problems. Psychotherapy apparently led to some decline in emotional reactivity and to a diminution of symptoms of tuberculosis (Grinker and Robbins, 1954).

Physicians and psychologists associated with patients in hospitals and wards for tuberculosis patients have often noted sharp changes—both favorable and unfavorable—with vicissitudes of emotion, both positive and negative (Papania, 1968). In support of a psychosomatic position is the report that psychotherapy alone has been sufficient to effect a cure in some advanced cases of pulmonary tuberculosis (Strange, 1965).

There are at least two distinct kinds of theoretical formulation that help to account for the possible role of emotionality in the genesis, development, exacerbation, and remission of physical disease conditions involving infection, such as tuberculosis. (1) As a consequence of pronounced or prolonged emotionality, that is, physiological changes to emotional stimulation, general bodily resistance is lowered. It may be due to excessive expenditure of or lack of availability of bodily resources—general bodily weakening. (2) As a consequence of pronounced or prolonged emotionality there may be particular physiological changes that occur to maximize the predisposition of an individual to a specific kind of disorder such as a lung disorder. It should be emphasized, however, that these are merely gross theoretical possibilities, and there are few data at the present time indicating precise relationships between particular emotional stress situations and vulnerability to tuberculosis.

THE COMMON COLD—CORYZA

Apparently, a number of different viruses provoke the symptoms summarized as "common cold." Although most people are exposed, only a relatively few develop colds. This may be interpreted as due to innate physical immunity and vulnerability or perhaps it is related to an emotionally engendered physiological susceptibility.

It is likely that self-destructive tendencies may lead some people to expose themselves to situations likely to produce a cold. Such a cold is in part a function of explicit behavior and in that sense is influenced by psychological factors; but it would not be considered psychosomatic according to the definition that has been employed in this presentation. However, excessive dryness or congestion of the mouth, nose, and throat, which may be engendered via autonomic activity, provide coryzalike conditions and perhaps facilitate infection.

Colds are believed to be due to microorganisms—either bacteria or viruses or both. The survival, growth, and increase in populations of such agents in the mouth may be a function of emotionality. For example, emotional situations via autonomic mechanisms may influence the quantity of saliva secreted, the chemical nature of the saliva secreted, or the internal temperature of the mouth. It is not implausible that any of these variables could influence conditions conducive to the development of coryza-producing microorganisms and therefore of colds. In fact, Kaplan, Gottschalk, and Fleming (1957) have reported that they could predict accurately variations of the bacterial population in the oropharynx of a rheumatic patient from knowledge of the patient's emotional status. Likewise, changes in the hydrogen-ion concentration of nasal secretions also have been reported (Fabricant, 1946) to vary with emotional states. Since the pH (hydrogen-ion) level relates to reproductive facility, it is likely that the emotionally founded physiological changes may influence rate of microorganism proliferation.

Saul (1938) reported a study of 15 patients subject to unusually frequent colds and sore throats who became "entirely free from colds or had them with conspicuous rarity" on the basis of no treatment other than psychoanalysis.

It has been suggested that colds are at least in part psychosomatic and that the effects of emotionality via autonomic mechanisms may predispose an individual to colds, foster their development, and contribute to their treatment resistance.

A similar kind of formulation may be proposed regarding susceptibility to pneumonia. Major differences relate to the pathogen involved and the severity of the symptoms.

ATTITUDES AND ILLNESS EFFECTS

Physicians have often noted and reported that attitudes and expectations of patients influence whether they recover health or perish and perhaps also their rates of progress in either direction.

For purposes of exposition it may be expeditious to distinguish two kinds of attitude or point of view—positive expectation and negative expectation.

1. *Positive expectation* may be characterized by terms such as hope, hopefulness, confidence, or enthusiasm. It is a condition of psychological and physiological activation; this condition involves attitudes and overt behaviors as well as physiological processes, and the sum of them are oriented toward goal achievement—in this case the acquisition of better health. Hope involves the augmentation of life mechanisms—life-promoting and -sustaining physiological processes.

2. *Negative expectation* may be characterized by such terms as hopelessness, discouragement, apathy, or surrender. It is a condition of psychological and physiological deceleration; this condition also involves attitudes and overt behaviors as well as physiological processes, and the sum of them are oriented toward failure or defeat—in this case "debilitation" and death. Hopelessness involves a radical slowing down of physiological processes (or other deleterious alteration in physiological processes); in other words, it involves physiological processes that hamper or interfere with the promotion and maintenance of life.

The hypothesis that there is a difference in the physiology of these two kinds of psychological process—positive expectation and negative expectation or hopefulness and hopelessness—as well as their intergradations and variants is deserving of intensive and detailed research study.

Bettelheim (1960) reported that prisoners in concentration camps of Nazi Germany who gave up hope and withdrew from interpersonal and other environmental stimulation soon died. Nardini (1952) reported that some American prisoners of war in Japanese concentration camps during World War II were so discouraged by difficult conditions that they gave up, lying down to die, and succumbed in the absence of any obvious physical pathology. These reports are consistent with the concept of negative expectation proposed. Further, almost any physician with extensive experience can report cases in which observed physiological trends that should have doomed the patient to death were reversed, presumably by strong positive expectations. In any case, an understanding of the psychophysiology of the attitudes described—attitudes of hopelessness and hope—seems desirable because of its relevance for recovery from all illnesses, psychosomatic or otherwise.

GENERAL CONCEPTS REGARDING PSYCHOLOGICALLY INFLUENCED SOMATIC DISORDERS

Emotional stimulation can produce extensive physiological changes and influence a wide variety of biological structures and processes that in turn, if sufficiently intense or sustained, may provoke pathology.

In outline, the biological mechanism is relatively simple. Impulses resulting from stimulation of any sense organ are mediated by afferent neurons to the central nervous system, including those areas of the brain with a role in interpreting the stimuli affectively. Such areas presumably are in intimate association with medial brain structures including the limbic system, reticular formation, and especially the hypothalamus, which influence peripheral autonomic outflow. Although many structures may be directly affected by autonomic nervous system activity, a variety of indirect effects may be achieved via cardiovascular, glandular, and gastrointestinal influences particularly.

1. Various and extensive changes may be mediated via the cardiovascular system including patterns of vasoconstriction and vasodilation, amplitude and frequency of cardiac contraction, and blood chemistry involving not only adrenalin and blood sugar level but also eosinophil count and others. Edema, stenosis, and other conditions provoke complications.

2. Various extensive changes may be mediated via changes in quality and quantity of secretion of various endocrine and exocrine glands. Some of the pathological effects may be direct. However, others may be indirect. For example, variations in the composition of saliva may interfere with its digestive properties or with its neutralizing and antibacterial properties.

3. Alterations in enzyme production may also profoundly alter metabolic processes—mechanisms whereby various disease conditions may be influenced.

CHAPTER FIFTEEN

PSYCHOTHERAPY FOR PSYCHOSOMATIC DISORDERS

INTRODUCTION:
DEFINITION AND GENERAL OBJECTIVES

Psychotherapy may be conceptualized in many ways. Following is a general statement concerning psychotherapy with psychosomatic disorders. Psychological therapy for psychosomatic disorders involves the central idea that by means of psychological procedures in the clinical situation the psychotherapist may be instrumental in modifying in a constructive direction the physiological states of the patient that are emotion and in altering their biological consequences—to make those consequences less harmful and more beneficial.

The immediate goal of psychotherapy with psychosomatic disorders is the amelioration of the disorder processes and the disorder symptoms. An important further goal is modification of the individual psychologically so as to reduce the likelihood of recurrence of the immediate disorder or of any other psychosomatic disorder. Premises associated with this conception are that (1) the therapist can help the patient to control emotional expression—not only the more explicit behaviors, but also the more fundamental physiological reactions and (2) the therapist can help the patient to avoid—or otherwise deal effectively with—emotion-provoking situations. Such situations are both overt and internalized in the form of thoughts and conflictful action tendencies. (3) The therapist can aid in modifying the personality structure of the patient so as to reduce the frequency and intensity of those emotional states that may have disadvantageous biological consequences for him, while facilitating those conditions that are likely to have advantageous biological consequences.

Psychotherapy is, of course, a kind of special education—generally education of an individualistic or tutorial sort. Part of that education involves helping the patient to identify particular stimulus situations or conditions—people, objects, events, ideas, attitudes, and the like—that in the etiology of the psychosomatic disorder engendered the emotionality that in turn promoted his symptoms. With the identification of such stimulus conditions, the individual can be given directions in how to avoid such situations. He may also be given some information on handling such situations should they be encountered and some help in techniques of emotional control generally. Further, the patient may be given education and direction by medical personnel in control of symptoms through use of drugs and other medical procedures, although use of drugs and various medical procedures typically will provide only temporary relief rather than cure.

Research evidence such as that acquired by Mittelmann, Wolff, and Scharf (1942) supports the rationale for psychotherapeutic treatment of psychosomatic disorders. They found when they put normal subjects and ulcer patients into emotion-arousing situations, among other changes, increased mobility and acidity of the stomach occurred in all ulcer patients and some normal subjects. But what is most important for psychotherapy, they also found that acidity and motility of the stomach were *reduced* by stimulus situations conducive to contentment. This may be a paradigm for other autonomic changes that occur under conditions of contentment and satisfaction and that serve to stabilize or normalize physiological functioning. Psychotherapy with the psychosomatic disorders often is concerned with promoting such conditions.

PSYCHOTHERAPY AS A LEARNING PROCESS

Psychotherapy is essentially a learning process. In the case of psychotherapy involving psychosomatic disorders two assumptions are frequently made.

1. *Psychosomatic disorders are often derivatives of learning.* Psychosomatic disorders are functions of undesirable internal behaviors resulting from emotional stimulation; the undesired physiological reactions to such emotional stimulation produce aberrant or anomalous consequences. Certain biological results of reactions to emotional stimulation, then, are

pathological and disadvantageous to organisms; they are the psychosomatic disorders. In large part, the stimulation-reaction relationships leading to psychosomatic disorders are learned.

2. *Those stimulation-reaction relationships learned by the individual that result in pathological biologic consequences can be modified by further learning events.* This modification may be accomplished by (1) unlearning or extinction of undesired responses, (2) relearning the earlier acquired more adequate responses that had been subsequently superseded by "disadvantageous learning," and (3) new learning of more adequate or constructive responses.

In the psychotherapeutic situation the individual can express himself freely under circumstances in which he has an opportunity to function at a physiological level within the realm of the normal. Considering emotion-provoking stimuli under such conditions may serve to reduce their effectiveness or even to extinguish responses to them. This is one kind of therapeutic learning activity.

Further, in the background of the patient, overt behaviors typically have been associated with those implicit patterns that are emotion. In the therapeutic situation the same overt behaviors are less likely to occur, even when the implicit responses are to some extent revived. Thus, the explicit behavioral supports associated with the physiological reactions of emotion are removed from association with the physiological behavior. Eventually, such dissociation contributes to the dissipation or reduction of emotional behavior. This is another kind of therepautic learning activity.

In addition, a general premise underlying psychotherapy with psychosomatic disorders is the following: *If an optimal or at least an improved level of autonomic functioning can be achieved in the therapeutic situation or as a consequence of it, the altered level of autonomic operation can be extended and generalized to other situations.*

PSYCHOTHERAPY AND SOMATIC TREATMENT

With regard to psychosomatic disorders, the physiological difficulties and somatic pathology require treatment as well as the psychological problems. Even though *cure* is not achieved until the individual is psychologically changed, that is, even though the patient's implicit behavioral or emotional reactions to stimuli and their surrogates (images, ideas, conflicts, etc.) must be altered before cure is achieved, nevertheless, somatic treatment is typically desirable or even essential and generally is an accompaniment, if not a precondition, of psychotherapy. In fact, under certain circumstances, such as an asthmatic attack, an extreme cardiac reaction, perforation of a gastrointestinal ulcer, spontaneous abortion, intense migraine, severe menorrhagia, or pronounced conditions of ulcerative colitis, somatic treatment is of *primary* and critical significance. The avoidance of permanent incapacity—and even the patient's very life—may depend on prompt and effective somatic treatment.

Obviously, somatic treatment can be accomplished best when the physician knows of the patient's current psychological makeup, that is, when the physician knows the patient's major immediate emotional problems. A small sample of the somatic therapeutic procedures employed will be briefly mentioned, but no attempt will be made to indicate their relative effectiveness nor the conditions that encourage or discourage the use of particular procedures nor the prognosis for improvement through employment of a particular method.

Likewise, in discussing somatic procedures involved in dealing with psychosomatic disorders, little attention will be paid to the use of analgesics employed to reduce pain, to antibiotics that are used to control infection, or to the sedatives and barbiturates that are often prescribed. Neither will much attention be paid to tranquilizers or antidepressants used to modify emotional reactivity. (All of these drugs are of course extensively used with psychosomatic disorders as well as with other psychological and organic disorders.) Instead, focus is on a few particular somatic techniques employed in the treatment of a few specific disorders.

It should be emphasized that somatic procedures merely relieve or reduce the somatic symptoms; they do not remove the fundamental cause. Also, improved functioning of the patient can best be accomplished by cooperation between a skilled psychotherapist and a skilled medical specialist.

Although sometimes psychotherapy may be so effective as to reduce the rate or stop the progress of the pathologic condition, it is rare that the biological condition—for example a structural pathology—can be reversed or eliminated exclusively via psychotherapy. Although symptom remission and even complete cure may occur, psychotherapy does not guarantee a permanent immunity against recurrences of the symptoms or the development of new psychosomatic manifestations under conditions of intense emotionality. In effective treatment, knowledge of the psychological and the physical functioning of the individual and their intimate association, particularly with regard to emotional factors and interpersonal situations, is necessary. A fundamental thesis of the position developed in this book bears repetition in considering treatment procedures: *The organism is a psychosociobiophysical unit.*

A major function of psychotherapy with psychosomatic disorders is to render the individual less emotionally reactive (or to change the direction of his physiological reactivity)—to reduce the likelihood of exacerbating the symptoms and to render him less vulnerable to other symptoms as a consequence of emotional reactivity.

In part, psychotherapy assists in modification of the basic personality structure so that the individual is less vulnerable to psychosomatic disorders. By changing self-attitudes from a negative direction (attitudes of personal inferiority and inadequacy and low self-confidence) to a positive direction (attitudes of high self-esteem, personal adequacy, and self-confidence), personality structure is simultaneously modified and the threshold for eliciting deleterious emotionality is raised. Psychotherapy also may involve the patient's developing skills for establishing and maintaining good interpersonal relationships and for resisting the effects of loss or threatened loss of such relationships. It involves conflict resolution.

Nevertheless, a major therapeutic consideration in the case of a psychosomatic disorder is treatment of the somatic manifestations of the disorder. Essentially that amounts to treatment of the symptoms. Thus, in the case of peptic ulcer, use of a bland diet, antacids, antispasmodics, and section of the vagus nerve to reduce acid secretion are standard kinds of treatment. In ulcerative colitis, liberal fluid intake, a nonirritating diet, and bowel antispasmodics are commonly prescribed. To survey completely the somatic procedures employed in treating psychosomatic disorders is far beyond the scope of this work. A brief sample of such somatic procedures, however, is overviewed in Table 15.1.

TABLE 15.1 Somatic Treatment of Psychosomatic Disorders

Representative Disorder	Somatic Treatment Procedures
Gastrointestinal system	
Peptic ulcer	Rest. Typically bland diet involving milk as the basis and several daily feedings of easily digested, palatable, nonirritating foods. Multivitamin capsules. Medication to minimize hyperacidity and intestinal spasm. Blood transfusion for hemorrhage of peptic ulcer. Surgical repair of perforation. Surgical removal of intractable ulcer (gastrectomy). Surgical section of autonomic fibers to gastrointestinal tract (vagotomy).
Ulcerative colitis	Bed rest, liberal fluid intake, nonirritating diet. Intramuscular injections of vitamin B-complex. Antispasmodics to depress activity of bowel.

TABLE 15.1 Somatic Treatment of Psychosomatic Disorders (*Cont.*)

Representative Disorder	Somatic Treatment Procedures
	Medication to thicken bowel discharges as necessary. Surgery: ileostomy or colonectomy as indicated for extensive bowel damage.
Cardiovascular system	
Anginal syndrome	Physical rest and avoidance of excitement critical. Limited activity and avoidance of overexertion prescribed. Low-fat diet may be helpful. Smoking is discouraged. Drugs to increase coronary blood flow by dilating coronary arteries may be desirable.
Essential hypertension	Administration of hypotensive agents. If obese, weight reduction may be desirable. Short-term periods of rest advised. Multivitamin tablets. Diet with restriction of salt; rice emphasized in a special diet that restricts sodium and protein content. Sympathectomy required only in malignant hypertension when less drastic methods have failed.
Respiratory system	
Bronchial asthma	Several drugs may relieve asthma symptoms— ephedrine, epinephrine, aminophylline, cortisone, hydrocortisone, and corticotrophin. Certain antihistaminic drugs may be effective in mild asthma.
Rhinitis	Alkaline spray to wash away mucinoid discharge. Electrocautery (or chemical procedures) to reduce hypertrophy of inferior turbinates. Surgical removal of hypertrophied portions of inferior turbinates.
Skin system	
Urticaria	Antihistaminic drugs, emollient baths, antipruritic lotions and powders. Cortisone, hydrocortisone, corticotrophin.
Acne	Keep entire body clean; squeezing, pinching,

Representative Disorder	Somatic Treatment Procedures

	and picking at lesions must be avoided. Steamed towels, antiseptic agents, antiseborrheic lotions. Greasy cosmetics to be avoided. Deep cysts and abscesses may be opened with thin scalpel. Sometimes multivitamin capsules recommended.
Genitourinary system	
Impotence	Hormonal substances such as testosterone and thyroid extract may be appropriate. Moderate ingestion of alcohol prior to attempted coitus.
Amenorrhea	Neostigmine methylsulfate may facilitate menstruation; thyroid medication may be helpful. Gonadotropins may be helpful, as may estrogen and progesterone.
Musculoskeletal system	
Rheumatoid arthritis	Cortisone, hydrocortisone, and corticotrophin treatment. Rest and avoidance of fatigue. Proper posture at rest is stressed. Salicylates. Transfusion to counteract accompanying anemia. Local treatment of joints with heat. Certain gold compounds are helpful.
Torticollis	Encourage patient to practice relaxation.
Endocrine gland system	
Hyperthyroidism	Application of techniques to reduce or suppress the production of excess hormones by the thyroid gland. Use of various orally administered drugs; subtotal thyroidectomy; radiation therapy.
Diabetes mellitus	Drugs to promote metabolism of glucose. Diet involving restricted carbohydrate intake. Insulin.
Sensory system	
Glaucoma	Various drugs to normalize intraocular tension.
Retinopathy	Treat the underlying more direct determinants, such as, hypertension, nephritis, and toxemia.

Assuming that the disorder is psychologically engendered, however, psychotherapy is generally the kind of treatment that is necessary to modify the fundamental determinant. Psychotherapy is an attempt to modify those aspects of the psychological nature of the individual that are presumed to be root sources or major determinants of the disorder.

RELAXATION

Jacobson (1938) hypothesized that a state of muscular relaxation was incompatible with anxiety. That thesis may be expanded to hold that *states of extensive muscular relaxation are incompatible with almost any sort of emotional arousal*. Although emotional arousal involves profound physiological deviations, such deviations are typically accompanied by skeletal activity and much muscular tension. Thus, these two sets of activities, as well as their initiating stimuli and their response-induced stimuli, tend to become intimately associated with each other. Therefore, if somatic relaxation can be promoted in the therapeutic situation, the autonomic accompaniments of such relaxation that are incompatible with emotional arousal will also be affected.

LEARNED AUTONOMIC CONTROL

Narrow and limited but, nonetheless, ingenious and apparently effective procedures have recently been instituted under the general rubric of "behavior modification techniques." These, like other kinds of psychotherapeutic procedure, involve learning and typically are devoid of an elaborate psychotherapeutic rationale, such as that apparent in analytic and psychoanalytic perspectives.

Representative behavior-modification techniques developed as related to psychosomatic disorders have involved the use of physiological instruments linked to display devices. The display devices provide information to the patient about ongoing autonomic operations and may be used by him to facilitate control of those internal activities. For example, information about blood pressure or heart rate may be supplied. The observer can look at especially amplified cues indicative of his own physiological reactions, make a variety of efforts at modifying such reactions, and obtain immediate "feedback" information concerning the consequences of his efforts. In time, he may be able to identify, select, and develop those sets, attitudes, efforts, and other central control devices that serve to produce desired levels of autonomic activity—as opposed to those internal control devices that do not result in change or that produce changes in the undesired direction. On the basis of observed display disclosures of internal reaction, or on the basis of other means of reinforcement or nonreinforcement, subvocal self-reports are developed. Modifications in subvocal self-report occur with modifications in internal reaction. In time such subvocal self-reports (or thoughts) become associated with particular internal reactions. Eventually, there may be self-directed or thought-directed autonomic responses—sets of internal or symbolic structures that regulate autonomic responses. With practice such responses can become automatic or "unconscious."

Sometimes autonomic responses may occur to overt stimuli without the subject being in any way aware of the response that was modified. For example, Shapiro and his colleagues trained subjects to modify their blood pressure. Each success—a decrease in blood pressure for some subjects and a rise in blood pressure for others—was indicated by a flash of light. Periodically, after a certain number of flashes, a reward was provided to successful male subjects—a glimpse of a nude pinup picture. Most subjects were unaware of the role performed by the flashing light and of the physiological response that was being monitored.

Experimental research concerning autonomic control was initiated many years ago in Russia. Recently Neal Miller (1969) and his associates, particularly DiCara (1970), have conducted a brilliant series of researches and reported dramatic success in the instrumental learning of autonomic responses in rats. Via stimulation of reward centers in the brain, discrete and specific responses—both increases and decreases—in heart rate, blood pressure, intestinal contraction, blood-vessel diameter, and rate of formation of urine were learned. Those researches have demonstrated that such visceral responses can be learned directly without any necessary mediation of somatic activity. Continued training with reward led to progressive deviation from initial base rates.

THE GOALS OF PSYCHOTHERAPY WITH PSYCHOSOMATIC DISORDERS

Following are some of the major goals of psychotherapy with psychosomatic disorders:

1. To help the individual recognize the role of emotions in the development and precipitation of illness generally and of his illness in particular.

2. To help the individual identify particular—or at least probable—

emotion-arousing situations and conflicts that operate for him.

3. To assist the patient in acquiring control over overt activities associated with emotional arousal. This includes not only training the individual to recognize emotional situations, but also training him to avoid such situations and, if they are encountered, to deal constructively with them. It also includes directing overt behaviors toward reducing or dissipating the energy resources and other physiological products generated by emotional reactivity, and directing behavior toward constructive activities and away from destructive responses.

4. To achieve modification in amplitude, duration, and frequency of deviations of autonomic reactions from pathogenic values to normal or optimal levels.

5. To help the individual to acquire, insofar as possible, direct control over his own autonomic reactions.

CHAPTER SIXTEEN

CONCLUDING DISCUSSION

A HOLISTIC POSITION

Certain disorders are primarily biological and others are primarily psychological; the holistic position in medicine and in clinical psychology has been extensively accepted, namely that *all biological disorders have psychological elements and all psychological disorders have biological elements that must be considered in both diagnosis and treatment.*

The disturbances with which we have been concerned, psychosomatic disorders, are *biological disorders,* that is, disorders of physiological functioning and anatomical structure, which are *determined for most part by psychological factors.*

Perhaps holism may be considered a kind of psychosomatic integration. Or even more broadly, the idea encouraged by a holistic position is that the organism is a *psychosociobiophysical* unit. There is no question that the potent stimuli eliciting emotional behavior typically have *psychological* and *social* significance, nor is there any question concerning the *biophysical* nature of the organism.

From the standpoint of emotional reaction, it may be said that *the body tends to respond holistically.* Anger involves the heart, bloodstream, respiratory mechanism, digestive tract including the bowels, endocrine glands, skin, and other bodily structures. So too do elation, fear, disgust, joy, hate, and a variety of other emotional reaction patterns. Emotion is rather diffuse and global autonomic behavior and in that sense can be regarded as holistic.

SUMMARY OF THE THEORETICAL
POSITION DEVELOPED

Following is a brief summary of the theoretical position developed in this book.

1. Emotion is behavior.
   (a) Emotional behavior is physiological behavior.
   (b) Emotional behavior typically involves the viscera extensively; the autonomic nervous system is the major mechanism for mediating emotional behavior.
2. Emotional reactions may be learned.
3. Emotional behavior is initially aroused by stimuli. Through associative processes, other stimuli, overt symbols, and central representations of emotion-provoking stimulus situations also evoke emotional reactions. Thus, certain physiological reactions are aroused by an increasing variety of circumstances.
4. If emotional reactions are sufficiently intense, sustained, or repeated, a durable physiological malfunctioning or an actual structural pathology may be engendered—a psychosomatic disorder.
5. There are individual differences in reactivity to various stimulus situations, and there are individual differences in suceptibility or vulnerability to psychosomatic disorders.
6. Emotional reactions may also be eliminated or unlearned.

Psychosomatic symptoms develop in emotional situations or as a consequence of emotional situations. Theoretically, any stimulus can become associated with any physiological reaction. Certain stimulus-situation and physiological-reaction combinations *initially* may be strictly fortuitous. Such stimulus-response combinations become strengthened merely by frequency or repetition of occurrence or by being reinforced—rewarded. Everyday gains that may serve as rewards to strengthen those stimulus-response combinations, which are psychosomatic symptoms, include escaping from work, avoiding unpleasant obligations, securing sympathy, obtaining a more comfortable existence, ceasing to be the recipient of criticism, and acquiring special services from others. In those ways psychosomatic disorders are fostered.

DELETERIOUS AND CONSTRUCTIVE EFFECTS
OF EMOTIONAL REACTIONS

Psychosomatic disorders may occur not only as an effect of negative emotion, but also as an effect of positive emotion such as joy, elation, or sex emotions. The profound emotional arousal in response to winning $50,-000. in the Irish Sweepstakes could lead to the rupture of a blood vessel in the brain; being honored by an elaborate and unexpected (surprise) party may lead to an asthmatic attack; or during the climax immediately following vigorous emotional arousal involving a highly gratifying sexual encounter, a psychosomatic cardiac problem could develop.

Further, emotional arousal—even arousal of negative emotions—may have a constructive effect. Examples include adrenal secretion combating an asthmatic attack; raised blood pressure assisting a person with very low blood pressure; and anger stimuli promoting glycogen liberation to counter the effects of hyperinsulinism.

PERSONALITY TYPES AND SPECIFIC PSYCHOSOMATIC DISORDERS

It has been proposed by some investigators and theorists, that particular kinds of personality are prone to display particular kinds of psychosomatic disorder. According to this point of view, different types of personality structure reflect themselves in different psychosomatic disorders. However:

1. Evidence available at the present time often suggests that individuals with *very similar* personality patterns are prone to *different* psychosomatic disorders.

2. There have been reports of individuals displaying more than one psychosomatic disorder at a particular time.

3. Research evidence suggests that different kinds or *different patterns of personality* are often associated with the same psychosomatic disorder.

4. Data support the position that there are no clear-cut personality types for any specific psychosomatic disorder.

5. Some individuals with "classic personality patterns," assumed in theory to be associated with particular psychosomatic disorders, never do provide evidence of any psychosomatic disorder.

Thus, Dunbar's hope of finding discrete personality patterns or characteristics uniquely associated with each type of psychosomatic disorder—and presumably a major determinant of that disorder—remains unfulfilled.

CRITERIA FOR A PSYCHOSOMATIC DISORDER

To be considered a psychosomatic disorder, at least three criteria must be met.

1. The disorder is not attributable to direct physical factors such as a mechanical blow, knife wound, microbial organism, exogenous toxin, or other similar determinant.

2. The disorder is a function of internal behavior—a function of behavior only minimally controlled, or at least for most part normally *not* directly controlled, by the organism. And such behavior in turn is attributable to emotion-provoking circumstances.

3. Emotionality involving potent "autonomic" changes is of a magnitude sufficient to account for the symptoms.

Obviously, the development of instruments, procedures, and units of measurement that permit more precise identification of variables than is possible at present will, in the future, permit better diagnoses.

SIGNIFICANT CONCEPTUAL AND RESEARCH DEVELOPMENTS

There are some formidable problems with respect to the determination of the relationships between emotion-provoking stimulus situations and the specific physiological reaction constellations elicited.

1. In a particular individual very similar physiological reaction constellations may occur in response to very different stimulus situations. The direct nervous system effects of stimulation should not be neglected in considering the reaction constellation.

2. The same individual may display very different physiological reaction constellations in response to objectively very similar stimulus situations.

3. There may be widespread individual differences in physiological reaction-constellations from situation to situation and from time to time.

If these three points prove to be rules rather than exceptions, firmly establishing the empirical findings supporting those principles will be critically important in delineating emotional behavior and in assessing the effects of emotional reactions on psychosomatic disorders.

As a matter of fact, Lacey and his associates (Lacey, Bateman, and VanLehn, 1953) have presented evidence to suggest that an individual will show rather similar patterns of autonomic response to a wide variety of stimulus situations. Their findings lend support to the first point considered above.

Gellhorn (1957) has developed a concept of autonomic tuning according to which the same stimulus may produce a predominantly sympathetic pattern of responses in one subject while providing a predominantly parasympathetic pattern of response in another. Likewise, an individual may react primarily with sympathetic responses at one time and with parasympathetic responses at another. Either division of the autonomic nervous system may be dominant and "sensitized" to produce responses depending on its being "set" or "tuned" or "adjusted" for reactivity to stimulation. Hypothalamic activity has been suggested as one of many variables that influence tuning of the autonomic nervous system; prior autonomic functioning and changes in the external stimulus situation are also influences. Gellhorn's conceptual scheme has a bearing on the second and third points mentioned above.

A number of investigators have conducted research investigations in the elucidation of the physiological reaction constellations characteristic of particular emotional stimulus situaions. For example, consider the following.

Wolf and Wolff (1947) found in their patient with an abdominal fistula that the stomach lining became pale under conditions of fear or apprehension and became red or inflamed under conditions of anger and resentment.

Ax (1953) used seven indicators of physiological reaction—pulse rate, heart stroke volume, breathing, facial temperature, hand temperature, galvanic skin response (GSR), and muscular action currents—under seminaturalistic conditions in which laboratory technicians by their behaviors and statements provided anger and fear situations while the subject's physiological responses were being recorded. Each of 43 subjects was placed in an anger and a fear situation once—about half in one order and the other half in the reverse order. Predominant in the anger reaction constellation were greater GSR, heart rate decrease, muscular tension increase, and diastolic blood-pressure rise. Predominant in the fear reaction constellation were muscle-tension peaks, skin-conductance increases, and respiration-rate increases. The differences most prominent in fear correspond to the action of epinephrine; those more prominent in anger correspond to action of both epinephrine and norepinephrine.

Funkenstein (1955) found that rabbits that depend for survival on their ability to run away (as in fear situations) show a predominance of epinephrine secretion. Lions and other aggressive animals (whose responses resemble rage-attack behavior) show a predominance of norepinephrine secretion.

Funkenstein, King, and Drolette (1957) exposed subjects to situations conducive to arousal of anger or apprehension. Some overtly expressed anger; others did not (and were said to express or turn their anger inward against themselves). Open expressions of anger and anxiety were associated with secretion of norepinephrine in the blood; the more controlled inward-directed anger was associated with secretion of epinephrine.

Studies such as these are the pioneering investigations that suggest a way to the acquisition of meaningful information concerning the nature of emotional behavior. Such studies are bound to provide some of the missing links needed for better understanding of the genesis of psychosomatic disorders.

A FORMULA FOR THE THRESHOLD FOR PSYCHOSOMATIC BREAKDOWN

The threshold for psychosomatic breakdown may be represented as follows:

$$BT = \frac{Emotional\ activation}{Biological\ assets}$$

BT is the threshold (breakdown threshold) for somatic breakdown to emotional arousal. Emotional activation refers to the value of emotional arousal, that is, to the strength or intensity, the frequency, and the duration of emotional arousal. Biological assets refer to the degree of biological strength or resistance, that is, the reciprocal of vulnerability to pathology.

The formula, it is hoped, will eventually be applicable to any biological structure so that the threshold of breakdown may be ascertained. The formulation, if it is to become useful, depends on investigators and clinicians eventually being able to quantify the two corresponding sets of values, perhaps to an arbitrary maximum of 100. Variable 1 refers to emotional activation, that is, to the deleterious effects of emotional arousal. Variable 2, biological assets, refers to the strength of a biological structure or function, that is, to its resistance to pathology. Whenever the magnitude of variable 1 exceeds the magnitude of variable 2, a psychosomatic aberration is the result.

Not only is the numerator or "stress" value—emotional activation—in a state of flux, but the denominator or "resistance" value—the biological assets—also is variable. Obviously, it is different at birth than at age 5, 25, 55, or 85. Certainly, it is different following an injury or illness than it is during a corresponding period of robust good health.

A worthy goal for researchers and practitioners in the field of psychosomatic disorders is to develop methods capable of carefully ascertaining the biological assets of particular individuals and to provide effective prescriptions for reducing emotional activation far below the critical level or breakdown threshold.

BIBLIOGRAPHY

Aldrich, C. K. *An introduction to dynamic psychiatry.* New York: McGraw-Hill, 1966.

Alexander, F. *Psychosomatic medicine: Its principles and applications.* New York: Norton, 1950.

Alexander, F. Emotional factors in essential hypertension. *Psychosomatic Medicine,* 1939, **1,** 153–216.

Alexander, F. Psychoanalytic study of a case of essential hypertension. *Psychosomatic Medicine,* 1939, **1,** 139–152.

Alexander, F. The influence of psychologic factors upon gastrointestinal disturbances: A symposium. *Psychoanalytic Quarterly,* 1934, **3,** 501–539.

Almy, T. P., Hinkle, L. E., Berle, B., & Kern, F. Alterations in colonic function in man under stress. III. Experimental production of sigmoid spasm in patients with spastic constipation. *Gastroenterology,* 1949, **12,** 437–449.

Almy, T. P., Kern, F., & Tulin, M. Alterations in colonic function in man under stress. II. Experimental production of sigmoid spasm in healthy persons. *Gastroenterology,* 1949, **12,** 425–436.

Alvarez, W. C. *Nervous indigestion.* New York: Hoeber, 1931.

Ambrose, G. & Newbold, G. *A handbook of medical hypnosis* (3rd ed.). London: Baillière, Tindall & Cassell, 1968.

Ax, A. F. The physiological differentiation between fear and anger in humans. *Psychosomatic Medicine,* 1953, **15,** 433–442.

Basowitz, H., Persky, H., Korchin, S. J., & Grinker, R. R. *Anxiety and stress.* New York: McGraw-Hill, 1955.

Behanan, K. T. *Yoga: A scientific evaluation.* New York: Macmillan, 1937.

Berger, A. S., & Simel, P. J. Effect of hypnosis on intraocular pressure in normal and glaucomatous subjects. *Psychosomatic Medicine,* 1958, **20,** 321–327.

Bettelheim, B. *The informed heart.* Glencoe, Illinois: Free Press, 1960.

Binger, C. A., Ackerman, N. W., Cohn, A. E., Schroeder, H. A., & Steele, J. M. Personality in arterial hypertension. *Psychosomatic Medicine Monographs,* 1945, No. 8.

Blaikley, J. B. Menorrhagia of emotional origin. *Lancet,* 1949, **2,** 691–694.

Blum, Lucille Hollander. Sterility and the magic power of the maternal figure. *Journal of Nervous and Mental Diseases,* 1959, **128,** 401–408.

Brady, J. V. Ulcers in "executive" monkeys. *Scientific American,* 1958, **199** (3), 95–104.

Brady, J. V., Porter, R. W., Conrad, D. G., & Mason, J. W. Avoidance behavior and the development of gastroduodenal ulcers. *Journal of the Experimental Analysis of Behavior,* 1958, **1,** 69–72.

Bridges, K. M. B. Emotional development in early infancy. *Child Development,* 1932, **3,** 324–341.

Burton, A., & Harris, R. E. (Eds.). *Case histories in clinical and abnormal psychology.* New York: Harper, 1947.

Bykov, K. M. *Cerebral cortex and internal organs.* Translated by W. A. H. Gantt. New York: Chemical Publishing Company, 1957.

Cameron, N. *Personality development and psychopathology.* Boston: Houghton Mifflin, 1963.

Cannon, W. B. The mechanism of emotional disturbance of bodily functions. *New England Journal of Medicine,* 1928, **198,** 877–884.

Cannon, W. B. *Bodily changes in pain, hunger, fear and rage: An account of recent researches into the function of emotional excitement.* New York: Appleton, 1920.

Cannon, W. B. *The wisdom of the body.* New York: Norton, 1939.

Cason, H. The conditioned pupillary reaction. *Journal of Experimental Psychology,* 1922, **5,** 108–146.

Chambers, W. N., & Reiser, M. F. Emotional stress in the precipitation of congestive heart failure. *Psychosomatic Medicine,* 1953, **15,** 38–60.

Clarke, C. A. *Genetics for the Clinicians.* Philadelphia: F. A. Davis, 1964.

Cohen, M. E., White, P. D., & Johnson, R. E. Neurocirculatory asthenia, anxiety neurosis or the effort syndrome. *Archives of Internal Medicine,* 1948, **81,** 260–281.

Collip, J. B. Hormones in relation to human behavior. In E. D. Adrian (Ed.), *Factors determining human behavior.* Cambridge, Massachusetts: Harvard University Press, 1937.

Conger, J. J., Sawrey, W. L., & Turrell, E. S. The role of social experience in the production of gastric ulcers in hooded rats placed in a conflict situation. *Journal of Abnormal and Social Psychology,* 1958, **57,** 214–220.

Cushing, H. Peptic ulcers and the interbrain. *Surgery, Gynecology and Obstetrics,* 1932, **55,** 1–34.

Daniels, G. E., O'Connor, J. F., Karush, A., Moses, L., Flood, C. A., & Lepore, M. Three decades in the observation and treatment of ulcerative colitis. *Psychosomatic Medicine,* 1962, **24,** 85–93.

Darrow, C. W., & Heath, L. L. Reaction tendencies relating to personality. In K. S. Lashley (Ed.), *Studies in the dynamics of behavior.* Chicago: University of Chicago Press, 1932.

Darwin, C. R. *The expression of emotions in man and animals.* London: J. Murray, 1872.

Dekker, E. & Groen, J. Reproducible psychogenic attacks of asthma. *Journal of Psychosomatic Research*, 1956, **1**, 58–67.

Dekker, E., Pelser, H. E., & Groen, J. Conditioning as a cause of asthmatic attacks. *Journal of Psychosomatic Research*, 1957, **2**, 97–108.

Deutsch, F. Psychoanalyse und Organkrankheiten. *Internationale Zeitschrift für Psychoanalyse*, 1922, **8**, 290–306.

DiCara, L. V. Learning in the autonomic nervous system. *Scientific American*, 1970, **222** (1), 30–39.

Doswald, D. C., & Kreibich, D. K. Zur Frage der posthypnotischen Hauptphänomene. *Monatshefte für praktische Dermatologie*, 1906, **43**, 634–640.

Dragstedt, L. R. A concept of the etiology of duodenal ulcer. *American Journal of Roentgenology*, 1956, **75**, 219–229.

Dreyfuss, F., & Czaczkes, J. W. Blood cholesterol and uric acid of healthy medical students under the stress of an examination. *Archives of Internal Medicine*, 1959, **103**, 708–711.

Dublin, L. I., & Spiegelman, M. The longevity of American physicians, 1938–1942. *Journal of the American Medical Association*, 1947, **134**, 1211–1215.

Dunbar, H. Flanders. *Emotions and bodily changes.* New York: Columbia University Press, 1935.

Dunbar, H. Flanders. *Emotions and bodily changes* (3d. ed.). New York: Columbia University Press, 1946.

Dunbar, H. Flanders. *Psychosomatic diagnosis.* New York: Hoeber, 1943.

Duncan, C. H., Stevenson, I. P., & Ripley, H. S. Life situations, emotions and paroxysmal auricular arrhythmias. *Psychosomatic Medicine*, 1950, **12**, 23–37.

Ecker, A. Emotional stress before strokes: A preliminary report of 20 cases. *Annals of Internal Medicine*, 1954, **40**, 49–56.

Engel, G. L. Studies of ulcerative colitis. I. Clinical data bearing on the nature of the somatic process. *Psychosomatic Medicine*, 1954a, **16**, 496–501.

Engel, G. L. Studies of ulcerative colitis. II. The nature of the somatic processes and the adequacy of psychosomatic hypotheses. *American Journal of Medicine*, 1954b, **16**, 416–433.

Engel, G. L. Studies in ulcerative colitis. III. The nature of the psychological process. *American Journal of Medicine*, 1955, **19**, 231–256.

English, O. S., & Finch, S. M. *Introduction to psychiatry* (3d ed.). New York: Norton, 1964.

Enos, W. F., et al. Coronary disease among United States soldiers killed in action in Korea. *Journal of the American Medical Association*, 1953, **152**, 1090.

Erickson, M. H., Hershman, S., & Secter, I. I. *The practical application of medical and dental hypnosis.* New York: Julian Press, 1961.

Evans, E. *A psychological study of cancer.* New York: Dodd, Mead, 1926.

Fabricant, N. D. Effect of emotions on the hydrogen ion concentration of nasal secretions in situ. *Archives of Otolaryngology*, 1946, **43**, 402–408.

Faulkner, Jr., W. B. Influence of suggestion on size of bronchial lumen: Bronchoscopic study and report of one case. *Northwest Medicine*, 1941, **40**, 367–368.

Feldman, S.S. Anxiety and orgasm. *Psychoanalytic Quarterly*, 1951, **20**, 528–549.

Folkow, B., & Von Euler, U. S. Selective activation of noradrenaline and adrenaline producing cells in the cat's adrenal gland by hypothalamic stimulation. *Circulation Research,* 1954, **2,** 191–195.

Fowler, E., & Zeckel, A. Psychophysiological factors in Ménière's disease. *Psychosomatic Medicine,* 1953, **15,** 127–139.

French, J. D., Porter, R. W., Cavanaugh, E. B., & Longmire, R. L. Experimental observations on "psychosomatic" mechanisms. I. Gastrointestinal disturbance. *A.M.A. Archives of Neurology and Psychiatry,* 1954, **72,** 267–281.

Freund, W. A. Zur Naturgeschichte der Krebskrankheit nach klinischen Erfahrungen. *Zeitschrift für Krebsforschung,* 1905, **3,** 1–33.

Friedman, M. *Functional cardiovascular disease.* Baltimore: Williams & Wilkins, 1947.

Friedman, M. & Rosenman, R. H. Association of specific overt behaviour pattern with blood and cardiovascular findings. *Journal of the American Medical Association,* 1959, **169,** 1286.

Friedman, M., Rosenman, R. H., & Carroll, V. Changes in the serum cholesterol and blood clotting time in men subjected to cyclic variations of occupational stress. *Circulation,* 1958, **17,** 852.

Fuller, J. L., & Thompson, W. R. *Behavior genetics.* New York: Wiley, 1960.

Funkenstein, D. The physiology of fear and anger. *Scientific American,* 1955, **192** (5), 74–76.

Funkenstein, D. H., King, S. H., & Drolette, M. E., *Mastery of stress.* Cambridge, Massachusetts: Harvard University Press, 1957.

Gantt, W. H. The origin and development of behavior disorders in dogs. *Psychosomatic Medicine Monographs.* New York: Hoeber-Harper, 1947.

Garma, A. On the pathogenesis of peptic ulcer. *International Journal of Psycho-Analysis,* 1950, **31,** 53–72.

Gellhorn, E. *Autonomic regulations: Their significance for physiology, psychology and neuro-psychiatry,* New York: Interscience Publishers, 1943.

Gellhorn, E. *Autonomic imbalance and the hypothalamus.* Minneapolis: University of Minnesota Press, 1957.

Gilbert-Dreyfus. Paradoxical obesity: A psychosomatic syndrome (L'Obésité paradoxale syndrome psycho-somatique). *La Presse Médicale,* 1948, **56,** 249–250.

Goldman, E., & Ulett, G. A. *Practical psychiatry for the internist.* St. Louis: C. V. Mosby, 1968.

Gorton, B. E. Physiological aspects of hypnosis. In J. M. Schneck (Ed.), *Hypnosis in Modern Medicine* (2d. ed.). Springfield, Illinois: Charles C. Thomas, 1959.

Grace, W. J., & Graham, D. T. Relationships of specific attitudes and emotions to certain bodily diseases. *Psychosomatic Medicine,* 1952, **14,** 243–251.

Grace, W. J., Seton, P., Wolf, S., & Wolff, H. G. Studies of the human colon: Variations in concentration of lysozyme with life situations and emotional state. *American Journal of Medical Science,* 1949, **217,** 241–251.

Grace, W. J., Wolf, S., & Wolff, H. G. Life situations, emotions and chronic ulcerative colitis. *Journal of the American Medical Association,* 1950a, **142,** 1044–1048.

Grace, W. J., Wolf, S., & Wolff, H. G. Life Situations, emotions and colonic functions. *Gastroenterology,* 1950b, **14,** 93–108.

Grace, W. J., Wolf, S., & Wolff, H. G. *The human colon.* New York: Harper, 1951.

Grace, W. J., & Wolff, H. G. Treatment of ulcerative colitis. *Journal of the American Medical Association,* 1951, **146,** 981–987.

Graham, D. T., & Wolf, S. Pathogenesis of urticaria. Experimental study of life situations, emotions and cutaneous vascular reactions. *Journal of the American Medical Association,* 1950, **143,** 1396–1402.

Greene, W. A., Jr., Young, L. E., & Swisher, S. N. Psychological factors in reticuloendothelial disease. II. Observations on a group of women with lymphomas and leukemias. *Psychosomatic Medicine,* 1956, **18,** 284–303.

Grimm, E. R. Psychological investigation of habitual abortion. *Psychosomatic Medicine,* 1962, **24,** 369–378.

Grinker, R. R. *Psychosomatic research.* New York: Norton, 1953.

Grinker, R. R., & Robbins, F. P. *Psychosomatic case book.* New York: Blakiston, 1954.

Hall, C. S. The inheritance of emotionality. *American Scientist,* 1938, **26,** 17–27.

Hansen, K. Analyse, Indikation und Grenze der Psychotherapie beim Bronchialasthma. *Deutsche Medizinische Wochenschrift,* 1927, **53,** 1462–1464.

Harrington, D. D. Ocular manifestations of psychosomatic disorders. *Journal of the American Medical Association,* 1948, **133,** 669–674.

Hartman, H. R. Neurogenic factors in peptic ulcer. *Medical Clinic of North America,* 1933, **16,** 1357–1369.

Health, Education and Welfare Trends. Washington: U.S. Department of Health, Education and Welfare, 1962.

Herrmann, F., Prose, P. H. & Sulzberger, M. B. Studies on sweating. IV. A new quantitative method of assaying sweat-delivery to circumscribed areas of the skin surface. *Journal of Investigative Dermatology,* 1951, **17,** 241–249.

Herxheimer, H. Induced asthma in humans. *International Archives of Allergy and Applied Immunology,* 1953, **3,** 192.

Hillarp, N. Evidence of adrenaline/noradrenaline in separate medullary cells. *Acta Physiologica Scandinavica,* 1953, **30,** 55–68.

Hinkle, L. E., Conger, G. A., & Wolf, S. Experimental evidence on the mechanism diabetic ketosis. *Journal of Clinical Investigation,* 1949, **28,** 788–789.

Hinkle, L. E., & Wolf, S. Experimental study of life situations, emotions and the occurrence of acidosis in a juvenile diabetic. *American Journal of Medical Science,* 1949, **217,** 130–135.

Hinkle, L. E., & Wolf, S. Importance of life stress in the course and management of diabetes mellitus. *Journal of the American Medical Association,* 1952, **148,** 513–520.

Hoelzel, F. Fear and gastric acidity. *American Journal of Digestive Disturbances,* 1942, **9,** 188.

Hofling, C. K. *Textbook of psychiatry for medical practice* (2d ed.). Philadelphia: Lippincott, 1968.

Hokanson, J. E., & Burgess, M. The effects of three types of aggression on vascular process. *Journal of Abnormal and Social Psychology,* 1962, **65,** 232–237.

Hokanson, J. E., & Shetler, S. The effect of overt aggression on physiological tension level. *Journal of Abnormal and Social Psychology,* 1961, **63,** 446–448.

Hollingworth, H. L. General laws of redintegration. *Journal of General Psychology,* 1928, **1,** 79–90.

Jacobson, E. *Progressive relaxation.* Chicago: University of Chicago Press, 1938.

Jones, M. C. The elimination of children's fears. *Journal of Experimental Psychology,* 1924, **7,** 383–390.

Kaneko, A., & Takaishi, N. Psychosomatic studies on chronic urticaria. *Folia Psychiatrica et Neurologica Japonica,* 1963, **17,** 16–24.

Kaplan, S. M., Gottschalk, L., & Fleming, D. Modification of oropharyngeal bacteria with changes in psychodynamic state. *A.M.A. Archives of Neurology and Psychiatry,* 1957, **78,** 656–664.

Kapp, F. T., Rosenbaum, M., & Romano, J. Psychological factors in men with peptic ulcers. *American Journal of Psychiatry,* 1947, **103,** 700–704.

Kazansky, V. I. *Cancer.* Moscow: Foreign Languages Publishing House, 1955.

Kisker, G. W. *The disorganized personality.* New York: McGraw-Hill, 1964.

Kissen, D. M. Relationship between primary lung cancer and peptic ulcer in males. *Psychosomatic Medicine,* 1962, **24,** 133–147.

Kolb, L. C. *Noyes' modern clinical psychiatry* (7th ed.). Philadelphia: Saunders, 1968.

Kracht, J., & Kracht, V. Histopathology and theory of shock thyrotoxicosis in the wild rabbit, virchows. *Archives of Pathological Anatomy,* 1952, **321,** 238–274.

Kraines, S. H., & Thetford, E. S. *Managing your mind.* New York: Macmillan, 1943.

Kreibich, C., & Sobotka, P. Experimenteller Beitrag zur psychischen Urticaria. *Archiv für Dermatologie und Syphilis,* 1909, **97,** 187–192.

Kroger, W. S. Evaluation of personality factors in the treatment of infertility. *Fertility & Sterility,* 1952, **3,** 542–551.

Lachman, S. J. A behavioristic rationale for the development of psychosomatic phenomena. *Journal of Psychology,* 1963, **56,** 239–248.

Lachman, S. J. *Emotional reactions: A behavioristic definition of emotion and a group of tables.* Detroit: Wayne State University, 1969. (Mimeographed.)

Lacey, J. I., Bateman, D. E., & VanLehn, R. Autonomic response specificity. *Psychosomatic Medicine,* 1953, **15,** 8–21.

Leigh, D. Sudden death from asthma. *Psychosomatic Medicine,* 1955, **17,** 232–239.

LeShan, L. A basic psychological orientation apparently associated with malignant disease. *Psychiatric Quarterly,* 1961 (April), 1–17.

LeShan, L., & Worthington, R. E. Some psychologic correlates of neoplastic disease: A preliminary report. *Journal of Clinical and Experimental Psychopathology,* 1955, **16,** 281–288.

Lewis, J. H., & Sarbin, T. R. Studies in psychosomatics: The influence of hypnotic responses on gastric contractions. *Psychological Bulletin,* 1942, **39,** 596–597.

Lewis, N. D. C., & Engle, B. (Eds.). *Wartime psychiatry.* New York: Oxford, 1954.

Liddell, H. S. The influence of experimental neuroses on the respiratory function. In A. Abramson (Ed.), *Somatic and psychiatric treatment of asthma.* Baltimore: Williams & Wilkins, 1951.

Lium, R., & Porter, J. E. Etiology of ulcerative colitis. I. Preparation, care and secretions of colonic explants in dogs. II. Effects of induced muscular spasm on colonic explants in dogs. *Archives of Internal Medicine,* 1939, **63**, 201–225.

Loeser, A. A. Effect of emotional shock on hormone release and endometrial development. *Lancet,* 1943, **244**, 518–519.

Ludwig, A. A. Rheumatoid arthritis. In A. W. Freedman & H. T. Kaplan (Eds.), *Comprehensive textbook of psychiatry.* Baltimore: Williams and Wilkins, 1967.

Macht, D. I. Influence of some drugs and of emotions on blood coagulation. *Journal of the American Medical Association,* 1952, **148**, 265–270.

Mackenzie, J. N. The production of the so-called "rose cold" by means of artificial rose. *American Journal of Medical Science,* 1886, **91**, 45–57.

Maher, B. A. *Principles of psychopathology: An experimental approach.* New York: McGraw-Hill, 1966.

Mahl, G. F. Effect of chronic fear on the gastric secretion of HCl in dogs. *Psychosomatic Medicine,* 1949, **11**, 30–44.

Mahl, G. F. Anxiety, HCl secretion, and peptic ulcer etiology. *Psychosomatic Medicine,* 1950, **12**, 158–169.

Maier, N. R. F., & Glaser, N. M. Studies of abnormal behavior in the rat. V. The inheritance of the "neurotic pattern." *Journal of Comparative Psychology,* 1940, **30**, 413–418.

Malmo, R. B., & Shagass, C. Physiological study of symptom mechanisms in psychiatric patients under stress. *Psychosomatic Medicine,* 1949, **11**, 25–29.

Mann, T. *The magic mountain.* New York: Alfred A. Knopf, 1927.

Marañon, G. Contribution à l'étude de l'action émotive de l'adrénaline. *Revue Française d'Endocrinologie,* 1924, **2**, 301–325.

Marchbach, A. H., & Schinfeld, L. H. Psychosomatic aspects of infertility. *Obstetrics and Gynecology,* 1953, **2**, 433–441.

Marcussen, R. M., & Wolff, H. G. A formulation of the dynamics of the migraine attack. *Psychosomatic Medicine,* 1949, **11**, 251–256.

Marcussen, R. M., & Wolff, H. G. Therapy of migraine. *Journal of the American Medical Association,* 1949, **139**, 198–200.

Masserman, J. H. *The practice of dynamic psychiatry.* Philadelphia: Saunders, 1955.

Masserman, J. H., & Pechtel, C. Conflict-engendered neurotic and psychotic behavior in monkeys. *Journal of Nervous and Mental Diseases,* 1953, **118**, 408–411.

McDonald, R. D., & Yagi, K. A note on eosinopenia as an index of psychological stress. *Psychosomatic Medicine,* 1960, **22**, 149–150.

Menninger, K. *Man against himself.* New York: Harcourt, Brace, 1938.

Menzies, R. Conditioned vasomotor responses in human subjects. *Journal of Psychology,* 1937, **4**, 75–120.

Meyer, K., Gellhorn, A., Prudden, J. F., Lehman, W. L., & Steinberg, Anita. Lysozyme in chronic ulcerative colitis. *Proceedings of the Society of Experimental Biology and Medicine,* 1947, **65**, 221–222.

Miminoshvili, D. I. Experimental neurosis in monkeys. In I. Rurkin (Ed.), *Theoretical and practical problems of medicine and biology in experiments on monkeys.* New York: Pergamon Press, 1960.

Miles, H. H. W., Cobb, S., & Shands, H. C. *Case histories in psychosomatic medicine.* New York: Norton, 1952.

Miller, N. E. Learning of visceral and glandular responses. *Science,* 1969, **163,** 434–443.

Mirsky, I. A., Futterman, P., & Kaplan, S. Blood plasma pepsinogen. II. The activity of the plasma from "normal" subjects, patients with duodenal ulcer and patients with pernicious anemia. *Journal of Laboratory and Clinical Medicine,* 1952, **40,** 188–199.

Mittelman, B. M., & Wolff, H. G. Emotions and skin temperature. Observations on patients during psychotherapeutic interviews (psychoanalytic interviews). *Psychosomatic Medicine,* 1943, **5,** 211–231.

Mittelman, B., Wolff, H. G., & Scharf, M. Emotions and gastroduodenal functions. *Psychosomatic Medicine,* 1942, **4,** 5–61.

Nardini, J. E. Survival factors in American prisoners of war of the Japanese. *American Journal of Psychiatry,* 1952, **109,** 242–248.

O'Neill, D. Uterine bleeding in tension states. *Journal of Obstetrics and Gynecology, British Empire,* **59,** 1952, 234–239.

Ottenberg, O., Stein, M., Lewis, J., & Hamilton, C. Learned asthma in the guinea pig. *Psychosomatic medicine,* 1958, **20,** 395–400.

Papania, N. I. *Personal communication.* 1968.

Pattie, F. A., Jr. The production of blisters by hypnotic suggestion: A review. *Journal of Abnormal and Social Psychology,* 1941, **36,** 62–72.

Pavlov, I. P. Lectures on conditioned reflexes. (Translated by W. H. Gantt.) New York: International Publishers, 1928.

Philipp, R. J. *An experimental investigation of suggestion and relaxation in asthmatics.* Unpublished doctoral dissertation. Kingston, Ontario: Queens University, 1970.

Platonov, K. I. *The word as a physiological and therapeutic factor.* Moscow, USSR: Foreign Languages Publishing House, 1959.

Poussaint, A. F. Emotional factors in psoriasis: Report of a case. *Psychosomatics,* 1963, **4,** 199–202.

Prugh, D. G. Variations in the attitudes, behavior and feeling states as exhibited by the play of children during modifications in the course of ulcerative colitis. *Research Publication of the Association for Research in Nervous and Mental Diseases,* 1950, **29,** 692–705.

Prugh, D. G. A preliminary report on the role of emotional factors in idiopathic celiac diseases. *Psychosomatic Medicine,* 1951, **13,** 220–241.

Rao, H. V. G., Krishnaswamy, N., Narasimhaiya, R. L., Hoenig, J., & Govindaswamy, M. V. Some experiments on a "yogi" in controlled states. *Journal of the All-India Institute of Mental Health,* 1958, **1** (2), 99–106.

Razran, G. The observable unconscious in current Soviet psychophysiology: Survey and interpretation of experiments in interoceptive conditioning. In L. E. Abt & B. F. Riess (Eds.), *Progress in clinical psychology.* Vol. IV. New York: Grune & Stratton, 1960.

Ripley, H. S., & Wolff, H. G. Life situations, emotions, and glaucoma. *Psychosomatic Medicine,* 1950, **12,** 215–224.

Roessler, R. L., & Brogden, W. J. Conditioned differentiation of vasoconstriction to subvocal stimuli. *American Journal of Psychology,* 1943, **56,** 78–86.

Rundquist, E. A. Inheritance of spontaneous activity in the rat. *Journal of Comparative Psychology,* 1933, **16,** 415–438.

Russek, H. I., & Zohman, B. L. Relative significance of heredity, diet and occupational stress in coronary heart disease of young adults: Based on an analysis of 100 patients between the ages of 25 and 40 years and a similar group of 100 normal control subjects. *American Journal of Medical Science,* 1958, **235,** 266–277.

Sadler, W. S. *Practice of psychiatry.* St. Louis: Mosby, 1953.

Saul, L. J. Psychogenic factors in the etiology of the common cold. *International Journal of Psychoanalysis,* 1938, **19,** 451–470.

Saul, L. J. Hostility in cases of essential hypertension. *Psychosomatic Medicine,* 1939, **1,** 153–216.

Sawrey, W. L., & Weisz, J. D. An experimental method of producing gastric ulcers. role of psychological factors in the production of gastric ulcers in the rat. *Journal of Comparative and Physiological Psychology,* 1956, **49,** 457–461.

Sawrey, W. L., & Weiss, J. D. An experimental method of producing gastric ulcers. *Journal of Comparative and Physiological Psychology,* 1956, **49,** 269–270.

Schlaegel, T. F., Jr. *Psychosomatic ophthalmology.* Baltimore: Williams & Wilkins, 1957.

Schoenberg, M. J. Remarks on psychosomatic factors in glaucomatous hypertension. *Journal of Clinical Psychopathology,* 1945, **6,** 451–452.

Schunk, J. Emotionale faktoren in der pathogenese der essentiellen Hypertonie. *Zeitschrift für klinische Medizin,* 1954, **152,** 251–280.

Seitz, P. F. D. Infantile experience and adult behavior in animal subjects. II. Age of separation from the mother and adult behavior in the cat. *Psychosomatic Medicine,* 1959, **21,** 353–378.

Selye, H. The general adaptation syndrome and the diseases of adaptation. *Journal of Clinical Endocrinology,* 1946, **6,** 117–128.

Selye, H. *The stress of life.* New York: McGraw-Hill, 1956.

Shoemaker, R. J. A search for the affective determinants of chronic urticaria. *Psychosomatics,* 1963, **4,** 125–132.

Sim, M. *Guide to psychiatry.* Baltimore: Williams & Wilkins, 1963.

Sines, J. O. Behavioral correlates of genetically enhanced susceptibility to stomach lesion development. *Journal of Psychosomatic Research,* 1961, **5,** 120–126.

Slawson, P. F., Flynn, W. R., & Kollar, E. J. Psychological factors associated with the onset of diabetes mellitus. *Journal of the American Medical Association.* 1963, **185** (3), 166–170.

Stern, C. *Principles of human genetics.* (2d ed.) San Francisco: Freeman, 1960.

Stevenson, I., & Ripley, H. S. Variations in respiration and in respiratory symptoms during changes in emotion. *Psychosomatic Medicine,* 1952, **14,** 476–490.

Stokes, J. H., Kulchar, G. V. & Pillsbury, D. M. Effect on skin of emotional and nervous states: Etiologic background of urticaria with special reference to the psychoneurogous factor. *Archives of Dermatology & Syphilology,* 1935, **31,** 470–499.

Strange, J. R. *Abnormal psychology: Understanding behavior disorders.* New York: McGraw-Hill, 1965.

Sulzberger, M. B., & Wolf, J. The treatment of warts by suggestion. *Medical Record,* 1934, **140,** 552–556.

Tryon, R. C. Individual differences. In F. A. Moss (Ed.), *Comparative psychology* (revised edition). Prentice-Hall, 1942.

Tuft, H. S. The asthma, eczema, urticaria, rhinitis syndrome. *Pennsylvania Medical Journal,* 1959, **62,** 177–180.

Tupper, W. R. C. Psychosomatic aspects of spontaneous and habitual abortion. In *Psychosomatic obstetrics, gynecology, and endocrinology.* Springfield, Illinois: Thomas, 1963.

Turnbull, J. W. Asthma conceived as a learned response. *Journal of Psychosomatic Research,* 1962, **6,** 59–70.

Waddell, W. R. The physiologic significance of retained antral tissue after partial gastrectomy. *Annals of Surgery,* 1956, **143,** 520–553.

Wallerstein, R. S., Sutherland, R. L., & Lyons, J. Some psychosomatic considerations in Addison's disease. *Psychosomatic Medicine,* 1954, **16,** 67–76.

Wenger, M. A., Bagchi, B. K., & Anand, B. K. Experiments in India on "voluntary" control of the heart and pulse. *Circulation,* 1961, **24,** 1319–1325.

White, R. W. *The abnormal personality* (3d ed.). New York: Ronald Press, 1964.

Wittkower, E., & Edgell, P. G. Eczema: A psychosomatic study. *Archives of Psychosomatic Medicine,* 1953, **15,** 116–126.

Wittkower, E., & MacKenna, R. M. B. Psychological aspects of seborrheic dermatitis, with a foreword. *British Journal of Dermatology and Syphilology,* 1947, **59,** 281–293.

Wittkower, E., Rodger, T. F., & Wilson, A. T. M. Effort syndrome. *Lancet,* 1941, **1,** 531–535.

Wolf, S., & Wolff, H. G. *Human gastric function.* New York: Oxford University Press, 1947.

Wolf, S., Cardon, P. V., Jr., Shepard, E. M., & Wolff, H. G. *Life stress and essential hypertension.* Baltimore: Williams & Wilkins, 1955.

Wolf, S., Pfeiffer, J. B., Ripley, H. S., Winter, O. S., & Wolff, H. G. *Annals of Internal Medicine,* 1948, **29,** 1056–1076.

Wolff, H. G., & Wolf, S. *Human gastric function: An experimental study of a man and his stomach.* Fair Lawn, New Jersey: Oxford University Press, 1943.

Yeakel, E. H., & Rhoades, R. P. A comparison of the body and endocrine gland (adrenal, thyroid, and pituitary) weights of emotional and nonemotional rats. *Endocrinology,* 1941, **28,** 337–340.

Yeats-Brown, F. C. C. *Yoga explained.* New York: Viking, 1937.

Zeligs, M. A. Central angiospastic retinopathy: A psychosomatic study of its occurrence in military personnel. *Psychosomatic Medicine,* 1947, **9,** 110–117.

Author Index

195

Subject Index